Pandora's Pride

Pandora's Pride

by MAY GRUBER

Lyle Stuart Inc.   Secaucus, N.J.

Published by Lyle Stuart Inc.
Published simultaneously in Canada by
Musson Book Company,
A division of General Publishing Co. Limited
Don Mills, Ontario

Queries regarding rights and permissions should be
addressed to: Lyle Stuart, 120 Enterprise Avenue,
Secaucus, N.J. 07094

Manufactured in the United States of America

ISBN 0-8184-0374-8

For
DR. ANNA LESTER PHILBROOK
who first encouraged me to write
and then assured me that my words
would find their way into print.
Bless you, Nan.

Contents

Acknowledgment of Debt

To Patricia Eakins,
hands-off tutor in creative writing, whose integrity
and guidance helped me assemble my material.
To many willing persons in New York and New Hampshire
who typed, typed, typed pages and pages of copy.
To my husband, Samuel William Gruber,
who judges creativity by a single standard:
Is the work good? He liked what I wrote.
THANK YOU.

May Gruber

ONE

Casting the First Stitches

KNITTERS GATHER EVERY other year in Atlantic City when the National Knitted Outerwear Association holds its trade show. The last time I attended, one of the exhibitors, a yarn dealer, introduced me to a major competitor of my company, an elderly dandy with bulging belly and a carnation in his lapel. Surprise flickered across his face as he connected my name, my title and my company.

"What's a nice lady like you doing in the *shmatta* [rag] business?" he asked.

Inside I did a slow burn. Outside I kept my cool.

I don't feel oddball. In January 1976, after twelve years as president of my firm, I stepped aside to chair its board of directors. During my tenure the company's employees numbered more than 1,200 and its volume grew from $8 million to over $30 million annually. While the elderly dandy's stock, listed on the New York Exchange, plunged up and down, our stock, privately held, multiplied in value almost tenfold. Dun & Bradstreet has given us top credit rating, AAA1. A trio of banks has lent us all the cash we ever needed at prime rate.

I take pride in having performed a professional job.

Not long after this trade show, an earnest young woman named Chris approached me to ask me to take part in a panel discussion on women in business. Flattered by my first such invitation, I gladly accepted.

"I'm curious about one thing," she said. "For an article in *Fortune*, a writer surveyed 1,300 companies all over the United States. Out of 6,500 executives earning over $30,000 a year they found only eleven women."

We stopped to figure out the percentage—less than one-quarter of one percent!

"You are president of one of the largest sweater and sportswear companies in the country. How did you get there? Was it through your family? Was it through death? Was it on your own?"

She posed the questions matter-of-factly. They shook me.

"Yes," I managed to answer.

Yes, it was through family. I was born into a knitting-mill family. Even before my birth, my father had entered the world of *strickerei*, knitwear.

Yes, it was through death. My husband had headed our company for nine years. He died suddenly in 1964. Of the remaining partners I felt best qualified to succeed him and carry on.

Yes, it was on my own. I've been knitting sweaters, as it were, for fifty years, named the company Pandora, helped construct the master plan by which it grew. When my chance came to buy out the other interests, I hocked every asset I had and put myself in debt for years to raise the money.

To all the people who helped me on my way, I dedicate this story. May others get a lift from it as they climb their own career ladders.

I got my first job by lying about my age. At fifteen I wanted to work because I could not bear to sit home and twiddle my thumbs. During the month of July, I had vacationed with my family in the Catskills; after Labor Day, I was to register as a freshman at New York University. In August, that yawning space between, I faced some empty weeks.

On a Monday morning, quietly slipping out of our two-family house in the Bronx, I took the subway downtown to Herald Square. I had learned from an ad that Gimbel Brothers wanted saleswomen, experience not necessary.

"Your age?" the interviewer asked.

"Seventeen," I told her. "I've just graduated from Evander Childs High."

She questioned me. No, I had no plans for the fall. Yes, I was definitely considering a career in selling. She hired me.

"You'll be paid fourteen dollars a week. Report to the training office," she said.

With a dozen other rookies I was soon sitting in a brightly lit classroom for a two-hour course on the art of sales-manship. We were to address a customer with "May I serve you?"; answer her questions if we knew the answers or refer her to Information or a service desk if we didn't; call the section manager to handle complaints. We spent a long time learning how to fill out a sales check. Names and addresses had to be written plainly or printed. And we had to punch a time clock before we entered or as soon as we left the sales floor.

"Wear sensible shoes and a plain navy or black dress; no frills," said our teacher. "Nothing must distract your customer from the merchandise."

Our group then scattered to find our section managers. Mine, on the main floor, directed me to an open booth near the Broadway entrance. I was to sell advertised specials in a heavy-traffic area. That day they featured a half-dozen housedresses in three colors. Except for a lunch break, I was kept very busy waiting on women and writing sales checks. At five o'clock I punched out and plunged into the rush hour traffic. I reached home before six.

My mother was spreading newspapers on her freshly scrubbed kitchen floor. After she laid an extra sheet of the *Bronx Home News* in front of the gas stove, she turned the flame low under a big white pot and skimmed fat from the surface of the bubbling soup and chicken.

"I didn't see you all day," she said.

I chose not to answer. I wanted to wait for my father to walk in before springing my news.

"See if you can find Teddy," she said. "Tell him it's time to eat."

I found my kid brother at the candy store around the corner.

"I got a job," I announced when our family assembled for supper. "I'm selling at Gimbels."

Startled, my mother stopped serving, her soup ladle in midair. "You don't have enough to eat? Or a bed to sleep in? Or nice clothes to wear? What will I say to Aunt Jennie and Aunt Dora?"

Teddy sat still, turning his eyes from Ma's face to mine.

At last Pa broke in. "Let her." In the measured rhythm of reason, he continued, first in Yiddish, *"Sit ihr garnicht shotten"* (It will damage her nohow), then in English, "She wants to discover America, let her. Let her find out how hard it is to earn a buck." As usual, he had the last word.

I worked four weeks in August, collected fifty-six dollars, and felt all grown up shopping for college clothes with money I myself had earned.

I can still hear my mother's stock speech to my scandalized aunts: "Just like her father. Once she makes up her mind, who can stop her?"

The work ethic was drilled into me from my early years. Morris and Bertha Blum, my parents, knew no other way of life.

In 1905, my mother's father sent passage money for his wife and thirteen-year-old daughter, Bessie, to travel from a *shtetl* in Lithuania to the *goldene medina*, the Promised Land. He, his son and an older daughter, Jennie, had preceded them. By train and boat, mother and daughter went from Chelm to Leeds, in England, where they stayed for two weeks with a close relative. They then crossed over to Germany and sailed from Bremen.

One morning, hearing a great hullabaloo, they ran to one side of the ship and saw a Big Lady standing in the harbor. Soon after, they were reunited with their family.

Jennie, older than Bessie by seven years, steered the *muzinka*, the baby or darling of the family, through the immigration formalities.

"Where it says name," Jennie counseled, "don't put down Bessie—so old-fashioned. Instead, put down Bertha. It's more American."

The pretty teen-ager struggled to copy Jennie's block-lettered BERTHA. Thus, she entered the United States as Bertha Greenberg. She was to recall one other vivid incident of that day.

"A new bridge just opened," said Jennie's sweetheart, a distant cousin. "We want to show it to Bertha."

"Is it safe?" asked her mother.

Assuring her of its safety, the couple took the thirteen-year-old for a walk across the Williamsburg Bridge. When they reached the halfway point Jennie, leaning firmly on her sweetheart's arm, jumped up and down several times to test the strength of the span. Laughing and feeling very secure, the three of them recrossed the bridge and strolled back to Delancey Street.

For ten weeks Bertha attended school that fall. Then a recession hit the family. Her older brother lost his job in a coffin factory, and her father lost some of his Hebrew pupils. He made little enough as *shamus* of his *shul*, or synagogue sexton. Jennie could spare no extra cash; she was saving money to get married.

So, at fourteen Bertha borrowed a friend's working papers, to prove she had reached sixteen, and went to work for three dollars a week, learning to stitch shirtwaists together. In the sweatshop she was exhausted by the pace, her eyes were strained by the harsh gaslights, and she sometimes had to work until eight or nine at night. Twice she registered for night-school courses. Twice she dropped out.

By the summer of 1909 Bertha had advanced to sample maker at the Triangle Shirtwaist Company. After eighteen months, a foreman who was going to start his own business persuaded her and her friend Lena to leave with him.

The girls soon wondered whether they had done the right thing, because the new boss's pay checks kept bouncing. "I would run to the bank early, and my checks went through," my mother later told me. "Other girls had to deposit theirs over again."

She added one other consideration. "We were working by gaslight. At the Triangle we had had electric light. We talked about going back."

They did not discuss it for long, however. Six weeks after Bertha switched jobs, on Saturday afternoon, March 25, 1911, tragedy struck the Triangle. As girls got ready to leave work, but before the owners had unlocked the doors of two of the lofts, flames burst from a bin jammed with greasy rags on the eighth story of the supposedly fireproof building. The blaze spread quickly to the ninth and tenth floors. Some of those who made it to the elevator crashed to their deaths when the supporting cables were consumed by flames. Some were trapped on fire escapes that buckled; some jumped to their deaths; still others were burned alive. One hundred and forty-six workers lost their lives.

From the sidewalk, authorities collected scattered arms, legs and torsos of twenty-eight girls. Before being buried in a mass grave, these parts were exhibited on long tables in a morgue. Also stretched out were corpses charred almost beyond recognition. Bertha went to the morgue to see if she could identify any of the bodies. She recognized three girls she used to work with, including the head of a pretty Italian girl who had sewed at the very next Singer to hers. Then she saw a sight that sent her in flight from the room.

A month before she left the Triangle, she and her co-workers had taken up a collection for a girl who had just announced her engagement. They put together forty-nine cents and had a little party for her. A photographer snapped a picture of the girls grouped around their Singers. Then they presented the bride-to-be with a pair of garters decorated with fur pompons.

At the morgue, Bertha had glimpsed a pair of fur pompons on a single garter on a solitary leg.

In 1907 Morris Blum emigrated to the United States, completing an odyssey that began when he was eleven in the sleepy village of Radzymin, in Poland. Morris (then Moishe) was the younger son of Rafael Fuczyna. Rafael, his wife, Naomi, his son Motl (older by two and a half years than Moishe) and his three daughters all ate, drank and slept their religion. The family lived in a two-story house near the rabbi, and Rafael seemed to want to exceed the rabbi in his fervor. When Rafael marched down the street, in long black caftan and broad-brimmed black hat, the young men of the village marched behind him. In the synagogue he led in singing hymns and sang the loudest in predicting the return to Zion.

Two versions are told of my father's odyssey. In my mother's account, one Sabbath, when all the other male Jews were *davening*, praying, in the synagogue, Moishe decided to take a ride on the back of a pig. The animal couldn't shake him off and ran amok through its Christian owner's vegetable garden.

"The goy heard the noise, came out waving a stick and started to chase Pa." Imagining the scene, my mother would laugh. "He couldn't face his father—the old man was so religious—he couldn't face the townspeople, and he surely couldn't face the farmer. So he ran away from home."

According to my father, he could foresee no future for himself in Radzymin and he had had enough religion to last him his lifetime. He decided to join his three cousins, the Tzudikers, in Warsaw, forty versts away. Mortcha, Phil and Abe, the three sons of his Mimeh Fageh, his Aunt Fay, his mother's sister, had left earlier for the big city to apprentice themselves in different trades.

The four boys lived together, ate together and starved together. Moishe found no trade that suited him. He tried cobbling, but no shoemaker he. He apprenticed himself to a tailor; again he failed.

Their mothers worried about them. One Passover, after Moishe had just turned fourteen, Fageh and Naomi prepared matzoth and kosher delicacies for their sons in Warsaw. After the mothers celebrated their own seders in Radzymin, they delegated sixteen-year-old Motl to deliver the food packages.

Slim Motl, with his high cheekbones, hollow cheeks and sad-looking face, donned his new overcoat and boarded the train. He had no trouble locating the foursome. Hungry, cold and penniless they welcomed him and the food he brought. They even licked their lips the next day over the leftovers. On the third day, though, they faced their customary starvation.

On this bleak morning a lovely dark-haired, dark-eyed beauty walked over from the next block and presented a package to Mortcha, the eldest.

"Your kindness brightens a black Passover, Rachel," said Mortcha as he unwrapped leaves of matzoth and a jar of honey.

In no time the youngsters had wolfed this down as well. By afternoon their hunger pangs had returned.

"How handsome your overcoat is!" Moishe remarked to his brother.

In the next few minutes he persuaded easygoing Motl to part with his prized possession. Running to a pawnbroker, Moishe traded it for six rubles. That evening they sat down to the finest meal of their Warsaw experience.

The next morning, minus his overcoat, Motl returned to Radzymin. "The police stripped me of it on the train," he explained to his parents.

After that holiday season, Moishe did not linger long in Warsaw. Heading west and earning his keep day by day, he traveled from farm to farm, city to city, until, at last, he crossed the border into Germany. There, Berlin drew him like a magnet.

In 1904, this city was buzzing with the excitement of *strickerei*, knitwear. Germans were perfecting automatic knitting. Seventeen-year-old Moishe wangled a job as assistant to the head mechanic in a knitting mill. He hauled bundles of yarn or pulled the carriage of a flat knitting machine back and forth, back and forth. But he also had the rare privilege of tinkering with and exploring the latest attachments for making the *strickmaschinen*, the knitting machines, more automatic.

Ordinarily, Moishe, a Polack, a Jew, would have had a hard time landing any decent job, let alone one in *strickerei*. Each new invention for the knitting machines was closely guarded. Grudgingly, the owners might divulge such trade secrets, but only to a German youth, preferably a Protestant, and then might even pay him a minimal wage. Moishe's chances became possible only because the head mechanic, though a German, had taken a fancy to him. The new apprentice could barely live on the money he earned, and he served as a butt for frequent and vicious gibes. But he did have a job.

In the daytime he learned all he could about flat and circular machines. At night, by gaslight, in his dingy attic room, he read all the books on business he could lay his hands on. Whatever he absorbed reinforced his conviction that someday he would own his own factory, and that when he did he would treat a workingman with the respect due him. His arrogant bosses evidently did not read the same books.

Moishe Fuczyna endured the abuse as long as he could. At twenty he decided to move on, to New York, if possible. He borrowed a passport belonging to a Morris Blum; he borrowed some cash. His fellow workers took up a collection for him when they learned he was leaving. He journeyed to the bustling port of Hamburg to earn passage money. In July 1907, thanks to a price war between transatlantic steamship companies, he paid only ten dollars to embark on a cattle boat bound from Bremerhaven to New York.

On shipboard he befriended an older man, a Galician

house painter, traveling to an established family business in Detroit. The man had both cash and a sister, Rose. Before they parted, "Morris" had negotiated a loan. In return he had pledged to use it in the next few months to travel to Detroit, to meet and seriously consider a romance with Rosie.

Two of his Tzudiker cousins, Abe and Phil, greeted him at Ellis Island; they had emigrated the year before.

Mortcha, the eldest Tzudiker and the first of the three to arrive, had married Rachel. "Do you remember her in Warsaw?" asked Abe. "The girl with the dark hair and dark eyes who came on the black Passover when we had nothing to eat and brought us matzoth and honey?"

Mortcha and Rachel were expecting a baby any day. "She's carrying so big we think she'll have twins," Phil put in. "You're coming with us."

Morris and his two cousins, as in Warsaw, lived together, ate together and starved together—but on the Lower East Side.

With his technical skill, handsome, cocky Morris Blum could get jobs easily enough; keeping them became a problem. He resisted taking direction from German bosses, indeed from any boss. And then, a job meant employment only while the owner had orders to knit. In slack periods, Morris had to scrounge around for any work he could find. One such makeshift he reserved for dire emergencies. It meant going, hat in hand, to a man he despised, the owner of the Peyser Knitting Mills, on 14th Street.

Such an emergency arose during Morris's first winter in New York. He had been laid off. He and the two younger Tzudikers were down to their last cents. As they debated whether to spend two cents for three bagels or for a pack of cigarettes, their landlady evicted them for not paying the rent. Each took his last nickel, paid his fare on the subway and spent the night sprawled on the cane seats of the train.

Early the next morning Morris applied to the big-bellied

Heinz Peyser in his disorderly loft. Peyser knew of the young man's mastery of newfangled knitting machines and hired him instantly. That job, however, lasted only until Morris could recoup his fortunes.

"Machen sie zu dem fenster," Peyser yelled over to him one afternoon.

"Close the window yourself," answered his insolent knitter, who then scooped up his tools and stalked off the job.

In the next few days he found no work that suited him, so he took off for Detroit.

There his shipboard friend welcomed him. "Don't worry about a job," his host assured him. "We'll make a painter out of you."

Moishe tried to learn the art of the paintbrush; at the same time he was dating Rosie. Neither took his fancy. At work in a fine home one day, the novice stepped backward into a bucket of off-white paint and stepped out of it onto an Oriental rug. He fled the scene, as he had fled his childhood home.

Back in New York, Morris found steadier work, at a high-class knitting mill in Newark. The owner rewarded his talent. After a few months he was promoted to shop foreman at an unheard-of salary of seventeen dollars a week. He paid a modest sum to a kinsman with whom he now boarded, sent money to Radzymin for his brother, Motl, to emigrate to the United States and managed to save a little. But even this job did not last.

No boss could contain Morris Blum. Hungry, overambitious and impatient, at twenty-two he seized his first opportunity to go into business with a partner.

In the New Jersey plant he had dealt with Michael Schwer, a salesman for the Singer Sewing Machine Company. Kindly, cultured and capable, this gentleman had represented Singer first in his native Odessa, then in other cities of Russia, and now in the New York area. A thirty-three-year-old bachelor, Schwer had experience in sales, connection throughout the industry, talent in design and three hundred dollars in cash. He had, moreover, deep regard for my father's knowledge of knitting.

Schwer's would-be partner scraped together two hundred dollars. In August 1909, Schwer and Blum founded the S & B Knitting Mills.

As their first location they rented a storefront on East 11th Street, and moved in their first purchase, three secondhand circular machines, on which to knit yard goods.

The first order Schwer brought in, however, was not for yard goods, but for finished sweaters. "We don't know how to make sweaters," Schwer had protested to an insistent customer on Orchard Street.

"Knit the same yard goods," the customer replied. "Put two holes in, one at each side, and a big hole in the middle, and you have a sweater."

Once Schwer had accepted the order, the partners needed yarn. Within the hour Morris took the subway to a Brooklyn dealer.

"I want to buy fifty dollars' worth of yarn," stated the young businessman.

"What credit references do you have?"

"I can't give you any except my word and that of my partner."

The wool merchant, Mr. Rottenberg, questioned him at length. "I'll take a chance on you," he finally decided. "How do you want it delivered?"

"Tie it up in bundles," his newest account directed him. "I'm carrying it back on the subway."

Morris knit S & B's first yard goods, figured out patterns and did the cutting. Schwer had a relative with experience on Merrow machines. He bought a Merrow, and on it this relative sewed the cut pieces together. Before they had completed their first order, Schwer accumulated orders for more sweaters.

Morris returned to Rottenberg. "I have twenty-five dollars for you on account," he announced. "I need another fifty dollars' worth of wool."

He got it. Dragging more bundles of yarn, he went back to 11th Street. The routine of getting orders, pleading for yarn, filling the orders promptly, pleading for payment—all the while establishing a stronger credit rating—continued. For Morris Blum, the inside man, it meant working from five in the morning to eight at night, six and a half and sometimes seven days a week.

One Saturday night Morris actually left his knitting an hour early. Out of the blue a newly landed Radzyminer had showed up in the shop. He had no place to stay and appealed to my father.

"I can offer you only a bathtub to sleep in," said Morris. "But you remember Luffke. Let's go over and talk to him." He escorted the man to the home of their *landsman*.

Two girls happened to drop in while the men were there. They worked at the Triangle with Luffke's daughter. The young ladies were planning a picnic in Central Park the next day. One of them caught Morris's attention.

He looked once, he looked again. Bertha had wide blue eyes, set deep, skin like cream, and light, silky hair piled high. She was so slender he could have encircled her waist with his two hands. As they spoke, she flashed a twist of humor that tickled him.

He asked to take her home; he asked to see her again, then again. Making time for romance was complicated for him by the hours he worked.

"How he knocked himself out!" my mother once told me. "He did the work of three men."

She was being pursued by at least two other young men with serious intentions. One of them, Cousin Sam, not only came from the same *shtetl* she did, but also was a brother of the man who had married her sister, Jennie. But right away Bertha discarded all other beaux, Sam included, and dated no one but Morris.

He would go to see her each evening after he left his shop at eight o'clock. They sometimes visited friends.

"Everyone walked to wherever they had to go in those

days," my mother recalled. "We had no phones. If we didn't find someone home, we walked to the park at 7th Street and Avenue B."

Some evenings, while they were sitting on a park bench, Morris's head would droop and he would fall asleep. Gently, Bertha would nudge him awake.

Their big dates were on Sunday, when he might stop work at two in the afternoon. She would come early to 11th Street with their lunch in a basket.

"Do you have any coat sweaters that need buttons or pockets?" she would call out.

"There's a pile of them on the cutting table just back from the buttonholer," he might tell her as he tied a cone of yarn on with a weaver's knot. "I have to finish this stripe of knitting."

She would determine and mark the positions for the buttons, and sew them on by hand. Though he owned no buttonhole machine, he did have a Singer and the Merrow. Bertha, gifted on the sewing machine, would stitch patch pockets in place on the heavy Shaker sweaters just coming into vogue.

At last he would bring the machines to a stop. He would attack the grease on his hands with yellow Fels-Naphtha, scrub his nails with a stiff brush and wash even his armpits. Finally he would change his clothes and be ready to go.

He would carry the basket as they walked up to where the Fifth Avenue bus began its route at 23rd Street. He would pay a nickel apiece for the fare and up the stairs they would climb, to the top of the double-decker. Sometimes they would ride all the way to the lake at the end of the line, on 110th Street; sometimes they got off earlier to enter Central Park for their outing.

"We may be poor now," he told her, "but someday..."

"I believed him," she told me. "He was so smart. He could see a year in advance. Ahead of Schwer, he knew what yarns and stitches to develop for the next season. He could make those machines talk to him." She paused. "I knew that with his push he would make good someday. He had to."

In a yellowed album are pictures of my parents taken before their marriage. Bertha was photographed among fourteen girls sitting and standing behind Singer sewing machines. All are dressed in the then current mode: ruffled white Gibson-girl shirtwaists and full, dark skirts. My mother, her face framed by soft, light hair, sits near her friend Lena. I labeled the slim attractive young lady "Bertha the Sewing Machine Girl."

Morris, in a bow tie and wearing a straw hat set at a rakish angle, looks cocky and handsome; his eyes dominate the picture. Those eyes are set in a lean face, crowned by full, dark hair. I automatically recall Cousin Sam, my mother's rejected suitor. Blond, good-natured and smiling, he had a *milchidike*, a milklike, face. What a contrast to my *fleishidike*, like red-blooded meat, father!

Morris and Bertha "kept company" for a year and a half. They were married in June 1911. I was born in March 1912.

TWO

The Goldene Medina

BEING BORN ON the Lower East Side in the years before the First World War made a child feel different.

"Lucky, lucky, lucky..." murmured the air I inhaled.

My father first told me of my luck when I was only a few months old. On hot summer evenings neighbors would leave their stifling apartments. Sitting on campstools, empty kegs or seltzer boxes, they would form a semicircle in front of their tenements to banter in Yiddish. My father would come home to his supper later than anyone else's; he would eat; then he and my mother, with me in my carriage, would join the crowd.

One night he swept me up and bounced me high in the air, then dandled me on his knee.

"Aren't you lucky," he crowed, "that I'm no millionaire! If I were rich, your mother and I might have sailed on the *Titanic* with the Astors." He looked around. "And when the *Titanic* sank—and the water was icy, and everybody drowned—where would you be now, my fine young lady?"

How lucky I was to be alive in the *goldene medina!*

Sweatshops, hunger, sickness, even economic depression stacked up as mere trifles compared to what these green-horns had survived. From each new arrival flowed stories of bribing border guards, of fleeing from Cossacks and pogroms, of evading tax collectors, military service, prison, of being subjected to anti-Semitism, ghetto humiliation, demeaning labor. Along with my mother's milk, I sucked in these *bobbe meisen*, these grandmothers' tales.

Castle Garden, where some of these people had disembarked, immediately became corrupted to Kessel Garden. *Kessel* is a tremendous cooking kettle, in which a variety of ingredients simmers together. Kessel Garden had admitted them to a life-size melting pot. They hunkered down on the Lower East Side, earning the privilege of struggle. A message emanated from a man like my father. It said, "You lucky Pole! To have made it to the United States of America!"

There was one other piece of luck a *maidele* like me learned about early. I had a papa and I had a mama. Not every child had both.

My mother, for instance, could have died with the girls in the Triangle Shirtwaist Company fire.

As for fathers, they could get sick and die.

At thirty-two, Mortcha, the eldest Tzudiker, had died of tuberculosis and left a widow with seven children, including three sets of twins. Because the dead man had not yet acquired citizenship, Rachel was granted relief, later called welfare, of only twenty-nine dollars a month. Every Friday, Motl's wife, Dora, took freshly baked challah to her and, now and then, clothes outgrown by my cousins Sammy and Ettie. Regularly my father slipped her cash.

Sometimes fathers went away.

In the first year of my parents' marriage, Motl knocked at their door late one night. "I bring you Mendl," he announced to his brother, introducing an older, dark-bearded man, their first cousin. "He's just off the boat. I'm taking him to my landlady to find him a bed to sleep over."

Mendl spoke briefly to Bertha and compared notes with Morris about mutual relatives and friends back in Radzymin. He mentioned his wife, Malke, whom he had left behind with their three daughters and a fourth child on the way.

The next morning Motl knocked again at the door. With

him he brought a young, clean-shaven, stylishly dressed and very handsome fellow. To my mother he repeated the same introduction, "He's just off the boat."

"How many came off the same boat?" asked my mother. "You just brought one last night."

"It's the same Mendl," said the ever-serious Motl, for once breaking into a smile.

So it was. Overnight Mendl had shaved away his beard, discarded his old clothes in favor of new and simultaneously cast off all inhibitions. Though he had barely recovered his land legs, he asked where he could take dancing lessons.

Malke's two brothers, who lived nearby, disgustedly watched Mendl shed responsibility. They determined to bring their sister and her children to this country themselves, as quickly as possible. War intervened. After four years of harrowing hardships, Malke and her brood left Poland's ravaged countryside for America. While they were on their way, Mendl collapsed on a sidewalk and was rushed to the nearest hospital with a ruptured appendix. For days his life hung in balance.

Malke and the girls arrived at Ellis Island. No Mendl. That very evening her two brothers appeared at our apartment.

"Will you sign a bond for them?" the older one asked my father. "Only if we have the name of a businessman on this paper can Malke and the children wait at Ellis Island until Mendl recovers. Otherwise they'll be shipped back."

My father looked across to my mother; without a word he filled out a paper pledging $5,000 to the government if the family ever went on relief. Malke and her daughters never did; my father never had to lay out a cent.

When Mendl was released from the hospital, he took one look at his European wife and their four ragged daughters, herded them through customs, installed them in his apartment—and fled, to Chicago. The girls never saw their father again. The eldest lived with us for eight months.

I had really good luck; I had a papa and a mama.

Everyone understood, consciously or subconsciously, this

feeling of luck. The strong helped the weak when the second wave of immigrants followed the passage of the pioneers. And many newly arrived greenhorns did not neglect parents, family and *landsleit*, kinfolk, in the old country. Every month my father mailed a postal money order to his folks in Radzymin. My mother and her sister alternated in giving money each month to their parents here.

Morris had brought over his brother Motl in April 1910. Motl's wife, Dora, followed after the birth of their first child that summer. For the six months he was separated from his beloved and his infant son, melancholy Motl got scant comfort from his brother.

"Motl never smiled," recalled my mother, who at that time was dating Morris. "Now and then he would crack a joke, with a perfectly straight expression. The day Dora landed, I did not recognize him. His whole face was lit up like Chanukah lights."

She and her future sister-in-law took to each other immediately. In time, Dora became as dear to her as her own sister.

My father sent passage fare for his sister Elka, and signed other bonds for other countrymen. Years later he helped three young relatives through college. To *mishpochah*, relatives, in distress he and Bertha opened their hearts, their homes, their pocketbooks.

One sacred doctrine they instilled in me was: A family must stick together.

My particular family had another sacred doctrine, equally taken for granted: A patriarch rules the home. Moishe had fled from his father, a patriarch who had decreed the most orthodox regimen for his family. Yet how easily Morris slipped into the role of patriarch himself, decreeing laws for his own family.

He led; Bertha followed. From the moment I was conceived, she had structured my place in their picture. A man like Morris, upward bound, deserved the biggest, brightest and best-behaved child on the block. She and I must always enhance, never handicap, him.

She named me May. "A short, easy name," she told me later. "I copied it from the calendar to make sure I spelled it right."

The calendar hung in, of all places, a hospital. Not for Bertha a midwife or a home delivery! My father had insisted that she use a well-known doctor. That professional dared to charge five dollars; and later his fee went to $10. No matter!

She took me home to an unheated three-room railroad flat. I slept in a carriage, gift of Motl and Dora. That apartment was furnished mainly with wedding gifts. Bertha's brother David had given them their brass bed, Jennie the couch, her parents the *bedgevant:* four pillows, a half-dozen sheets, a European comforter and bedspread, linens, towels and a chamber pot. (The toilet was located one flight down, in the hall.) Pieces of carpet, cut glass and pans came from friends. For $1.25 the young couple had bought a coal-burning stove. By paying installments of $1 a week, they now possessed a round oak dining table with four chairs and a tall sideboard.

This home to which Bertha carried me was located one block east of where my father worked. Our household, after all, revolved around Morris Blum, partner in the S & B Knitting Mills.

For my father, no other field had the glamour of knit goods. He reveled in every facet of the business. In addition to his exhaustingly long regular hours, he might be called back at midnight, by a relief knitter with a bad dropout. Off he would rush. Those circular machines had to keep running.

He scoffed at religious holidays, observed no rituals and would go to work on the holiest of days if it meant getting out a rush order. Once he even went to work on the Day of Atonement.

Near noon that day, he caught the middle finger of his left hand in the carriage of a machine. Clutching the finger as it dangled, he ran to the nearest doctor. By chance, the man had come home from the synagogue for a brief rest. He sewed the skin together and set the bone. By some miracle the finger healed well. After that, though, my mother persuaded my father to observe Yom Kippur, at least.

He poohpoohed light-headed fools like Mendl who took dancing lessons, those who played too much pinochle and those who ran around from one party to the next. He knew, my mother knew and I grasped that he could not afford to dribble away one drop of time, energy or money. As if by osmosis, I absorbed his credo.

To get ahead of the next fellow he had to outcreate, outproduce and outsmart him as well as outguess trends. A new stitch developed first, a new fiber conquered first, a new style presented first—to achieve these challenged him, even as he delivered retail orders in full and ahead of schedule and managed to buy yarn at a lower-than-market price. Morris was competing hard. I, too, must compete hard.

Almost from my first breath my mother enveloped me in the world of *strickerei*. I slept in a sweater she had knit for me. My toes were covered by booties she had crocheted for me. During the night I was kept warm under an afghan, her handiwork. To fashion these she had plied together ends of yarn my father brought home from his shop.

My mother functioned as a self-sacrificing helpmate. A wife had to look nice, cook well, keep a clean home and manage her weekly house money, too. She had twenty-five cents to put in the gas meter, five cents for ice and seven cents for a scuttleful of coal for the stove. Nine cents went to the grocer for two quarts of milk, ladled into a tin pail. She had to cajole bones from the butcher for my father's dog, Peyser. She made sure I looked nice, too. From a peddler with a pushcart she bought ten cents' worth of white eyelet-embroidered broadcloth and, for an extra five cents, a sash and a hair ribbon of just the right shade of blue satin. Late into the night she treadled her Singer to sew my dress. She did not neglect her husband's shop either. Afternoons, while I slept outside in my carriage, she found time to do hand finishing there.

One day "Uncle" Schwer had her pose for a photograph.

He snapped her in a long Shaker coat with a deep sailor collar. She stood half-turned, her hands in the patch pockets, the wide belt crossed over in front, long fringe dangling from its ends. Schwer claimed she looked so lovely that her picture helped him open accounts with R. H. Macy and Marshall Field.

Our knitting family sensed a huge pendulum swinging back and forth across the horizon. In one direction its swing would bring us good fortune; in the other, disaster. We had to rock with these cycles.

In 1912, the year I was born, we suffered poverty, sometimes not having enough to eat. By 1913, the partners had moved to an Avenue A storefront with twice the space of the old one. Behind a pair of whitewashed windows, on a grease-soaked floor, stood five machines—to the three circulars had been added two semiautomatic flats. Whenever the flats stopped, a hired knitter pulled the carriages back and forth, made the necessary changes and set them going again. The mill was filling orders for more and more Shakers. Business was looking up.

By 1914, S & B Knitting Mills occupied half a large loft in a building on Broadway. At the same time, my father moved our family to a sunny three-room apartment in the Bronx.

Some happy images from the 159th Street days come to mind. We had our own bathroom—on the left as we entered. Straight ahead was a large, bright, comfortable kitchen, our favorite room. Next came the dining room, largely ignored except when company came. Beyond it was the bedroom, where my small bed—no crib for me—stood in one corner.

In the kitchen we ate at our round oak table, which was protected by a white oilcloth cover. My mother and I had breakfast and lunch there together. For supper we always waited for my father. He would arrive long after seven and spend much time washing up. There was little conversation until after he ate his main course. When he needed something, he never called my mother by name. Instead, he would grunt or motion to get her attention. Ma, who called him Morris (Mawrrriss) or Moishe, kept quiet, too, and busied herself anticipating his needs.

As a typical meal she might serve him chicken soup, then the upper quarter of the chicken with mashed potatoes and sweet-and-sour cucumber salad. He would finish up with stewed pears or a fruit compote. With his glass of tea, he would munch on a thick slab of pumpernickel, liberally smeared with chicken fat.

Between sips of tea and bites of pumpernickel, he would begin to talk of the day's happenings. Often he grumbled about Schwer, the *richtike*, generous, spender. My mother always defended Schwer. She was accustomed to acting as peacemaker. Pa might grimace, but he would let Ma soothe his ruffled feathers. I would breathe sighs of relief, for I could bear no slurs against my beloved Uncle Schwer. My dearest possession had come from him.

One stormy afternoon two big cartons were delivered from F. A. O. Schwartz. How much brown paper, excelsior and shredded newspaper Ma and I had to pull out! From one package came a round brown table, and from the other a pair of matching chairs—all scaled to my size. Twisted iron framed the top of the table and its legs. The chairs had twisted iron backs just like those I had seen in the ice-cream parlor. The card read, "To May, on her 3rd Birthday. From Uncle Schwer." I loved them.

After supper Pa would sit in his rocker with an apple and a paring knife. I would draw up one of my ice-cream-parlor chairs to sit beside him. Gently rocking, he would peel the apple while I held on to one end of the skin and watched to see how long and unbroken a ribbon he could dangle. As he sectioned out a wedge of apple for me he would tease me. From him issued a steady flow of jokes and ridicule, waiting for my retorts and sparks to fly. And yet there were moments as perfectly amazing as an endless ribbon of apple peel dangling from a child's fingers, the whole apple naked before it was cut.

I used to bathe with my father. He loved to get into a hot tub with a stiff, long-handled scrubbing brush. He would scour the skin of his back until it turned an angry pink. With Packer's tar shampoo he would massage his scalp vigorously until he changed the heavy liquid into a yellow foam crown. I still remember his elbow flexing up and down as he worked the brush over his shoulders. I remember the thicket of black hair on his chest and the dark tufts of hair in his armpits. I remember the sudsy water and my delight in sharing it with him.

He stopped letting me bathe with him when I reached four or five. "You began to ask too many questions," my mother told me.

On a Saturday morning Pa sometimes took me along with him to the Factory. My hand in his, I would trot along beside him to the Third Avenue El. My bulky thighs got wattled sitting on the cane seats. Somewhere, we changed to a subway and got out at Prince Street. Passing a store where gold letters spelled out SUSSMAN—YARN DEALERS, we turned the corner to Broadway and headed for our building. An elevator operator in splendid livery took us up to our mill on the fifth floor.

First, I would search out Uncle Schwer. He always had a book, a gift in Schwarz wrapping or some shiny quarters stashed away. Hazel, in the office, would supply pencils, fat crayons and scrap paper. Al, the yarn man, would let me bounce on the overstuffed bundles of yarn. Claudia, the winder, gave me empty cones to stack in tottering towers. Her sister Anna, a stitcher, saved odd buttons for me. I could sew these on a rainbow of colored swatches of cutting waste.

I thrilled—and still do—to fat spools of yarn jiggling on the spindles of relentlessly revolving circular machines, the cones dwindling in size as the threads vanish through the carriage to reappear in waves of bright colors and bold Jacquard designs. In awe I would gaze at my Uncle Motl as he managed this magic, or at Emil, a swaggering giant of a man, as he ground a machine to a halt when he saw that a needle had dropped a stitch.

The pride and self-confidence of these people as they worked at their machines cast a spell over me. It enhanced the regard I later had for any worker at any work station.

Around noon my father took me for lunch. Sometimes Uncle Schwer joined us. We would walk a few doors north on Broadway to a cafeteria bright with dazzling lights, long white tables and a spotless white tile floor. I would eat quietly while my father and his partner talked business.

My father once made a pitch for that new yarn, rayon.

"I hate that shiny stuff. And what prices they charge!" Schwer objected, thoughtfully fingering his mustache. "Don't order too many pounds; just get a sample lot from Sussman."

"Dreck [Shit]!" my father agreed. "But what can you do when sweaters have gone pfft? I'll have to figure out a way to make long fringe for the bottom of the rayon dresses."

Someday I would follow my father's tracks, I thought. Someday I would start my own business—knitting, of course—and, of course, with a partner.

I pictured myself on an endless tightrope, my body wheeling, turning and flexing hidden muscles to keep myself perpetually in balance. I, too, would cope with each emergency, overcome each disaster and come out triumphant.

Three rules governed my upbringing. One said, "Bigger is better"; the next, "Be a good girl," and the third, "Bright is right."

I seemed bright enough to delight both my parents. At 11th Street I had crept early, walked early, talked early.

"You were forever going "kotchavay,'" my mother recalled one day. "Kotchavay" was my term for "across the way." "From the first minute you crept, you crept 'kotchavay' to my friend Lena's apartment. When you walked, you pulled me 'kotchavay on lemon shit.'" The latter meant "across the way on 11th Street."

"How your father carried on about you! To each one he had to tell every little trick of yours." Then she added, "He was very proud of you. He treated you almost as if you were a boy."

About being a good girl, I early grasped that my best

efforts would never fully satisfy my mother. She constantly compared me—with cousins, neighbors' children and friends. This one kept her clothes cleaner; that one never wet her bed; another obeyed her mama better. She deeply embedded in me a sense of my inadequacy to live up to what she expected.

Once, she confessed a trick she had used. "You would never hold my hand, even when you were two. You had to run ahead to the end of the block. There, at least, you would wait for me. But one day," and she laughed, "I really scared you."

Running ahead to a corner, I had collided with a small girl running from the side street, a girl exactly my size and pitch black. Never before had I seen a Negro. I sidled back to my mother.

"Who is this?" I asked, in Yiddish, naturally.

"She's a *maidele* who didn't listen to her mama."

Fifty-five years later, on a snowy winter's day, as I was crossing Fifth Avenue at 14th Street, a United Parcel Service truck, beating the traffic light, hit me. The impact sent my body flying through the air and sliding across the ice for forty feet. I landed on my skull, fractured it and regained consciousness in a hospital.

How could this happen to me? was my first thought. I waited for the green light. Honest, Ma, I was a good girl.

For "Bigger is better," nature had given me a physical edge. I grew quickly, grew tall, strong and solid. My size and my physique gratified my parents, certainly my mother, who sewed my clothes.

"Other women would buy more expensive materials. Then they wondered why on their children the dresses never hung right; but on you they fitted just so," she once said. "If their kids were skinny, the sashes would slide all over. When I put a black velvet sash on you, it stayed in place as if glued there. You had the fit built in."

She had my portrait taken while we lived on 159th Street. I stand on a dark, covered wooden bench with a broad armrest at one side. Three books are piled at an angle on the armrest. Holding a bunch of violets, my left hand rests on the books. My Buster Brown hair is swept back from bangs and caught up in a generous bow of white ribbon. Wide, light eyes look out solemnly from a full face. A heart-shaped locket, dangling from a chain around my neck, falls on the lace vestee of my white broadcloth dress. The dress has a blouse effect, formed by that wide sash of black velvet, resting firmly on my hips. A narrow ruffle of dainty lace edges the short puffed sleeves. A lace hem, as wide as the sash, ends in points, twenty-three of them, spaced every inch, across the front.

I look all girl, a sturdy four-year-old.

From this period one event, delicious but scary, comes to mind. One stormy, snowy winter evening my parents and the couple who lived across the hall decided to shop at a once-a-week outdoor market. These friends brought along Milton, their son my age. From some hidden storage space in the basement, Milton's father brought a sled to the sidewalk. Milton and I, in heavy winter clothes, were snuggled into a blanket. I kept my hands warm in a white fur muff.

Our sled was pulled across a broad avenue to the base of a long, steep hill. The two men took turns hauling us up, over cobblestones well covered by snow. At the top, around a turn, we unexpectedly came to a thronged square, illuminated by overhead strings of lights. Along three sides rough booths were lined up, each with its own merchant, merchandise and clientele. Released from the sled, Milton and I began running around to see what people were selling in each booth.

One of these held a tank filled with water in which live fish were swimming. Guarding them stood a burly woman in a heavy Shaker sweater with a knit scarf wound around her neck. For each customer she would dip her hand net into the tank, capture a fish, weigh it on a crude scale, then dump it out quickly to wrap it in newspaper. Milton and I could not pull ourselves away.

After a while our mothers came to her booth. As we watched, the woman caught two fish, wrapped each one separately, then together in one package. After this last purchase, Milton's father once more swathed us in our blanket cocoon and set us on the sled. This time, though, we shared the space with all the shopping. We started downhill.

The package with the fish in it wouldn't stay put. It lay still for a moment, then gave a sudden start. Every time it did, Milton and I giggled. The men were joking back and forth; the women, walking behind the sled, were laughing—all prompted by the dancing fish.

Back home, the women divided their bundles. At last we were alone in our own kitchen. My father sat in his rocker with a newspaper while my mother went to the sink. On a wooden board at one side of it she unwrapped the fish, which still twitched and jerked. In one hand she grasped a rolling pin, in the other a cleaver. Pow! She struck with the pin and stunned the fish. Next, with a mighty blow, she wielded the cleaver and severed its head.

The headless body flew to the floor, landing right at my feet. But it didn't stay there. With a great heave, it flew a distance, landed, and jumped again. I jumped, too. I jumped over to my father and held tight to his knee. The tail still wriggled when my mother picked it up and carried it back to the sink. When she began to scale and clean it, the fish lay quiet at last. And when it did, I dared to loosen my grip on my father's knee.

The scaredy-cat *maidele* alternated with a bold tomboy. Beginning with the mild days of spring, our double kitchen windows generally stood open. My ice-cream table, with its matching chairs, was positioned beneath them. My mother served me lunch there one day. This consisted of a mound of mashed potatoes, sprinkled with red paprika and oozing with butter, the center scooped out for a great blob of sour cream. I had finished and was drinking my milk and gazing at the fire escape outside the window. Suddenly, from overhead, I heard a voice in glorious song, embroidered with the chirping of a bird.

While my mother busied herself elsewhere, I ventured out on the fire escape and followed the iron steps up two flights, until I came to another open window, in an apartment identical to ours. Inside, I saw a large, blonde lady and, near the window, a canary in a birdcage. Both were singing their hearts out.

Mrs. Strazinski (known as Mme. Tetrazzini to me) welcomed me in, fed me cookies, and put on a concert for me. She poured forth an aria; the canary warbled along with her. After a while she and I went down the regular stairs and she restored me to my frantic mother.

Later that summer, on a broiling Sunday afternoon, with the same windows open, my father was trying to snooze. Again we heard singing. This time it came from below—a man's voice, completely off key.

"That dumb Polack!" muttered my father. "Why doesn't he shut up?"

I slipped out of the apartment, descended two flights to the street floor and rang the bell of an apartment in our line. A giant of a man in a white union suit answered my ring, overflowing the doorway.

"My papa says you're a dumb Polack," I told him, craning my neck to look up at him. "He says you should shut up." I turned on my heel and climbed back upstairs.

For a long time my parents did not understand why the tenant on the ground floor refused to talk to them.

In April 1917, the United States declared war on Germany. In May, Congress passed the Selective Service Act, to mobilize an army. And in July, Morris Blum received greetings from the United States Army. He was summoned to appear before his draft board.

My mother and I went with him when he reported. We entered a three-story house, set back on a broad lawn, one of a row on Eastern Parkway in Brooklyn. With many others, we waited in an anteroom to be called. When Pa's turn came, we found ourselves in a large room with an American flag draped across a bay of three windows. Behind a massive desk sat a stern official who asked my father many questions.

At one point my father hoisted me in his arms to show me to the man. We left; my mother and father seemed very sad.

Afterward they repeated every detail of the interview to Uncle Schwer. They held little hope of my father's staying. What would happen when he went overseas? Schwer volunteered to keep the S & B Knitting Mills afloat until his partner returned. My mother could work in the factory; I could go live with my grandmother.

Dramatically, just days before Pa's departure date, the government proclaimed a new ruling: married men with children were exempted from the draft.

May, the heroine, had saved Pa from having to cross the ocean to fight for Uncle Sam against the Kaiser. What joy! What thanksgiving! What a fuss was made over me!

This drama had been enacted against a change in setting. Before dawn one morning in early May, our family had stolen out of our flat on 159th Street. Very quietly, so as not to wake the janitor, we had tiptoed down the stairs and past his apartment. My father had used the rent money to put a deposit on a *cuchalein*, a do-your-own-cooking room, in Coney Island. When summer ended, my mother told me, we would move back to the Bronx—to a larger apartment, where I would have my own room.

My father's search for this next home had marked time while his draft status remained in doubt. By September, however, he had resumed looking. During the interval the housing situation had worsened radically. No more buildings were going up; people were not moving; rents had risen. My parents finally settled on a five-room flat on the top floor of a four-story walk-up in the North Bronx.

The apartment, on a windy corner, was too large, the rent too high and the location more distant than they had planned. Four of the rooms were bunched together: bedroom, parlor, dining room and kitchen. I slept in the bedroom, my parents in the parlor. Down a long corridor was a bathroom and, still farther down, at the entrance, a second bedroom. As a temporary measure, they rented this to "the boarder," a quiet man who slipped in and out unobtrusively.

When I entered school in February 1918, I skipped kinder-garten. "Such a big girl!" the admissions woman told my mother. "I'll put her in first grade."

All by myself I walked to and from school. Reaching Prospect Avenue one day, on my way home for lunch, I found the street thronged with people, as if everyone had emptied out of every house. Women were dancing with each other; men were throwing hats in the air. I saw one hat trampled on. The owner didn't even care; he put his arm around a woman's waist and twirled her around.

The fruit-store man on the corner was yelling, "The war is over! The war is over!" I skipped all the way home.

During the war days, when Pa took me to the mill on a Saturday, I would see lengths of khaki goods spewing from the circulars. After that magic day, olive drab disappeared. Shiny yard goods, instead, came pouring down in bright colors. At war's end consumers hungered for new fibers, novelty knits and vivid shades. The S & B Knitting Mills kept in step with fashion.

The partners took over the entire fifth floor of their building. When the floor below emptied, they occupied that one as well. No longer did they argue about whether to buy two or four machines. To fill the demand for jersey yard goods, they purchased banks of new equipment. They employed more people, and Michael Schwer and Morris Blum began to prosper.

Now my father could indulge us with luxuries. One day I came home from school to find a Steinway piano in our parlor. The spinster lady who gave lessons to my friend Blanche was promptly engaged to teach me. On another day the floor in our parlor was covered with a lush blue Chinese rug.

Ma and I had to outdo ourselves to achieve the heights to which Pa was rising. Ma, still slender and girlish, took pains with her appearance and with mine. She also worked hard adorning our home. One linen tablecloth she embroidered had ninety-two scallops and 974 eyelets.

I did my part, too. I excelled in school. But I had unex-pected assistance. A policeman's daughter lived next door to us. Three years older than I, Ruth loved to play school. We would set up class on the stairs from our landing, she the teacher, I the pupil.

We started with my reader. "Dickie Dare went to school," I sounded out. From there we went on to "On the way he met a cow. 'Moo, moo,' said the cow." By the end of the first week Ruth had steered me through the entire book.

We tackled arithmetic. Each day in regular school my teacher had us fill pages with one number at a time, beginning with zero. My play-teacher, meanwhile, was initiating me into plus and minus. While the class struggled to write sevens or eights, I asked Miss Kleppner about carrying numbers in subtraction.

I skipped half the first grade, skimmed through a second-year, rapid-advance class, and began third grade before I was seven. When I studied piano, I soon played harder pieces than Blanche, or even my cousin Ruth, Aunt Jennie's daughter. Each day my list of successes grew.

My mother topped me one spring. She delivered a baby boy!

With my brother's coming, my parents were transformed into strangers. The full force of it hit me when Aunt Jennie and I visited Ma in the hospital. Through the open door I saw my father cradling a dozen long-stemmed American Beauties in his outstretched arms. A nurse plucked these one by one from his bundle to arrange them in a tall vase. My mother beamed as she watched. She lay in bed, to the foot of which was hooked a bassinet. A baby was stretched out in it sleeping.

Never before or after did I see Pa come bearing roses. Never before or after did I hear him address my mother as Bertha. Nor had I ever seen him kiss, embrace or even touch her. Now he was talking and laughing with her. When he sat down by her bed, his hand rested on her arm. No trace remained of the stabbing skeptic or the constant critic. Unrestrained joy shone on his face; unaccustomed boasts dropped from his lips.

He, who never wasted a word, gloated over having the biggest baby on that floor, a *Wunderkind* the nurses had dubbed "the Prince," and over the fountains of milk that gushed from my mother's breasts to feed this nine-pound marvel.

Ma looked different, too. She had blown up like a balloon, from perhaps 120 pounds to some 200. With Aunt Dora's help, she had fashioned a navy-blue cape that expanded prodigiously with her during her pregnancy. I had thought she had a funny kind of sickness that would go away. It never did. She retained at least sixty pounds.

At the hospital my mother had a request to make. "We named him 'Tevya Mortcha,'" she told Aunt Jennie and me.

"Tevya after Theodore Roosevelt and Mortcha for the oldest Tzudiker," my father interrupted.

"We need a nice name for the Mortcha," my mother went on. "I don't like Theodore Mordecai. If this baby ever becomes famous and wants to drop the Blum, we have to give him an American name that would look good in lights, like those on a Broadway theater. What should it be?"

I suggested "Morton" and assured her that, whether my brother became a stage star or a band leader, the name Ted Morton would look great in lights.

The stardom my mother already assumed for my brother set me thinking. A woman, I realized, attained her greatest heights when she bore a child, especially a man-child. Someday I would have many children, nurse each one at my breast and pray for sons among them.

Then a jarring thought sprang up to blot this one out. When I was born, had my father wanted to welcome, not a daughter, but a Crown Prince?

For my first seven years Pa had treated me as he would have a son. Overnight I had been dethroned. Had I been born the wrong sex?

After she brought her infant son home, Ma and Pa moved into the bedroom; they moved the baby and his cradle in there, too. I was transferred to the bedroom now vacated by the boarder, that faraway room separated from the others by the lengthy corridor. What a fine reward, my mother assured me, for a big girl! I did not appreciate it.

Each night, Ma would come, bearing a glass of hot milk, to tuck me in. As I sipped it—slowly, to stretch out my private moments with her—the hot creamy milk would form streaky white patterns on the tumbler. I liked watching the random shapes. Sometimes I complained of a bellyache or a grippey feeling. Then my mother would lie down alongside me and rub my shoulder. Sometimes I even complained when I didn't hurt too badly. At last Ma would turn out the light and leave. I can still picture the snowflakes against my windowpanes in winter; they, like my milk, etched irregular patterns on the glass.

How isolated I felt! I began to keep on piece after piece of underclothing before donning my nightgown. First my underpants, then my undershirt, then I extended this to petticoat and stockings. One night Ma caught a glimpse of a black toe. After that she made me remove all the extras.

In the dark I lay panic-stricken. To go to the bathroom I had to leave my warm, safe bed and journey down a narrow, black hall. If you were not a one-hundred-percent good girl, boogeymen might get you. They crouched in the shadows inside and outside my room. For a long time I was terrified.

I reacted to my change in status in two ways. I revved up my motor to fight for a first-born's rightful place, but I also reverted to helpless little girl; I became a chronic bed-wetter.

My mother soon cast me in a new role, that of her chief assistant. When she first returned from the hospital, neighbors dropped in with food they had cooked, bread and cake they had baked and gifts for the infant. The policeman's wife next door loaned us an electric heater. The amply built grocery woman from the corner store below walked up four flights to tell my mother that she had only to rattle the ropes in the dumbwaiter shaft they shared, and "whatever you need I'll send up right away." Aunt Jennie, Aunt Dora and the neighbors continued to help my mother for several days.

After that she depended on me. But now I played only a minor character in our family saga.

"Take the baby for an airing," my mother would say.

Down four flights of stairs—bump, bump, bump—she would push the carriage, with the baby in it. Holding the front end and descending backward, I would help her. Then off I would go. Steering that carriage, I traversed strange neighborhoods, even crossed dangerous intersections. When I returned, I stowed the carriage in the stairwell for my father to bring up later and carried my brother up the four flights.

One autumn day a street photographer snapped a picture of Teddy and me. He sat erect and regal, with a smile; I firmly gripped the handle of his stroller. The man asked for my name and address, then surprised my mother with the picture. It showed I had wandered at least a half-mile from home.

Before Ted's birth, Pa had occasionally taken me with him to the movies on a Sunday afternoon. We had seen Alma Gluck and Efrem Zimbalist in *Humoresque.* I had cried. On another Sunday I accompanied my father on the subway to Broadway and 50th Street, where the size, magnificence and sparkling crystal chandeliers of the newly opened Capital Theatre had awed me.

No longer did I get such treats. Instead, while my mother prepared Sunday dinner, Pa wheeled Ted's carriage into Crotona Park. Dutifully, I trotted alongside. Pa would sit on a sunny bench talking to other men guarding other carriages. I would run to Indian Lake to play with children there.

The pattern was interrupted on one Sunday outing when my brother began to cough and cough, a racking cough that would not stop. Pa lifted Ted out of his carriage, but he still coughed. He gave him some sugared water; Ted kept coughing. He patted his back. Nothing helped. Frantically, he put the baby back in his carriage and, with me beside him, ran, literally ran, home. The doctor, when he finally came, diagnosed whooping cough. I remember that Teddy's cough lasted a long time. Even more vividly I remember my father running home like a scared rabbit.

"Help me carry the wash up to the roof," my mother would ask.

Laundry took up a big chunk of her day. All dirty wash, including sheets and my father's shirts, had to be scrubbed and pounded on the corrugated washboard. On the stove, covering two burners, a huge copper-bottomed cauldron boiled away. Now and then, with a long-handled wooden spoon, my mother stirred the diapers in it.

She would wring out a great load of clothes and heap them into a wicker basket. Each of us would grasp a handle and haul it up one flight to the roof. Holding one or two clothespins in her mouth, Ma precisely positioned each piece on the lines. First came diapers, then Teddy's shirts, socks and bellybands, followed by all the rest. Sparkling white, the parade of clothes whipped in the wind, ready to pass inspection.

"Bring down the wash," I heard later. Into the same wicker basket I would heap laundry and pins. On top I would pile diapers, each one carefully folded.

On a fine afternoon, women met on the roof. Hanging their wash or waiting for it to dry, they exchanged small talk. My mother and I often hoisted baby, carriage and campstools up there to join them.

One late afternoon on the roof we heard a terrible commotion from the inner courtyard. I ran to the edge with the rest. My mother looked at the scene and pulled me back. A small boy had fallen out of a third-story window. Crouched over his smashed, still body was his mother, letting out bloodcurdling shrieks. A growing crowd encircled her.

The janitor phoned for the police. When they came, they summoned an ambulance. Too late! The child had died immediately.

Much later I crept downstairs and stole into the courtyard. Every trace of the tragedy had vanished. Turning to leave, I saw, off to one side, a curious, glittering, dime-size object. I stared at it. It was the iris of an eye—the boy's eye.

"Run downstairs to the store," my mother would say. A year after the armistice, sugar was still being rationed. Our half a pound of brown sugar, in a neatly tied brown paper bag, could not be entrusted to the dumbwaiter. I had to run down and fetch it.

Then again, my mother sometimes yelled a large order down the shaft to the Cohens, and if they didn't fill it soon enough, I would be dispatched to hurry them along. I was accustomed to rambling in and out of the store at will.

One August evening, when my father was sitting with us in the sidewalk crowd next to the grocery store, Mrs. Cohen buttonholed him and drew him into the store. Gravely, she told him of seeing me sneak behind the glass-enclosed candy counter and steal some penny candy.

"Is this true?" Pa asked me.

I couldn't answer; I stammered with guilt. I had done it only two or three times.

"Get upstairs," he ordered.

As we climbed he began unbuckling his belt. In our apartment he gave me the first licking of my life.

Humiliated and unhappy, I sized up my situation. I had many more jobs and much less time for myself than I had had before Teddy was born.

How I missed having fun with my friends Blanche, Sadie and Emily! During the war we had had few new playthings and had improvised. We four had found empty spools, hammered four nails on each and vied to knit the longest horse rein. We had saved India rubber bands, carefully stretched the loops over a core and then over each other, and so constructed our own balls. Those rubber-band balls seemed to bounce almost to the sky. We invented rhymes and games to go with them. I owned a favorite potsy for hopscotch; Blanche and Emily specialized in playing jacks; Sadie would borrow her mother's clothesline for double dutch. Now that I was burdened with the baby carriage, I had little leisure to play with the girls.

I missed, too, the privilege of walking my teacher part of the way home from school. I had earned this by sitting in the first seat of the first row. Because of my brother, I now had to go straight home. As I left, I would see Solemitus, the girl behind me, waiting to escort Miss Fitzpatrick.

One day I stood on a corner that was half in sunshine, half in shadow. Beyond, extended an empty lot, fenced off from the sidewalk by a patchwork of boards. In the sunshine my brother lay sleeping in his carriage. In the shadow I stood brooding.

"The happy days of childhood!" I muttered. "Humph! I wish I were dead! Ma and Pa never listen to me.... They're so mean.... They don't understand and they never will."

I considered various ways of killing myself. Maybe I should jump from our roof. But I remembered the splattered body of the boy in the courtyard. Maybe I should swallow some of the lye in the can under the sink. It was marked POISON, with a skull and crossbones underneath.

"They'll feel sorry—when it's too late. But how can I leave this poor baby to those monsters? Who else can protect him from them?"

So, for the sake of my infant brother, I decided I would not do away with myself, not yet. I would battle for the recognition I deserved. I would show my parents. I would show everyone else.

Instead, my father did the showing. He came home early one day and waved a legal-looking document in my mother's face.

"We're moving," he announced.

"Where? When?" asked my mother, shocked.

"I bought a house in New Rochelle," he told us.

"You what?" she shrieked. "Where in New Rochelle? How could you do this without even asking me?"

"This weekend I'll take you there. A beautiful house with three bedrooms. You'll see it for yourself."

"How will I manage without a friend or a relative nearby? Where will I shop for groceries, for vegetables? Where will I find a kosher butcher? *Moishe, wie crechst du mit die krimma fees?*"

Morris may have been creeping with crooked feet, but he cut all her objections short. She would hire a maid; we could well afford one. He was buying a car; she would learn to drive. On North Avenue, not more than five or six blocks away, he had seen a grocery. May was a big girl now; she could run there on errands. On Thursday nights he would drive her to the kosher butcher. Once they had a car, they could visit the *mishpochah* in the Bronx.

"I want the best for my family," my father said.

Wherever Morris was creeping, we crept with him.

From the Bronx apartment we moved to a white colonial house with green shutters, located in New Rochelle's choicest residential section and near its finest grammar school, where at age nine, I would enter sixth grade. When the principal interviewed me, however, he placed me in a special class that completed sixth and seventh grades in a single year.

A Jewish kid from the Bronx, I soon discovered, is not quickly accepted by the WASP suburban establishment; nor does a nine-year-old mix easily with eleven- and twelve-year-olds. A classmate, for instance, handed out party invitations to all but four girls in our class. I was one of the four. For my birthday party, amid a pleasing buzz of attention, I handed out twenty invitations, omitting no one. Three girls showed up.

My parents could not or would not help me. Although Pa joined the Benevolent and Protective Order of Elks and downed beer with the best of his brothers, their benevolence and protection ended abruptly at the front door of the lodge. Never did one Elk stray outside his preserve into our home.

My mother made a full-time job of keeping our home scrupulously clean from top to bottom. No maid for her! "Any extra person around the house will only get in my way," she said to my father.

Pa splurged on an open green Studebaker. When he urged her to take driving lessons, she claimed, "I don't have enough hours in the day."

I have vivid memories of some of the early rides we took. Once we climbed an embankment ten or twelve feet above street level while my mother shouted, "Morris, the road is down there!" Another time, a chicken flew excitedly in front of the car, then plummeted down with a thud. As my father managed to brake the car, an old farmer, waving his straw hat, came running out of his house and yelled guttural curses in German. My father paid for the dead hen, of course.

Perhaps such episodes tended to discourage my mother. With one alibi or another she put off that first lesson, and did not learn to drive in New Rochelle.

She made few friends, except for immediate neighbors. She might have met a congenial group in temple, but neither she nor my father attended. She waited for others to seek her out. They didn't. We spent each weekend visiting Aunt Dora or Aunt Jennie in the Bronx.

I had begun to read books to Teddy and to play games with him.

"Play with Teddy upstairs," my mother said one stormy day. "I have to wash the kitchen floor."

Obediently, I helped Teddy climb the flight of stairs. We began a game of tag in the upper hall. Crouching and making weird noises, I would spring toward him from one end. Giggling and squealing, he would run for the bathroom door at the other end.

He swerved once to see how close I was getting. Teetering too near the stairwell, he toppled headlong down the curving flight, his body crashing on each step. He lay on the landing and howled.

"What did you do to him?" screamed my mother as she rushed from the kitchen.

"I didn't do anything," I said. "We were playing and he fell backward."

"Did you throw him down the stairs? Listen how he's screaming."

"I didn't, Ma. I was yards away when he fell."

She began to comfort Teddy, ran to call the doctor, came back to comfort him some more, ran back to call a taxi. During the wait for the cab, while my brother moaned, she phoned my father.

"I'm leaving work," he told her. "I'll get to the doctor as fast as I can."

The physician took his time examining the two-year-old, while my mother and I stood by anxiously.

"A fractured left shoulder," he reported at last. "He should stay overnight in the hospital. He'll be all right," he reassured my mother.

Just then my father rushed in. "What happened?" he asked.

"May threw him down the stairs," my mother told him.

"I didn't! I didn't! I was nowhere near."

I clamored in vain. Bertha, the caretaker of Morris's precious son, had to find a face-saver. I later heard "May threw him down the stairs in New Rochelle" repeated and repeated.

By the second autumn in New Rochelle I was beginning to be better accepted by my peers. At ten, representing my school, I won second place in a citywide spelling bee. My classmates, the teacher, even the principal seemed proud of my achievement. A girl I liked handed out invitations to her birthday party including everyone in her room. I hesitated to accept, but after her mother telephoned mine and insisted that I come, I went, and had a fine time. I had made instant friends with the Harvey twins across the street. By winter I had another close friend, two blocks away. Amy and I would take our sleds and go sliding down Coligny Hill, the steepest one nearby.

One treasure I held dear above all. From a neighbor, Pa had gotten a fox terrier puppy. I cuddled him, looked into his soulful eyes, set in the white blaze on his brown forehead, and claimed him for my own.

When I ran to Bohack's on North Avenue to buy a five-cent loaf of Grandmother's Bread, Prince ran along with me.

When I explored the forest around the lake behind school, Prince trotted over the rocks and nosed through the underbrush around me. Sometimes on Sunday my father caught bass or carp, with his bare hands, in the lake and clubbed them. I took charge of the burlap bag into which he threw them, while Prince yipped with excitement. On weekday afternoons, when I played with Lillian and Louise Harvey, Prince, of course, romped with us.

One spring day the twins and I were exploring the woods at the corner. I collected some shiny odd-shaped stones; Louise dissected mushroom growths; Lillian had climbed the low branches of a tree. Prince was off chasing chipmunks. Suddenly we became aware of old Mrs. Van Winkle, from the dark house on the far side of the woods.

"You're on my property," she shrilled. "I want you off."

Prince barked.

"Be quick about it," she rasped.

Prince jumped up, putting his paws on her coat. I called him off, and we left.

Mrs. Van Winkle did not rest her case there; that evening she phoned. "Your dog nipped me," she told my father.

"I'm very sorry," my father apologized, using his most contrite voice. "I'm surprised. He's never done such a thing before."

"I'm filing a complaint," she said, and hung up.

"He just jumped on her coat," I told Pa. "Let her show you where Prince nipped her. She can't. She's always crabbing."

"I'm not starting up with any neighbors," my father said.

"What are you going to do?" I asked anxiously.

"You'll see," he replied. "Hold your horses."

That Saturday afternoon Pa announced that we were going on a picnic. We drove a great distance and came to a heavily wooded area.

"We'll eat here," he decided.

Ma spread an old khaki blanket on the ground and placed treats from her hamper on it. We ate; we stretched our legs. Pa played with Prince, throwing sticks for him to fetch.

"Get in the car," he suddenly ordered.

Obediently, we got in, except Prince, who was still chasing after sticks. My father hurled a last stick. It went far. Prince raced after it. Pa cranked the starter of the car until the engine caught and jumped in. With a jerk we lunged off, leaving Prince behind.

"Stop the car!" I shrieked. "He's running after us; he can't catch up."

Pa said nothing. He stepped more heavily on the gas.

"Please stop the car," I pleaded. "Listen to the way he barks." I began to cry.

My father said nothing, just drove faster.

Prince's barks grew fainter; I cried louder.

That's something I can never forget.

In June, at the age of eleven, I graduated from Mayflower Elementary School. To commemorate the occasion, we posed for a family portrait. Center front, in an armchair, sat my father. My brother perched beside him on a pedestal, grinning, one foot under the other. Proud and placid, my mother stood at the rear to the right. Balancing her in the left rear, scowling, I clutched my beribboned diploma.

That scowl may have reflected my response to my parents' pressure. At times, though, I may have misjudged their demands.

My graduation had been marred for me. Top honors had gone to our class president. Judging by marks alone, I should have won second honors. But my name had not been called out at the ceremonies. I puzzled over how to explain this to my parents. Should I blame anti-Semitism or my not belonging to the "in" group? Though they said nothing, I felt I had failed them.

One Sunday, shortly after this, we visited Aunt Jennie— "going to the opera," my father called it. While playing with my cousin Ruth, I could overhear the grownups talking over tea. My father mentioned my graduation—with never a word about my not having been named salutatorian. My mother bragged about my being the youngest in the class. I could hardly believe my ears. They didn't sound the least bit disappointed. What relief I felt!

Aunt Jennie walked down with us to our Studebaker when we left. I started to kiss her good-bye—then kept on kiss, kiss, kissing her nonstop, hugging and clinging to her.

"A real kissing bug," she said. She didn't stop me, just held me tight.

Unexpectedly, my parents deposited me at a sleep-away camp. I remember it was July 4, because I arrived at Camp Allegro in the midst of a fireworks display. Only on Labor Day did I learn why I had been shipped off. My parents had gone househunting.

After two years in New Rochelle, my father had surrendered. Early in September he drove us to the new house—in the Bronx. I saw a two-family, red-brick dwelling, one of four identical free-standing units. Construction had not yet been completed. For the month before we could occupy the upstairs apartment, I was to commute to Evander Childs High School.

What an adventure that was! I took the North Avenue trolley to the New Rochelle station of the Boston & Westchester line, traveled to West Farms in the Bronx, there hopped on a crosstown trolley to Fordham Road, and walked the rest of the way. In the afternoon I reversed the process. Once, when I had missed the trolley, I dared to hitch a ride on a truck to the train stop. By October, when the family moved to our new home, I was well settled in my classes.

With the shift in setting and the glamour of high school, my home responsibilities eased considerably. I was taking five subjects; my mother had great respect for their difficulty. I did my homework on the glass-topped dining-room table under the crystal chandelier, with my English and algebra textbooks and Caesar's *Commentaries* sprawled out around me. My mother allowed nothing and no one, not even my brother, to interrupt. I could not help with the dishes, wash my own stockings, sew, mend or cook. My mother did it all, because May had to study.

I took piano lessons again, but for only a year, because homework consumed more and more of my day. Recognition of my efforts came once, in a school assembly of some 1,500 students. The principal asked me to rise and commended me for earning the highest average in that marking period, 94.6 percent.

My grades in my junior year descended rapidly from this rarefied height. I had discovered boys!

At age twelve, I had blushed on getting my first letter from a boy. He had left the resort where we were both vacationing a few days earlier. I was handed his letter at the dining-room table, with the eyes of all the guests on me.

In my early teens I agonized at neighborhood dances. Would anyone ask me for the next waltz or fox trot? Would I have to sit out the number like a wallflower?

When a thirteen-year-old associates constantly with girls of fifteen or sixteen, she acquires values her parents may not prize. My friends dated, some even with college men. They used make-up, plucked their eyebrows and wore earrings. They knew the Charleston steps, the black bottom shuffles and all the latest dances. Some of them wore tight-fitting sweaters or revealing dresses, and even rolled their stockings. They discussed whether to neck, pet or "make out" with their dates. Necking, I knew, meant from one's neck up; petting or making out I could only imagine. Feeling awkward, I stood on the fringes, looked on with hungry eyes and could not wait for the day I would catch up.

Two events hastened that day. My father treated me to a luxurious dark raccoon coat. Soon after, a schoolmate walked into our homeroom with her hair chopped off and her ears showing. We gaped at her overnight transformation from Ella-sit-by-the-ashes to date bait. Swiftly I adopted this latest fad. Wrapped in my classy fur coat and sporting a boyish bob, I itched for my first date.

When my mother and I traipsed in and out of shops looking for clothes for me, I scrapped with her. I wanted, not sensible, but more glamorous clothes, like those my friends were wearing.

"Why can't I be sixteen?" I spit out at her "Why do I have to be only thirteen?"

When my social life did begin booming, I barely managed to stay on the honor roll.

That raccoon coat had not happened by chance. My mother had a handsome nutria coat, our family a new car, our home new furniture, heavy rugs, expensive drapes and furnishings. Our money worries had vanished.

Morris Blum and Michael Schwer had achieved remarkable success with S & B Knitting Mills. In the postwar years the demand for wool jersey, balbriggan and duvetyn had sky-rocketed. A craze for printed tricolette—christened "trico-shit" by my father—coincided with a vogue for King Tut prints. I recall a dress my mother made of this material, one of the last she made for me. Due to a slight oversight when she cut the pattern, Tutankhamen, who sat on his throne over my front, was, in the rear, standing on his head.

These goods produced extravagant profits for the firm, and the knitting boom went far beyond the partners' wildest expectations.

In 1924, they suffered their first reverse, a slight one, due to a downturn in the economy. It gave them pause; they reassessed their status. After all their hard work, why run risks? They could afford to—and agreed to—cash in.

The two men dissolved the S & B Knitting Mills in 1925. Some of their equipment was grabbed up by another knitter. My father warehoused the rest and disposed of it in the following months. Michael Schwer, not yet fifty, and Morris Blum, thirty-eight, retired.

Uncle Schwer stayed retired. His investments yielded enough dividends for a year-long cruise around the world, exotic gifts for all of us on his return and luxuries for himself for the rest of his days.

My father invested in and became a consultant to another knitwear firm. Long before his one-year contract ended, he grew disillusioned with the owners.

"A bunch of blow-hards," he stormed, refusing their pleas to renew his contract. My mother must have agreed; she did not try to dissuade him.

He withdrew his money, and next acquired a huge apartment house in Jersey City. With his remaining cash, he, with two partners, bought and managed several neighborhood garages. One of these partners played poker with him. The other, a dour, unattractive man, willingly worked nights. Instead of grumbling about Schwer, Pa now complained about these two.

Pa's changed schedule gave him much more time to oversee me and my romances. One big crush, for instance, was Steve Johnson, captain of Evander's football team. When he came calling, ostensibly to be tutored in algebra, I introduced him to my parents.

"A goy and a *gap* [a dunce]," summarized my father, whose *ferkrimte ponam* (twisted face) did not encourage me to invite Steve again.

Nor did the next young man strike Pa's fancy. I had met Benjamin Zion Levitsky, a law student, at a party. Behind his back I had promptly labeled him "Benzine." My father did not laugh. He considered Ben too old, too serious and too sophisticated for a fourteen-year-old.

A third suitor was thrown bodily out of the house. Pa had strolled into the sun parlor to check on my caller and found him stretched out, feet and all, on the day bed.

This kind of episode continued until after my graduation. "That sweet, persuasive something," read the caption under my picture in the *Oriole*, our senior album. The compliment by the class scribe took me by surprise. Any sweetness or powers of persuasion I possessed seemed to exert little influence on my parents.

Once I had graduated, I felt ready to break out of the mold into which they had cast me.

At fifteen I got my first job, selling at Gimbels.

At fifteen I entered New York University.

At fifteen I met Sol.

THREE

A Courtship

AT A NEIGHBORHOOD Thanksgiving dance, a tall, lanky blond with a baby face, green eyes and a lock of hair falling over his forehead asked me to dance. I left my friend Millie's side to accept. He placed his large, firm hand on the small of my back and off we sailed to the strains of "Me and My Shadow."

I, who thought myself graceless, found I was light and easy on my feet. Sol Sidore led with surety, finesse and a rhythm so infectious that he carried me along. As we floated, he began to parody the words of the song. I slipped in some ad libs of my own. It made him laugh, such a hearty belly laugh that we stopped dancing. Enjoying our amusement, other couples stopped to form a circle around us.

He asked me for the next dance. We danced together all evening. When the evening ended, he got my raccoon coat from the checkroom, helped me into it, and asked to take me home.

Our taxi dropped Millie off on the way. In front of the eight steps that led to my front door, he and I stood chatting.

"What do you do?" I wanted to know.

"A draftsman," he answered. He was working for a coke-oven firm on Union Square; evenings he attended architecture classes at Columbia University.

"You work on 14th Street," I exclaimed, "and I go to Washington Square."

"How about meeting me for lunch Tuesday in Greenwich Village?" he asked.

"I don't date babies," I told him.

He ransacked his pockets for paper to prove his age: twenty.

"How old are you?" he questioned in return.

"Not sixteen, but not eighteen either," I coyly replied.

He tried to kiss me good night. I averted my head. "I'm tired of fooling around," I told him. "I'm saving my kisses for the man I marry."

He swallowed that, told me when and where to meet him on Tuesday, and watched until I disappeared into the vestibule. I wafted upstairs, grinning and hugging myself with delight.

About my age I had only skirted the truth. Within the next month, Sol found out I was fifteen. But I made some discoveries, too. I asked him his I.Q. This guy had scored even higher than I had. I noted with interest that the five-year age difference between us was just the same as between my mother and father. I was amazed to learn that our birthdays fell only two days apart; mine on March 6, his on March 8. Obviously, fate must have brought us together!

By New Year's Eve he had proposed. I accepted. We kissed for the first time. On my middle finger he placed his signature ring, the one bearing his monogram, s o s, etched in silver on black onyx, with a diamond chip.

Nine weeks later I had a party to celebrate reaching Sweet Sixteen (my mother claimed it was my third such party). That evening Sol drew me out of the gathering in the parlor and presented me with my own ring, a companion to his. It bore the letters m a y, etched in silver on black onyx, with a diamond chip.

I sat on his lap while he removed his too-big ring from my right hand and slipped this custom-made one on the fourth finger of my left hand. At that instant the phone on my desk rang.

"I have two tickets for a Broadway musical for next Saturday," a young man's voice said on the other end. "Will you go with me?"

"So sorry," I happily told him. "I've just become engaged."

When we sauntered back to join the others, I showily scratched my nose with my left hand so all my friends would notice the ring.

From the first instant of that first dance I had sensed my luck. That feeling stayed. I had a sweetheart of my own. I belonged somewhere and to someone. Each time the telephone rang and I heard his dear voice, it renewed my yearning to share his strength and warmth.

During our courtship Sol gradually briefed me on his background. His grandmother Sara Maryashe, widowed very young, had landed in this country with four children, one of them a too-beautiful teen-age daughter named Rebecca. To support her family, Sara worked hard, long hours flicking feathers from chickens. She worried, too, about finding a male protector for Becky, a husband to look after her.

Benjamin, or Barney, Sidore, a junk dealer who owned his own horse and wagon soon fell in love with the girl. A bit older, he had the virtue of being an "Amerikaner," a big plus in those days. Becky, barely seventeen, married Barney at her mother's urging. Their first son was born before she reached eighteen. He died, but two other sons, Lou, then Sol, followed before her twenty-first birthday.

After that Becky put obstacles in Barney's way. "I remember Mom had me sleeping between them in their bed," Sol told me. "Pop started to climb over me, like some kind of animal, trying to get at her."

Pop must have succeeded in the next dozen years, because Becky bore him two more children, daughters.

The couple fought over sex; they fought over money. Becky could never live within a budget. Barney could never bring home enough cash. He began to gamble at cards, hoping to win a lot the easy way. Instead, he lost steadily. He tried harder, staying out till all hours. She would track him down, drag him off, or try to smash up the card game if she could. The two of them bruised each other badly.

"As kids we were very, very poor—so poor you can't possibly understand," Sol explained. "It was bad enough when they lived together. One time, though, she left him."

Mother and children moved out to a cold-water flat in Brooklyn and spent a freezing winter there. They could not afford wood for the stove.

"Lou worked as an errand boy in a grocery store after school. The man there was very nice about giving him food to take home," Sol recalled. "I sold newspapers at the El station, and kept my oldest kid sister with me, where I could keep an eye on her. She sold shoelaces and Tootsie Rolls. That's why we call her Tootsie to this day.

"I remember big holes in the bottoms of my sneakers, and my mother making newspaper soles to fit inside. We had no money to buy new shoes. It was tough, but in time we could have managed."

In the midst of this bad time, Auntie Annie came calling one night, with Sol's father, like a bashful bridegroom, slinking behind her.

"She persuaded them to get together," Sol continued, "while Lou and I begged Mom not to go back with him."

The couple did move back together, but their home remained a fractured one, with Becky frequently throwing Barney out. If he could not satisfy her money needs in the early years of their marriage, how much more did their woes multiply as her tastes grew more sophisticated!

"My mother loved quality things," Sol told me at another time, "fine table linens, china and silver, Oriental rugs. She wanted to buy shoes for the girls at Best & Company. My mother owns every record Caruso ever made. "As for Pop," he added, "he thought it all nonsense. He came from rough country people. To him, women were meant for farmwork, housework, cooking and bed.

"What a mismatch!"

As soon as Lou graduated from grade school, he got a job as a Wall Street runner. Sol kept going through high school. He longed to go to Syracuse University for an engineering degree. Instead, he settled for working during the day and going to school at night.

Sol's mother prevailed on a distant relative, an architect, to employ Sol as an office boy while he was enrolled in a drafting class. After he became a draftsman, Sol registered at Columbia.

He showed me some plates he had drawn for a design course. I admired them.

"I don't know," he said, shaking his head disparagingly. "I wonder if I have what it takes."

Just as my father dominated his household, Sol's mother dominated hers. Over the years, Sol became her chief support. Equally crucial for her, he provided a listening ear when she poured out her troubles. Sol idolized his mother and scorned his father. Somewhere in the world, he felt, an ideal father must exist. Since I blindly accepted my father as Mr. God, Sol also adopted him.

My father did not reciprocate. He looked with critical eyes at the newcomer.

The sympathy and respect Sol felt for his mother he extended to all women, indeed to anyone in distress. I tasted Sol's unfamiliar tenderness and clung fast to the sensitive soul who offered it. Pa considered this sissy stuff.

Sol demonstrated his affection. He hugged me, kissed me and showered me with daily phone calls and thoughtful gifts. When we sat together, we held hands. When we walked together, he hooked my arm in his. My parents shunned such outward displays. I had never known the physical expression of affection from either of them. Sol's warmth thrilled me. My father turned away from us in disgust.

Sol called his mother Fatso and, to differentiate, called mine Skinny. He addressed my father as "ole man," taking care to stress the subtle shading between "old" and "ole." I, who had never had a nickname, became Honeygirl, sometimes varied with Mug or Runt. I tagged him Toothpick.

"Kinderspiel [child's play]," scoffed Pa.

Sol had one "sin" directly attributable to his mother. Because of her, both sons had *weibische,* wifely, skills. When each of her daughters was born, she made the boys help her. They knew how to burp and diaper a baby, how to cook and, if need be, iron.

On one of our early dates, I walked in to greet him while trying to snap the wrist of my dress. As I pushed, the snap fell off in my hand.

"Give me a needle and thread," said Sol. "I'll sew it back for you."

To my father such a schmo had no manliness at all.

Even worse in my father's eyes, Sol sought my opinion and made no major move without consulting me. At this Pa showed utter loathing.

Sol's ultimate flaw was his membership in an organization known as the Mantle Club. This group had a code of ethics by which its members pledged to abide. Two or three times a week they met for what later were called consciousness-raising sessions. They recited personal experiences to prove that "principles pay."

I grew jealous of this competitor for Sol's free evenings. By every feminine wile, I tried to wean him from attending so often. I did not succeed. In the tussle, though, I gained even greater respect for my guy. I couldn't push him around.

My father did not share my respect. "When you give your word," he mocked, "who needs mantles, schmantles?"

One basic difference between them was that Pa saw every man as a rival to be outsmarted and outpaced, and Sol lived by such beliefs as "Love thy neighbor" and the value of asking "How can I help you?"

I enjoyed the way my sweetheart put his philosophy into practice. Forever, I had been dreaming up bright ideas, only to have them ridiculed. Not so with Sol! If one of these clicked with him, he would carefully weigh the risks. Did it stand a fifty-one percent chance of success?

"Plan your work and work your plan," Sol would caution.

We would then proceed to adjust my concept to practical shape, flesh it out with minute detail, and hedge it with an alternative.

"Must we always plan ahead?" I asked.

"When you do, you have something firm to hold on to," he explained. "You can always change or cancel out at the last minute."

Following his system, after we began to go steady we opened a joint savings account. Each of us stowed away five dollars a week for the dream home we would furnish when we married.

With a skeptical eye, Pa watched us. I walked on eggs during the early days of Sol's courtship. Would my father dismiss this boy friend, as he had dismissed others before?

He couldn't. My mother stepped in—firmly. "I like Sol," she said, "I think he's good for May."

Pa may not have eliminated Sol from the scene, but he did not eliminate himself, either. He kept a watchful eye on our wooing. Sol and I dated three times a week—on Wednesdays and over the weekends. Whether we went out to dinner, to a movie or to a social gathering, it was home before midnight.

Sol first checked on my brother, peeking into his room at the far end of the parlor. He had presented Teddy with a pencil-flashlight, so that he could read under the covers after my mother had put his lights out.

"Fast asleep," he would whisper to me.

So we would try to smooch on the living-room couch. Hardly had we settled down when my father would emerge from the long black corridor to the bedrooms. From the dim outline of his figure, draped in droopy underdrawers, would come a bellow.

"Did Toothpick go home yet?"

"Not yet," I would stall. "In just another few minutes."

He would retreat, only to emerge and bawl out this question at regular intervals.

As a variation on this routine, Sol's mother sometimes called. "You know, Solly," she would tell him, "I can never fall asleep until both my boys are home."

After a steady barrage of this single- or double-barreled pressure, Sol would finally say good night.

Soon after we met, Sol shifted his job and his locale. All over the city, apartment houses were springing up. He became an architectural draftsman for a Bronx firm heavily involved in this building boom. His income soared, but his job kept him working days, overtime, weekends—except for Saturday mornings, when he took a surveying course at New York University's uptown campus.

On Saturdays I had my own job, working as an extra selling pocketbooks at Avedon's, a Fifth Avenue specialty store. On Sundays I often accompanied Sol to his Fordham Road office. I would read a school text while he completed the last specs for some rush job. One complicated project, I remember, was a house designed for a steep slope; the basement at the foot of the hill stood five stories below the entrance at the top.

One Sunday, Mother's Day, he put in no overtime. Instead, he took me home to meet his mother. (I met his father much later.) She was a short woman with hair drawn back in a tight knob; slender, graceful legs supported a top-heavy, busty frame. She inspected me with wide, gray-green eyes heavily fringed by dark lashes; my father would have labeled them bedroom eyes. She showed scant enthusiasm for her son's girl friend.

Sol gave her the gift we had brought. She unwrapped it and became furious.

"A housedress?" she said. "You mean I should stay home and do my housework?"

"We bought the same thing for my mother," I said.

"I don't want it," she declared. "Take it back."

After this inauspicious start, she launched herself onto another topic, one dear to her heart. "Gold I pour down his throat," she complained. "Pure sweet cream I feed him, and look how skinny he's getting!"

"With or without gold," I replied, "Sol looks fine to me."

"A *stinkerke*," she said, turning to her son. "Doesn't she care about your health? Get her out of here."

Sol's mother had reason to be annoyed. At the Thanksgiving dance where we had met, Sol, a six-footer, weighed 137 pounds. He had steadily lost weight since. When the scale dipped below 130 in June, Fatso insisted that he visit the family doctor, an old Italian.

"Three times I pulled you through pneumonia," said Dr. Fortunato. "Now you try to get the TB?"

The doctor questioned further. He learned about Sol's job, his organization meetings, his college course, then about me.

"You want to burn yourself out?" asked the old man. "With overtime and staying out every night in the week and the girl, you will get yourself sick." He pondered a moment. "Why don't you marry her?"

"Her folks think she's too young. They say she must first finish college."

"For three months you must not see her at all," the doctor ordered. "Build yourself up; rest. I will give you some medicine. After you reach 150 pounds, come back to me, and I will tell you about seeing her again."

Sol told me all about it, over the phone. He had cajoled the doctor into letting him phone me once a week and write each day. We were forbidden to date.

Meanwhile, I had found a summer job. I was selling hosiery in a store on Fordham Road, the very street on which Sol worked, a half-mile east.

At noon on a scorching summer day I waited on a customer in the cool of the shop. Sol, meanwhile, was leaving his office to catch a crosstown trolley on his way home for lunch—an extra-nourishing meal prepared by his mother.

"Yes, madam," I was saying, "at $1.95 a pair, you save fifteen cents when you buy three pairs for $5.70." Saying this, I slipped my hand into the sole and held the ankle of the stocking taut over my clenched fist. "The best colors?" I pulled out boxes of Grain, Seasan and Gunmetal and opened them for madam to examine. "I'll gladly measure the lengths for you," I assured her.

While mechanically reciting this spiel, I had kept my eye on my wristwatch. At exactly eight minutes after midday I excused myself, leaving the lady to decide which shades she preferred. I slipped from behind the counter to post myself in the doorway.

Three minutes earlier Sol would have boarded the trolley. As it came into view up the hill and passed my shop, I spied him and frantically waved. He saw me, waved his long arms, and kept waving as long as he had me in sight—perhaps twenty seconds. When the trolley passed the corner, I concluded the hosiery sale.

From Monday through Saturday, for three months of enforced separation, Sol and I caught only this glimpse of each other.

Near Labor Day he wrote me this letter:

"It makes me feel good and also raises goose pimples on my skin every time I see you from the streetcar. When you're not there, I feel an awful emptiness in the pit of my stomach, an ache just below the heart.

"I think I gained another two pounds. I'm almost finished with the whole bottle of tonic. My weight, I almost forgot, is 150 with my clothes on, but only 142 stripped.

"I'm going to ask Doc about seeing you. I'll find out, when I go tomorrow. I'm wishing Doc will give me an answer that will make me jump for joy. If we even met for lunch, we could have lots of fun.

"Oh, Doc, bring home the bacon!

"Tomorrow at two o'clock I'll call, and once more in a week I will speak to you."

He called. We were allowed to date again—although less frequently and with an earlier curfew. Doc had brought home the bacon.

That fall I registered for my sophomore year and reclaimed my Saturday job at Avedon's. I also renewed a friendship. In freshman Spanish, I had been seated, alphabetically, next to

Molly Bromberg. Every time I looked toward the professor, I had gazed past Molly's Grecian profile and dark straight hair. Soon we were meeting for lunch in the Commons; later we visited each other's homes. I journeyed from the Bronx to Flatbush, where I met her twin sister, her mother, her father, also Polish, also a manufacturer (of outdoor clothing) and a carbon copy of my own. She even had a kid brother. She, in turn, met my family and Sol.

Reunited, we compared notes. "Sol and I laid a deposit on a hope chest," I told her.

Molly, who had had several boy friends, informed me she was seeing only Sam.

"Sol and I each put away the same amount every week," I went on. "He finds it harder to put away his five dollars than I do."

I told her how Sol gave the biggest chunk of his pay check to his mother and spent the rest freely. Since his scare about his health, he had joined an athletic club. I, on the other hand, earned four dollars each Saturday, received four dollars allowance and won at least two dollars from my mother each week at two-handed pinochle.

"I'm selling my tickets for the football games. I need every cent I can lay my hands on," I told her.

"I'm selling my tickets, too," Molly said. "Sam works every Saturday and Sunday afternoon."

Sam, she told me, was determined to reach his goal: to pass the bar, to become the best lawyer he possibly could— and to do this without money. He had developed a three-stage plan of action. He had graduated from City College with a degree in pharmacy. Next, he had got a job in a drugstore on the night shift. Finally, he had registered for the day section of St. John's University Law School. All night, between filling prescriptions, he pored over his casebooks.

"Sol is not going back to Columbia," I confided. "His mother blames me for his dropping out of architecture."

Molly changed the subject. "I want you to meet Sam," she said, and invited us to a gathering at her home.

Sol, no longer working weekends—the building business had slacked off—and fresh from a game of four-wall handball at his club, picked me up at Avedon's. We ate, then traveled to Molly's and met her friends, including Sam, who showed up very late from work.

He and Sol made a striking contrast. Both were tall, the only physical characteristic they shared. From his afternoon of sports, a sauna and a rubdown, Sol had a healthy, ruddy glow. Sam had the pale, sallow complexion of the student buried in his book. The dark, limp hair on Sam's bullet-shaped head bobbed above a big, loosely jointed frame. Sol, fair and slender, moved his body with graceful ease. Sol had a bubbling, outgoing manner, whereas Sam seemed quiet and reserved.

Not only did Sol and Sam become buddies, but formed a natural foursome with us.

One Sunday evening that winter we got together for dinner in a downtown restaurant and thrashed out some problems each of us faced.

Molly was thinking of dropping out of school to go to work for her father. He had no backup in his business except her uncle, with whom he constantly argued; her younger brother had his heart set on medical school; her twin sister was training as a kindergarten teacher.

"My dad really needs me," she said. "I can help him out and save some money for when Sam gets his degree and we get married."

Sam seemed to agree with her reasoning. "Once I get established," he told us, "I don't want my wife working. Until then, Molly," and here he smiled, "you may have to support me."

We smiled with him. Just then the waitress came for our dessert orders. Sol hesitated between two favorite desserts, both chocolate: chocolate éclair and chocolate pudding.

Molly and I then talked about sororities. Now in the upper half of my sophomore year, I was joining one. I finally felt I had caught up with my classmates, whatever their age.

Sol broke in. "May and I have gone steady for over a year already," he said. "I can support her right now. How do I get around the ole man?"

"Build up a case," Sam advised. "Make him listen to you."

At our birthday time in March, Sol cornered my father. The two sat alone in the sun parlor. Formally, Sol asked Pa's consent to our marriage when I had completed my sophomore year. Pa would have to sign the marriage license, since I was still a minor.

"First she finishes college," he said.

"I'll see to it that she finishes," promised Sol.

"I'll see to it myself," said my father, and cut off any further argument.

Meekly we reconciled ourselves to waiting another two years.

No sooner had Sol stated how ably he could support me and put me through school and no sooner had my father rebuffed him by stating that he would support and educate his own daughter than both men had their underpinnings knocked away.

The Bronx building boom had peaked, then collapsed. Sol lost all overtime, then his job. His bosses took the trouble, however, to place him with a prestigious Manhattan firm. He sat on a stool at a drafting board diagonally across from a famous architect, Henry Wright.

"He's doing plans for Radburn, a model community in New Jersey. What a break for that office! But," Sol went on, "I wish they would give me something more exciting than making layouts for garages. I'm bored stiff."

Six weeks later he would have welcomed garage layouts. The Manhattan firm had run out of work; Sol was handed his notice. A new job proved hard to find. His friends, some with degrees in architecture, could not find jobs either. In September he accepted temporary status as a draftsman with the New York State Department of Architecture. This entailed moving to Albany.

The giant pendulum I had seen on the horizon since childhood now gained momentum on its downswing. In November 1929, the Great Depression descended on us. With one wallop it knocked out my father. He lost every cent he had sunk into his Jersey City property. An absentee owner and inexperienced in managing real estate, he could not trim his overhead fast enough; he had to throw in fresh capital and then stand helplessly by while a bank foreclosed his mortgage. He was left a one-third owner of some marginal garages with two unappetizing partners—a poker pal and a Gloomy Gus in greasy coveralls.

In 1927, my mother had expressed horror when I got my first job. By 1929, she no longer protested. As a result of my father's reverses, I had to earn my own money for tuition if I hoped to continue in college.

That year I had a Saturday job at Lord & Taylor. I had a sweetheart 150 miles away. I accepted both as facts of life.

Our courtship zigzagged over this rough detour. Sol and two fellow draftsmen bought a junk heap of a car for thirty-five dollars. In this, when finances permitted, they drove from Albany to New York City on alternate weekends. On the other weekends Sol usually phoned. At least every other day he wrote.

"Do you think it safe to take so long a ride in the Battlewagon?" I asked in one letter. "With those cracked plastic curtains, you must freeze as you chug, chug, chug all the way to Albany."

"It's better than sharing a berth on the Hudson River line with the bedbugs," Sol wrote back. "Can you persuade your ole man to let you come up for Christmas? On a holiday when everybody has something to do or someone to go with, it can get so lonesome. Maybe Molly can come with you. If not, my landlady told me she would act as chaperone."

"I won't even ask," I replied. "You don't know how hard Pa is trying to get us to break up. He doesn't want me to tie myself to one guy, especially one so far away. By the way, I'm getting suspicious of that landlady, Mrs. F. You sound too impressed with her, with the husband who loves her up and their baby Sammy, with whom they're forever romping on the floor. She might give you ideas."

Back came his answer. "Don't think your dad isn't reasoning logically—if I wasn't so much in love with you, he'd have surely persuaded me last Sunday afternoon that we should break up. But you're too dear to me, Runt. I'm so in love with you I think I'm going crazy. I can't sleep at night, and when I do, I wake up thinking of you. I keep on thinking of a home of our own, and having you as my wife, and some babies— our life together and dreams and more dreams. Don't say 'castles in Spain,' and I don't need Mrs. F. to give me any ideas. I'm not giving you up!"

This brand of torture had gone on for six months when a most unlikely savior came to Sol's rescue. His in-again, out-again father, Barney, reappeared on the scene. A small, slight, sinewy man with dark eyes protruding from shadowy sockets, he pulled some political strings. Through a contact at a Bronx Democratic club he reached Charles Buckley, a Tammany bigwig. Barney, a faithful ward heeler, was given a job for his son.

In April, Sol transferred to the New York City Department of Transportation. He was assigned to drafting plans for the projected Eighth Avenue subway. We resumed our courtship.

In June 1930, I searched for a summer job, but far more people were searching for far fewer jobs. By chance, in early July, I noticed a small sign in a neighborhood dress shop, one of a chain. It said, SALESLADIES WANTED. Immediately, I inquired.

An opening existed, to be sure, but at a modest wage and at a branch in a neighborhood where I had never ventured, lower Third Avenue in the South Bronx. I accepted gladly.

Walking in the sun from the El station to the address given, I passed a wino in smelly rags skulking in a doorway and a woman pushing a decrepit baby carriage as she hugged the shade of the pillar-supported El structure. Across the street, a department store, its windows a half-block long, was crowded with flashy fashions and ablaze with fluorescent lights that pulsed on and off.

Reaching the right address, I saw three women seated in the entrance to a long, narrow shop. The manager rose to question me. I found it hard to meet her gaze, because she had one eye that wandered and often crossed with the other. Homely and hawk-nosed, she introduced herself as Miss Essie. Then she introduced Cooper, a hard-faced peroxide blonde, and Dotty, a younger, shapely, adorable-looking girl with long, corkscrew curls.

Cooper immediately commented, "Now they're sending them from the nursery."

"Shut up," said Dotty.

Miss Essie, with a dirty look at both of them, began to dig into my past experience. "Department store!" she exclaimed, with obvious contempt, and questioned me no further. The thunder of a train overhead drowned out her voice as she outlined the hours of my shift. She had accepted me.

Willing or unwilling, I had enrolled myself in an offbeat school with a tough faculty. What an education they were to supply in the next eight weeks!

I learned first about customers. They were neatly made up and decently clad or had painted faces and tinselly clothes. Slips and petticoats, when worn, looked fresh and clean or were held together by safety pins or were even bloodstained.

Then I learned about the people who paid the bills. A woman sometimes took money from a wad securely pinned in the cleft of her brassiere. Often a husband waited outside. From a purse he grudgingly peeled bills, counting them twice over. Once in a while a man in a car waited while a floozy, wafting strong perfume, dashed in, grabbed a dress, threw over a ten- or twenty-dollar bill and ran back to the car.

I learned next about the staff. Cooper had a husband whom she was forever punishing, claiming she would gladly go to bed with other men, especially black ones. Dotty had a husband, Frank, a solidly built Italian. She also had a lover, Nick—a slim, dark handsome man well connected through the Mafia with the Artichoke King. Miss Essie, usually shrewd and efficient, and after many long years a maiden, had still not given up hoping for a man.

When we met at 1:00 P.M. on a Monday, we exchanged gossip from the weekend.

Dotty, looking in a mirror as she tweezed her eyebrows, told us, "I went with Nick to Atlantic City Saturday night. We're in the hotel under the covers Sunday morning when somebody knocks on the door. 'Bellhop,' he yells. I didn't have a stitch on—I hid under the sheet.

"Luckily, when Nick opened the door he stood behind it. Boom, boom, boom, goes the guy into the room." With her index fingers she jerked the triggers of two imaginary pistols three times. "Then he runs off down the hall. We had no idea who put the finger on Nick."

Miss Essie cut her off. "A customer, girls. Who's up? No, it's just a looker; she's not coming in."

Ignoring Dotty, Miss Essie went on. "You know where I was this morning? At my dentist's. And did he give me a loving!" She crossed her arms over flabby, dangling breasts and clutched her own shoulders, swaying with her eyes closed to express ecstasy.

"I had no date Saturday night, so I went by myself to a movie," Cooper said. "When I came back I knew my husband was in the house already. So I stood outside the door and went smack, then another couple of smacks." She stood on her toes and made kissing sounds.

"Did your husband hear you?" I asked.

"He'd have to be deaf not to hear me," said Cooper. "That bastard! He made believe he was sleeping in the living-room chair."

I was just telling them that my father was to call for me in the car that evening, because Sol had a meeting, when a real customer interrupted.

"Who's up?" asked Miss Essie.

Dotty and, even more effectively, Cooper had taken me in hand to show me how to land a sale. I had lost several. Once, I had spent too much time with a customer. She had walked out because she couldn't pick her favorite; too many of the dresses looked good on her. Miss Essie was threatening to fire me when the other two stepped in with their course of instruction.

"Don't ever say, 'Oh, madam, how lovely this looks on you!'" Cooper told me, and mimicked my tones. "Instead say, 'How do you like this?'"

"What if she says, 'I don't like it'?" I asked.

"Get it off her and try the next one," Cooper answered.

"No use wasting your energy if she doesn't like it," Dotty put in.

"But if she says, 'I do, except—' then you have her," Cooper went on. "If the color bothers her, tell her how it brings out the color of her eyes. If she worries that it makes her look fat, tell her what a gorgeous shape she has in it. If it's too long, put three pins in front, pull it up in back, and show her how stunning she'll look when she wears it at the right length. Each time, find out what she objects to and take care of the objection."

"And don't show her too much," Dotty said.

"You lose a sale when she has to choose—you know that," Cooper went on. "Once she doesn't like something, take it away, so it doesn't mix her up. Once she's settled on something, finish the sale then and there. Unless she needs more than one, why show her anything else?"

"It doesn't matter whether you like it or not," Dotty added. "What counts is how she likes it on herself."

Absorbing their constant and candid criticism, I began to do better. One morning, when I had scored four sales out of four customers, even Miss Essie softened up.

No summer-school credits were granted for my course in retail selling, but it paid off handsomely for me that fall. I was working as a Saturday extra in junior dresses at B. Altman. The buyer, a dark-haired kewpie doll, gave no helpful hints.

Instead, she stalked around her domain in superhigh heels, always modeling a dress carried in the department.

"Probably graft she sweet-talked from the manufacturer," one of the girls murmured to me.

The buyer's only show of emotion came late on Saturday afternoons, when the merchandise manager marched into her tiny office to compare the current day's sales with those of the same day in the previous year. Her color would rise as both heads bent over the "Beat It" book, the figures from the previous year that had to be surpassed.

One Saturday, our department experienced an unexpected slow spell. The buyer minced around stiffer and more frozen-faced than usual; her manager looked in on our area several times. I minded my own business, which had been very good that day. I had some out-of-towners and concentrated my Dotty-Cooper techniques on them.

A late customer with a large multiple sale kept me in the fitting room long after the closing gong sounded. I walked into the buyer's pocket-sized cubicle last with my sales summary. She and the merchandise manager were tallying the day's totals. Judging from their worried faces, she had obviously not met her figures. When she looked at the fat envelope I handed her, the relief on her face, then his, was beautiful to behold.

On subsequent Saturdays, my figures remained impressive. I knew those two higher-ups were keeping tabs on me. All through the year they made me feel respected and secure in the job.

Throughout 1931, in the depths of the Depression, Sol and I had much to encourage us. Sol, back home, was firmly slotted in his municipal civil service job. I was still in school. We looked forward to being married when I graduated.

We sloughed off some low-key grumbling from his mother. Sol's brother had been married the previous June. Dramatically, on the day after the wedding, his father-in-law had dropped dead. Lou and his bride, Ann, were summoned home from their Canadian honeymoon to attend the funeral.

Then, to comfort Ann's mother, the couple had moved in with her.

It distressed Fatso that Lou had no home of his own, that he seemed forever in debt. Starting out at fourteen as a runner on Wall Street, he had pulled himself up to the position of trader. He was earning good money. Yet he was squandering it, in his mother's eyes, on expensive trinkets for Ann, paid for on the installment plan. Sol sat through Fatso's long monologues on the subject. When I visited, I sat through them, too.

During the same period, my father also was wearing a sour expression. Fewer cars were being stored in his garages. To meet competition he had to charge lower monthly rates. He was drawing less money and bickering more with his partners.

Sol and I made light of their complaints. Instead, we treasured our own happiness. In the spring, we set the date for our wedding, October 11, and moved ahead in high gear.

Along with graduation in June, I had to pass the tests for a teacher's license. Far too late I had discovered how useless my major, Latin, was; no city test was being offered in that subject. Why, oh, why, had I never considered teaching typing and shorthand? Instead, I must try for a substitute's license in mathematics, my minor.

I had to work from June to mid-September if I wanted a trousseau. Sol, meanwhile, had to put in overtime. He needed to store up enough leave and money for a three-week honeymoon; we would settle for not one day less. In more than three years of saving, by putting away ten dollars each week, Sol and I had accumulated enough money to furnish our own home. In September, we would lease an apartment and select our furniture.

Sometime in May, I approached the friendly merchandise manager at Altman's for summer employment. I was placed full-time in the bathing-suit department, with a transfer promised after July 4 to the College Shop.

Next, I took the New York City written test for math substitute and squeaked through. For the physical test, I queued up last to read the eye chart. As those before me called out the letters, I memorized the ones too small for me to distinguish. I passed.

Then came a blow. The English Department suddenly sprang to life. Compared with other colleges, too many of N.Y.U.'s graduates were failing the oral test for teachers. The administration decreed that all applicants must be screened with a preliminary speech test. Deeming this a mere formality, I went to a public-speaking professor, auditioned for him—and promptly flunked.

"You mispronounced *law* and have an 'ng' defect," he explained.

I went home utterly crushed. A few hours later I rallied and refused to accept his verdict. I locked myself in the bathroom and stayed there until the little hours of the morning, examining my lips, tongue and tonsils in the mirror. This went on until I mastered "aw" and recited "the cataract strong goes dashing along." I went to sleep dreaming of "singing" and "swinging" and "ding-a-linging."

Early the next day, the very last day for these tests, I returned to the professor and demanded a retrial.

He refused. "We don't have time to give everyone a second chance."

I would not be brushed off. Grudgingly, he listened. Most graciously, however, he passed me. When I took my oral test the next week, I sailed through the very "cataract strong goes dashing along" that had first stymied me. I had won that coveted scrap of paper, a math substitute's license for the City of New York.

As for Sol, whenever his squad leader, who relied heavily on him, had extra hours to hand out, he favored Sol. We began to breathe more easily.

My father cashed in a Morris Plan Building & Loan bond for $5,000, his last one. He and my mother rented the swanky Royal Palms, in mid-Manhattan. I arranged for engraved wedding invitations. My mother went with me to order my wedding gown, a fitted one in ivory velvet. My sorority sisters surprised me with a bridal shower.

Every piece was falling unbelievably well into place.

On the Tuesday after Labor Day, Sol was waiting for me when I emerged from the employees' entrance at Altman's. I wasn't expecting him.

"What's wrong?" I asked as I took in his stricken face.

"I've been laid off," he said. Eight hundred men had lost their jobs. New York City was suspending all further construction on the Eighth Avenue subway.

In a daze, we walked to a nearby drugstore. We found stools at the counter, sipped coffee, talked. What would this mean to us? What could we do about it?

Sol had been recommended for the job of moneychanger at one of the newly opened stations of the Eighth Avenue line. This paid $28.50 per week. He would have to act quickly, because these jobs were being grabbed up. My substitute teaching would pay $7.50 per day. If, by luck, I got the thirty days required to renew my license, this would amount to $225 for the year. Teachers, however, avoided staying home sick during the depression. Would I get thirty days?

Later that evening we broke the news to my parents. The four of us pulled up chairs around the dining-room table. My father came up with an unexpected proposal: we should go into business together! We—my father, mother, Sol and I— should start a knitting mill as four equal partners.

Pa wanted to get rid of his garages. He could borrow $3,000 on his life-insurance policy; he would furnish his technical skill and business expertise.

Sol and I would invest our nest egg, $1,642. Instead of renting our own apartment, we would share my bedroom in my parents' home for the time being. The three of us would work full-time. My mother would fill in at the factory mornings, reach home in time to greet my brother when he got home from grade school, keep house, and prepare meals for us.

Sol and I drew away to discuss this by ourselves. "Sounds great," he said, "but let's talk this over with Fatso."

"I don't like it," Fatso said. "Louie still doesn't have his own place—it's going on for the second year. Now they're talking about having a baby, not about having their own apartment. What can I say when you come to me, Solly, and you don't have your own home either?" She began to crack her knuckles. "Can you do something else?"

We went through the alternatives, my impatience mounting because she didn't appreciate what a golden opportunity my father was offering us.

"I promise you, Mom, that the very first chance we have," said Sol, "we'll pull out and set up housekeeping on our own."

"When you promise, I take your word," she told Sol. So, reluctantly, she gave us her blessing.

We returned to my father. "It's a deal, Mr. B," Sol said.

The two men shook hands.

In October, we were married in style. Gifts poured in, overflowing our hope chest. Out-of-town relatives poured in, including Abe and Esther Tzudiker, from Boston, whose daughter was to be one of my bridesmaids. We found places for all of them to stay.

Late in the afternoon on Sunday, October 11, we posed, rather stiffly, for our wedding portrait at a studio, then were driven to the Royal Palms.

While guests were arriving in long gowns and black ties we had to round up two witnesses for the *ketubah*, the Hebrew marriage contract. Uncle Schwer and a slight red-headed man from Sol's side signed, and the rabbi handed me the scroll.

"You notice they give it to the woman," Sol said as I fondled it.

"I'll hold on to it in case you change your mind," I told him.

The rabbi we had selected was an outsider. We had watched him conduct another wedding and been inspired by the talk he gave the young couple. Now, after bridesmaids, ushers and the rest of the bridal party had taken their places, we stood before him. After we made our vows under a *chupa*, or canopy, I recognized the sermon he was giving us. Parrotlike, he was repeating the speech he had used at the other ceremony.

Sol lifted my veil; we kissed; he crushed the traditional glass under his heel; we marched down the aisle. Passing a frail soprano perched on the top step of a tall ladder behind an ivied screen, where she warbled "Ah, Sweet Mystery of Life," we formed the head of the receiving line.

I remember waiters serving endless courses and I remember dancing with Sol between courses. Shortly after midnight, we slipped away with relief and taxied to our downtown hotel.

The next morning, I telephoned my mother while we waited for the train to take us on our honeymoon. About to ride off into the unknown, after sleeping under a strange roof, with that strange species, a male, I burst into tears as I said, "Hello, Ma."

Sol and I spent our honeymoon at a newly built winter lodge in upstate New York. Our genial innkeeper was phasing out the farm his father had left him and accommodating a dozen guests, who came to view the fall foliage or stalk deer in the hunting season.

Sol and I hiked along the country roads, over meadows, through woods. We climbed across stiles, under barbed wire, or stepped from tie to tie on railroad tracks. Sometimes we ended up at a steep, narrow waterfall that splayed into a wide, rocky basin. We'd climb to its crest and sun ourselves on a broad, flat rock. Lying there one day, we settled on the size of our future family: at least six children, spaced two or three years apart.

Some afternoons we helped Willy, the ancient farmhand, round up the cows and take them to the barn or dig up the last potatoes. On other days we helped the innkeeper's brother as he electioneered for county judge. We nailed dozens of his posters to telephone poles and billboards along the state highway and in the village. On the way back we gathered hickory nuts.

In the lodge's Great Room, birch, cherry or seasoned oak logs spit flames in the fireplace. Other guests gathered to share hot tea and good talk, and to help us dry and shell the hickory nuts. Through picture windows we gazed at a blue-green lake with an islet in the middle like the hazel pupil of a giant eye.

Sol snapped one picture of me that I kept for a long time. Hands in the pockets of pepper-and-salt tweed knickers, I stood on a knoll. My boyish bob was accented by the white collar of a mannish shirt showing above the V neck of my Argyle-bordered sweater. Knee-high patterned socks and high white sneakers completed this outfit. A smile lit my face.

As for the way Sol looked, what a ribbing he took on our return! In three weeks, Toothpick had gained seventeen pounds.

FOUR

A Businesswoman

ON THE FIRST Monday in November 1931, my father drove Sol and me down to the Nile Knitting Mills on Wooster Street. On the way he explained the name. Before we left on our honeymoon we had agreed to the name Juvenile Knitting Mills. Finding that name already legally registered, Pa simply lopped the first four letters off.

A creaking elevator carried us to the topmost loft of a cast-iron building. At the far end of a splintered floor stood four flat knitting machines; a mechanic in oil-stained overalls crouched over one of them. Some hanks of baby-blue yarn encircled the reels of a winding machine nearby.

Under a skylight, an oblong pressing table waited for action. A long, battered cutting table occupied the middle. Closer to the entrance we saw some Merrow machines and a Singer already set up at work stations. In front of those stood some secondhand tables and chairs. Nearer to us, a space for an office had been partitioned off. It contained one roll-top desk and one wooden swivel chair with arms.

"The landlord gave me a rent concession until November 1," Pa told us. "Robaczynski is letting us have the machinery on easy installments. I've already established a line of credit at the bank." He had done likewise with a yarn dealer he knew from the old days.

Willingness to extend credit to him came on two grounds: as a former principal in the S & B Knitting Mills he had an impeccable reputation; and he had represented himself as sole owner of the new operation.

"My name would be mud," he explained, "if they thought I couldn't finance a two-bit operation like this." Looking at Sol, he added, "We can't damage what little standing I have. For the time being we must keep any mention of our partnership hush-hush."

Sol looked startled but seemed to accept the condition with becoming restraint.

Pa had contacted a children's clothes jobber for orders. The jobber (a middleman selling our goods to retailers under his own label) had given him sweater-and-beret sets in toddler sizes two to four to duplicate. As soon as samples were approved, we would get contracts for production.

I was to run the stitching-room section; my mother was to do trimming and finishing on a part-time basis. The plant would operate on one shift except for knitting. The machines had to keep going on two shifts.

"I'll supervise everything during the daytime," said my father, and then he asked Sol, "Will you come down around four o'clock and take over from then until midnight?"

My bridegroom looked sideways at me. With grace, he said, "Why, sure, Mr. B. If I have to, I have to."

Almost overnight, Sol had been transformed into a husband, a relief inside man, and a very silent partner. Almost overnight, I had been transformed into a wife and an executive in a knitting business.

Millions of us struggling through the Great Depression bore its mark ever after. At the same time, the Depression created an opportunity I, a woman, could never have grasped in happier days.

The tidal wave cradled me and helped me swim far and fast. Only the rescue counted. Both my father and my husband respected my input. I could ask a million questions. I could help Sol collect "memos" in his little black book.

"The trouble with America," my father ridiculed, "is that they all know how to read and write."

Even he did not ridicule me too severely. After all, we had nothing to lose.

The Nile Knitting Mills had no trouble finding experienced help. On the day shift we had the knitter-mechanic, who made samples on a dinky (a miniature flat machine used for collars, trim, swatches, and so forth) and ran down the regular orders. We also hired a few operators, a finisher and a floor girl. On the night shift we employed a knitter and a part-time winder, moonlighting after his regular job in Brooklyn.

When Sol came in, he wrote up the orders in the most suitable knitting units. He weighed out bundles of yarn for these orders. The winder reeled the bundles from hanks into cones. Each morning my father ran to the machines to check the quality as well as the weight per dozen of the night's knitting—a major concern.

Fanny, the floor girl, an anemic, pimply youngster, steamed whatever came off the machines. All knit goods had to be steamed, lest they curl and refuse to lie flat after the stripes were separated. I got deep cuts in the outer edges of my pinkie fingers from the sharpness of the separating thread. Fanny and I stacked up bodies and sleeves and carried them to the cutting table.

There, my father, wielding heavy Wiss shears, did all the cutting himself. In between, he might go out to harass the jobber for payment due us or to wheedle more orders. He might check the yarn dealers for a bargain on an odd lot of yarn. He might drop in on our bank to renew a note. Always, though, he had to leave enough cut work for the Merrow operators.

I matched and separated collars for each bundle of bodies and took them to the next stop, where four-fingered Nick and his wife, Angela, working as a Merrow team, pushed through order after order. If the style called for inside or patch pockets, it went to the Singer operator, Pauline. For buttonholes, she would use an attachment to her Singer; we couldn't afford a Reese buttonhole machine. The finisher could sew on buttons, bows, or any other trim. I can still see my mother's fair hair, streaked early with gray, in the glare of an unshielded electric bulb as she pulled in the ends and trimmed each garment.

Taking them from her, I jerked each seam straight, carefully laid the garments one atop the other in a uniform pile, and took them to the table alongside the Hoffman press. During the night Sol flattened each sweater, inserted a round cardboard into each beret, and steamed them. The sets were then folded into packs of a dozen, and the packs were stowed into cartons for shipment in the morning.

Once a month the sharp accountant I knew from my father's garage days appeared, to make up a profit-and-loss statement. We carried the lowest possible overhead; we drew subsistence pay; we did much of the work ourselves; my husband worked by night, I by day. With all that, we were making no money. The accountant confirmed what we had already guessed. The jobber was paying us barely break-even prices.

For ten weeks Sol had drawn terminal pay from the Department of Transportation. For the first few months my father had cashed checks from the two partners he had left behind in the garages. In the spring, though, we felt the squeeze. What to do?

In my childhood I had heard how Uncle Schwer had captured healthy orders from Marshall Field and Macy's to keep the S & B Knitting Mills rolling.

"How about my going to Macy's and getting an order?" I asked one day.

"*Grosse knacker* [large noisemaker]," said my father.

Sol and I went to a Prince Street beanery.

"On fifteen cents a day, with a nickel for a cup of coffee, I'm better off with soup," he told me. "For the dime I could get a sandwich, but with the soup I get two pieces of bread anyway."

Then he brought up the subject of Macy's. "You go right ahead and try it, Mug. I'll get the night knitter to run down samples in the next size range, three to six. I'll use different colors and position the stripes differently. That way we won't get in trouble with the jobber and you'll get your chance."

In the morning I found the samples. Grudgingly, my father cut them. I had the fronts, backs, sleeves and collars sewed together, finished and pressed. With three samples, I set out to attack R. H. Macy & Co.

I ascended to jammed buying offices on the eleventh floor. The only woman, I waited my turn for hours with a hundred salesmen, watched them bounce like yo-yos in and out of cubbyholes, and at last heard my number called for the children's buyer. I accosted a grim-faced merchandise woman sitting behind a tiny table. Her placard read ROSE LIPPERT. Her features softened as she looked quizzically at me and my offering. Soon she took pencil and pad and started writing. I thought she was copying the style numbers. No. Instead, she handed me an order for 400 dozen at $6.75 a dozen.

I looked at the paper; I looked at her. "You don't know me," I said. "How do you know we'll deliver the goods?"

"I'm sure you will." She nodded, with a smile.

"Thank you," I managed to utter.

Out of the store, into the subway, then up the stairs I flew, holding tight to that incredible paper. What a reception I got! Even my father was impressed.

My father labeled the 4,800 sweaters "hot dogs" and began to crank them through the process. The knitters went on overtime, to produce our bread and butter—the infants' sets for the wholesaler—and these children's garments for Macy's.

For hours, Pa would stand at the cutting table, with no interruption, getting "elephant's knees." A callus formed on his thumb knuckle as he chopped away with the weighty scissors. I worked all day until dusk; Sol worked all night until dawn. In stifling heat that summer, under the open skylight, he pressed "hot dogs" and, later on, the reorder "pups" that followed. Toward dawn he packed toddler's sets into cartons, sweaters into larger cartons, made out bills, and left respectable shipments for pick up by the trucker.

After depositing those first checks from Macy's, we found small black numbers appearing on our monthly profit-and-loss statements. With increasing confidence, I got more orders from Miss Lippert. The numbers grew bolder and heavier. Then, abruptly, the bubble burst.

We did not know that a manufacturing lull fell just before Christmas. Stores placed no orders for children's sweaters until the next back-to-school season. Overnight our retail customer disappeared.

To aggravate our despair, our wholesale customer had walked out on us the month before. He showed up in our mill one day, red-faced and shouting, with two men trailing him. He scooped up every infant sweater and beret, had his two men pack them into cartons and drag them into the elevator, and stomped out too angry to explain.

Too late we learned that he had given us his least desirable size range. Novices like us accepted work in sizes two, three, and four. A Brooklyn contractor had knit the same sweaters, without berets, for him in the three-to-six size range, sweaters just like the ones I had sold to Miss Lippert. With Macy's advertising our sweaters for ninety-four cents each, we had undercut our jobber most cruelly. My father, who preached that you always leave doors open behind you, found this one nailed shut.

Once the machines stopped knitting, we laid off help. But we still had to carry overhead; our black figures quickly slid back into red. One frosty Saturday morning in January, three of us sat in the office waiting for my father's friend, the yarn man, to show up. He had promised to bring a prospective customer. We listened for footsteps on the stairs; they never came.

In the midst of this crisis, my father pulled a merger out of thin air. He negotiated with an old established firm famous for its registered cashmerelike "Valcuna" yarn. Dan Rheinauer, crusty, stiff-collared president of New York Knitting Mills, envied Pa's low overhead and technical know-how. Once an agreement had been worked out, Rheinauer promptly moved from his expensive uptown premises to our humble loft. Blum, the inside partner, found a niche for Sol in production and inventory control. He himself had to tackle the job of hatchet man. He had no place for me as a forelady, or for my mother as a finisher.

I found a temporary job at Altman's during their Great Midwinter White Sale. How narrowly, though, Sol and I had escaped complete disaster! We had dreaded the worst; instead, we found an unexpected bonus: Sol was drawing a regular salary.

"I'll work like the hammers of hell," he told me, "but we're getting out of here." "Here" referred to my bedroom, where we had slept for sixteen months. Sol had in mind the promise to his mother, that we would have our own home at the first opportunity.

"How can we?" I asked. "So far you haven't seen four pay checks."

"As soon as I do..." he said.

He did draw four consecutive pay checks. With the fourth, we moved into our very own one room and kitchen in Greenwich Village, not three blocks from our factory. On my last day at Altman's I paid $8.88 for a mattress, thanks to my ten percent discount. It was delivered on April 1 and went on the Murphy bed that leaped out of a closet. We set our lonely hope chest in the one huge room and put a drop-leaf maple table in the kitchen. Until the arrival of the two chairs we had ordered, we sat on wooden crates.

The first morning there I rose early to cook farina. Carefully, I stirred some of the cereal into water heated in the top section of my double boiler. Inserting the top into the bottom, I placed the boiler over a low flame and covered it tight. Nothing seemed to happen, except for a peculiar smell.

Sol came out of the bathroom, sniffed, investigated, and broke into a loud guffaw. "You have to put water in the bottom of that thing," he said.

At suppertime I resolved to redeem myself. I set the table with cheerful pink china, a gift from Sol's mother. I diced fresh fruit to begin our meal and cut greens for the salad.

When Sol opened the door, I placed four rib lamb chops under the broiler.

We seated ourselves on the packing cases to savor our first dinner in our own home. We talked, ate the fruit, lingered to talk some more.

"The lamb chops!" I cried, springing up. I stared at four blackened blobs on the broiling rack.

"That's all right," Sol consoled me. "I like burned lamb chops."

Alone for the first time since our honeymoon, we discovered our own private world. We could giggle, indulge in horseplay, sleep late on Sundays and not ever worry about the creak of bedsprings. We could even entertain friends.

Our first guests were Molly and Sam. They came bearing cookies—chocolate, of course. We had to let down the Murphy bed and slide the hope chest over alongside it, so that the four of us had places to sit.

We talked about Molly and Sam's situation. Married the year before us, they had rented their own apartment immediately. Law, however, had yielded so meager a living that Molly had persuaded both Sam and her father that Sam join the family business.

"Imagine me standing at a steaming table pressing lumber jackets," said Sam. "Then I had to put them on a hand cart, wheel them to the freight elevator and push them across the sidewalk to a truck. After one week, I walked out."

"It's not for him," declared Molly. "We'll have to live on whatever he makes at law."

A picture of Sol came to my mind, the gusto with which he had pressed "hot dogs" by the hundred all night long under the open skylight in last July's heat wave.

"Help me get some tea ready," I said to Molly, and we went into the kitchen.

"Two months have passed," I heard Sol saying, "and Mr. B. has never mentioned one word to Rheinauer about our partnership. Everybody thinks the ole man is doing his son-in-law a big favor, to find me a job there."

I had known my father's subterfuge had bothered Sol; I had not realized how much.

Sam made a wry face. "Either he's stalling," he told Sol, "or maybe he sized it up right when you first started out. It *might* have killed his credit line then. It may hurt his leverage with Rheinauer now. But," he advised, "watch for the earliest chance to have it spelled out."

Molly and I arranged pink cups and saucers, chocolate cookies, spoons and napkins and began to drag the table from the kitchen. The men jumped up to finish the job. We drank tea, and the subject of my father's unfulfilled commitment was dropped.

It was never raised again during the merger period. For the next few months I often slipped over to the Wooster Street loft on the pretext of bringing Sol his lunch. I heard mutterings that spelled trouble.

My father resented the pruning and firing he had to do. "Rheinauer's dirty wash," he called it. Most of the staff were loud-mouths, in his opinion. Mostly, though, he chafed at playing second fiddle. Rheinauer not only wore starched collars, but also, with regained business health, was growing more stiff-necked.

Pa bellyached under his breath; he vented his gripes on Sol. Usually Sol could find excuses for everyone, even my father, but not this time.

"Your ole man preaches, 'You can say anything you want to anyone, provided the two of you are alone. You never bawl a man out in front of a third party,'" Sol bitterly related. "He goes into Rheinauer's inner sanctum, rushes out and starts yelling at me in front of the knitters. I don't have to take that crap from anyone."

My mother and I had always gentled flareups between Pa and Sol. Anxiously, I now got between them, and felt the pressure from both. I developed colds. A nervous sneeze, sometimes a dozen in a row, stayed with me. I couldn't shake it.

To heighten my unease, retail orders were trickling in too

slowly. One day, Sol's lunch in hand, I bumped into the sales manager, who was carrying a sample case and frowning.

"Business over the counter stinks," he complained as we rode up on the slow-motion elevator.

"I don't understand why," I said. "With your Valcuna yarn, you have a beautiful line. I bet I could sell it."

"Really? Where would you go?" he asked.

"I'd take a quick trip around New England," I answered.

"Suppose I get a line together for you..."

"Sure," I agreed. But I felt like an amateur backed into a corner by a pro when I repeated the incident to my husband and my father.

"Not a bad idea, that trip," Sol said. "The machines are hurting for work, and that hotshot isn't feeding them orders."

Pa laughed. "He caught you where the hair is short," he taunted. "Now, *chochom* [wise guy], you have to go through with it."

By late afternoon Sol and I had mapped out an itinerary; looked up stores and buyers in Boston, Providence, Hartford and New Haven; assembled sweaters with swatches and price tags, and folded them into a double-strapped black packing case.

I telephoned cousin Abe Tzudiker in Boston, to ask if he'd meet me and put me up for one or two nights. I promised Sol that he would hear from me each evening.

My cousin and his wife met me with open arms. On the way to their Dorchester home, Abe stopped off at a favorite bakery for pumpernickel hot from the oven. When we reached their tenement, I sat with them, sipping coffee, dunking the fresh-baked bread, and briefing them on my schedule. Abe promptly revised it.

"You don't have Grover Cronin on your list," he told me. "It's a high-class store in Waltham. I'm taking tomorrow morning off—my insurance business can wait—and I'm driving you there."

He did. I made my way inside the specialty store. Finding

the sweater buyer on the selling floor, I introduced myself and quickly laid out a half-dozen of my most tempting numbers on her counter.

Attracted by the lush feel of the Valcuna, she called over Mr. Cronin himself. He, too, approved. After a quick trip to the car, I showed the rest of my samples. While Cronin and I chatted cordially, the buyer wrote out an order, had him scan it, and signed it. I thanked them and jubilantly left.

"I broke the ice," I announced while Abe adjusted his spectacles to inspect the paper. "What a good-size order! Thanks to you, my trip has been paid for already."

Abe dropped me off in downtown Boston to tackle three or four super-size department stores there. No reception equaled the warmth of my first one, but I did land a few orders, among them a most respectable one from Filene's, and some appointments for the following day. That evening I reviewed my progress with my sympathetic audience. Abe took my suitcase with him to his office the next morning. Whatever time I finished, he would meet me, have supper with me and see me off. We did not rush this farewell meal— I had so much to tell him—and it was quite late when I caught the train to Providence.

Suitcase in one hand, sample case in the other, I got off the train in the dark. At a dimly lit ticket booth, the agent directed me to a commercial hotel nearby. I registered in its seedy lobby and took a rickety elevator upstairs to my room. To reach it I had to pass an open door, through which I glimpsed a man in shirt sleeves and suspenders riffling a pack of cards. Empty chairs and ashtrays waited. Quickly I averted my eyes, marched to my room next door to his, entered and locked and chained the door. Then I tested the bolt on the connecting door.

In my shabby room, with its peeling paint, I sat at a scratched-up desk to review my plans for the next day. As if no wall existed, I could hear every sound in that next room. There were at least four voices. I heard chairs pushed around and cards dealt out. I knew they were passing a bottle around; I could hear each slurp and each burp. The voices grew louder and more boisterous, with more and more laughs and arguments as the game grew hotter.

Too scared to leave the room to phone Sol, I propped a chair under the knob of the connecting door, undressed and silently slipped into bed. For hours I lay as still as I could; I couldn't fall asleep. Near dawn the clack of the cards stopped, the voices trailed away, and, in the sudden hush, I managed to doze off.

Otherwise, Providence left kind memories: two stores, two orders. In Cherry & Webb I found the salesmen's sample room tucked away under the roof; in Gladding's I descended to an out-of-the-way corner in the subbasement to display my merchandise.

I phoned Sol as soon as I got to Hartford. His voice was encouraging as I reported my successes, but I skipped over my terror of the night before.

In the dusk Hartford looked more inviting than Providence, the hotel seemed friendlier, and registering by myself came easier. The next morning my line clicked with the buyer at G. Fox. She handed me my largest order of the trip. In New Haven, on my last day away, I scored one more hit and made the noon train to New York.

Riding back, I totaled my dozens and grouped them by style. They added up to decent quantities for each type of knitting machine. At Grand Central I hailed a taxi impatiently. Hardly noticing the heaviness of the bags, I trotted up the six flights of stairs at Wooster Street and burst into the loft. Sol ran to me, hugged me and kissed me in front of the whole factory.

I hauled out my sheaf of store "paper" and flaunted it before him and my father. The two men looked over the orders.Then Pa grabbed them and headed for the door to Rheinauer's office. He didn't bother to close it, and everyone within earshot could hear his views about so-called big shots who brought in nothing but excuses, whereas a *pisherke* like May became an expert traveling saleslady in five days.

My small victory only aggravated a steadily worsening situation between Morris Blum and Dan Rheinauer. I stayed out of their way for the next few months and looked around for a practical project to fill my unaccustomed leisure. Still sneezing, I decided to go back to school. Enough of ancient history and Greek! I had to find out about buying, selling and mastering the techniques that make cash registers ring in department stores.

Late in May, I competed with several hundred candidates, who jammed the rooms and stairways of a Columbia University building. The Graduate School of Business Administration and B. Altman jointly were offering a two-year work-study program leading to a master's degree. The salary earned by working at Altman's almost covered the tuition charged by the school. I won one of twenty bitterly fought-for places.

"They screened us with a math test," I told Sol. "Lucky for me they didn't try chemistry or physics."

Each morning, beginning in September, I attended classes on Morningside Heights. At noon I took the Seventh Avenue subway to 34th Street, gulped down a quick lunch, and ran two long blocks to Altman's. I interned in the store for four hours each afternoon. On a stagger system, groups of us were put through the paces of receiving, stock-keeping, buying, selling, advertising, and even comparison shopping. I learned about and gained respect for the intricate infrastructure that supports a selling floor.

Courses at the university were conducted by Dr. Paul Nystrom, a lean, tall, gray-haired man. Head of a research association for a group of large department stores, he knew his subject inside out. He lectured on Economics of Fashion and Economics of Retailing. In clear, concise language he had written the textbooks we used. He held me spellbound.

I would try to repeat his theses verbatim to Sol. "Make a quality product in a popular fashion, deliver it at the right time and at a fair price," said this crisp-speaking professor, "and you're bound to succeed."

"Fashions come and go in cycles," he stated. "Those who latch on to them too early get high prices but low volume; Johnny-come-latelies get high volume but bargain-basement prices."

As if on a surfboard, you had to catch the fashion on the upswing before it crested, ride the wave, judge the moment to let go, then hitch on to the next surge before you were beached.

Sol posed a question. "Let's say a new firm gets started. How does it get enough customers even if it guesses right about fashion?"

One day I brought home Nystrom's answer to that one, the old cliché about building a better mousetrap. New York Knitting Mills had a winning mousetrap in their Valcuna yarn. If and when we started out again on our own, Sol and I must invent a supermousetrap.

Pa had cut costs and made increasingly respectable profits for New York Knitting Mills. As he did, he grew less and less civil to his partner. Rheinauer, for his part, had regained his swagger along with his business health. The sputterings of these two strutting roosters swelled to an angry crescendo. One day it reached a climax. They split up.

In September 1934, about twenty months after merging, we found ourselves outside New York Knitting Mills. We had gained a valuable edge, though. My father had reaped a handsome cash settlement. He had won back his reputation as an efficient knitter and had made many more contacts in the industry. Sol had streamlined effective internal systems. I had soaked up much knowledge about the retail market. Our fourth partner, my mother, carried a fairly light load, with Ted still in high school, but she offered what skills she had.

Awaiting my father's signal, the four of us stood poised for action.

FIVE

Four Partners

WE RENTED A LARGE, bright floor on East 20th Street. We were wedged between a feather-hat maker overhead and a blouse manufacturer below.

"Figure out a British-sounding name," Pa instructed me.

Using *B* for Blum and *S* for Sidore, I came up with Brook-and with Shire. My father had Sam, who was zealously building up his law practice, register the name and file papers of incorporation for the Brookshire Knitting Mills.

"Mr. B. requested that I list him as sole owner," Sam warned Sol.

Sol grabbed hold of my father. "What are you doing to us, ole man?" he asked. "When does my name appear?"

"Zei nicht kein yold [Don't be a stubborn ass]," answered my father. "Give the baby a chance to crawl, then to stand by himself. We have to establish our credit all over again. Have a little *gedult,* a little patience."

"Let a year or two pass," Sam counseled; I concurred. Reluctantly, Sol agreed to have *gedult.*

My father lost no time in calling on women's-wear jobbers; placing orders for the most advanced types of knitting machinery; re-establishing our standing with the banks and with yarn dealers. Sol followed up on promised dates for delivery of equipment, checked on electricians and plumbers, and interviewed and hired help. He had never given up attending his Mantle Club meetings at least one night each week. To my delight, he also now registered for a night course at N.Y.U.

"Maybe I'll complete my degree," he told me. "Engineering and law are two valuable disciplines for any businessman."

I bowed out of my executive training at Altman's but continued Nystrom's courses at Columbia. Except for the three mornings I went to class, I again took charge of the stitching floor. My mother took her seat among the finishers. Within six months, she retired.

"You don't really need me here," she said. "Emma can pull in ends twice as fast as I do." Emma, a tall, willowy beauty, had been sitting beside her. "I know I shouldn't, but I worry about Teddy alone at home."

Emma and the other hand-finishers formed only one section of a well-orchestrated work force. Sol had hand-picked good people. Al, whom I remembered affectionately from my childhood visits to the S & B Knitting Mills, managed the Brookshire yarn inventory. He worked from 5:00 to 11:00 P.M. and looked after the second-shift knitters. A Jew, he had married the Italian girl, Claudia, who used to wind the S & B yarn. Claudia became our Brookshire winder.

"Don't tell me the date you two got married," my father would tease them. "I know you tried out a *forspeis* [appetizer] on the yarn bales when you were supposed to be putting in overtime."

As our master mechanic, Julius, "the Dutchman," ruled with an iron fist over the flat machines. Between his capable son and three tall, handsome nephews, he supplied all the apprentices we could use. Jack, the night knitter, worked alongside his stepson Billy.

I co-ordinated the flow of work among the operators, most of them Italian girls. Bundles of sleeves and bodies went from Emily, a cutter, to Lucy, the Merrow sample maker. Other bundles went to Singer operators or covering, crocheting or other specialized machines. Sometimes loopers had to attach collars first.

Once the sweaters were completed, I passed them through finishing, to be trimmed or to get hand-sewn touches. The bundles went next to Pat, Lucy's cousin, a wiry young man, who worked the press. Finally, the garments were folded, packed and shipped.

From the beginning we were busy, with substantial orders from jobbers. Our reputation as a superior manufacturer grew, steadily improving our financial statements. Then, a lucky fashion break came our way. Knit skirts to match sweaters suddenly became the vogue. We were equipped to handle the most complicated styles and stitches of these outfits. Instead of idling after Thanksgiving, Brookshire went full blast for all twelve months.

How bright a picture! But it had at least two flaws. By our second year, Sol had made no headway in formalizing the partnership, and I was still sneezing.

"The ole man keeps stalling for more time, keeps pulling that act about the banks," Sol complained. "I'm stumped. I don't know how to force his hand, how to get our fifty percent down in black and white."

"Let's talk it over with Ma," I advised. "She always sticks up for you."

She begged us to give Pa more time. "He gave you his word. He'll keep it. He always does."

I was torn between father and husband. And now I was sneezing full time. Yet I did not connect my mounting inner tension with the sneezing. Sol and I consulted an allergist. The medical man pricked my arm with a dozen serums. He even asked for a sample of our wool yarn, had that made into a serum and injected me. Nothing showed up; I had no allergy.

To add to the problem, I had my own pet peeve. Shopping in Gimbels on a Saturday, I had come across a sweater we had manufactured. A royal-blue mohair-and-wool slipover, its shawl collar was looped with a royal-blue-and-gold scarf. It had taken a lot of effort and engineering to expedite that particular style through our mill. I flipped the price tag over. Gimbels was charging four times what the jobber had paid us!

"When will we sell direct to the stores?" I asked Sol. "How long do we have to keep on selling to middlemen?"

Sol added his own fuel to my fire. "They buy from hole-in-the-wall makers and then use our quality garments to spice the lot."

"I don't say we should give up making 'mama' sweaters for the women's jobbers," I replied, "but we could also make snappy young fashions for college girls. We could go straight to junior departments ourselves."

"Maybe Jane would free-lance for us," Sol suggested.

Jane headed the design staff of our most valued customer. Since she created their women's styles, she would know exactly how to produce a distinctly different junior line. I had found her practical and easy to work with and admired her taste.

I jumped at Sol's inspiration. Then, mindful of Nystrom's better mousetrap, I said, "She'll have to figure out some angle that will make us unique."

My father bucked at hiring the "Big Swede," his name for the designer.

"You want to piss on the parade?" he asked Jane. "What if your boss smells this out?"

He turned to me. "What's your trouble? We're not doing good enough for you?"

He stopped short of a veto, though.

Mr. Paneth, the blouse man on the floor beneath us, had promised to carry our numbers as a sideline. Again I had to invent a name. No trace of "Blum" appeared in this title. For our new venture, I took the "Pan" of Paneth, tacked on the "dore" of Sidore and came up with Pandora, straight out of Greek mythology. At Sol's insistence, I handwrote the logo for our label.

In the next weeks, Pandora found the feature that made it stand out from any other junior line. We pioneered with

"Pandora Partners." Our sweater tops co-ordinated with fabric skirts—unheard of at that time. A white wool slipover boasted a Peter Pan collar of Dress Stewart tartan. The cardigan had binding of the same tartan. We completed the ensemble with a simple A-line skirt in the Stewart cloth. The three pieces dovetailed strikingly.

Out of the corner of his eye my father watched our progress; he did not shrink from voicing his opinion—again and again. Faithful to his knitting, he despised *schneiderei*, or cutting up woven fabric into *shmattas*.

Sol held his peace and signaled me to do the same. We weathered Pa's outbursts but, as the critical moment for launching came, we suffered a serious setback. Mr. Paneth backed out.

He had dallied from August to September about starting his selling trip. Then he confided, "It's not going to work out. My timing to hit the road doesn't match yours. After all, blouses are my bread and butter."

"I'm taking the line out myself," I told Sol. "It's aimed for the holiday season. If we delay any longer, the styles will get dated."

"I hate to see you go right now," he objected.

He and I had dusted off the master plan for our future family, drafted on our honeymoon and shelved for four years. We had even checked with a specialist that my sneezing would not harm any unborn baby or cause me to miscarry.

"Please let me go, Sol," I coaxed. "We've told no one. I'm not even sure myself yet—and I'm feeling fine."

He held out for a while, then yielded.

On that trip I wrestled with not one, but two sample cases, as well as my suitcase. In Pittsburgh, then called the "Smoky City," a buyer ribbed me about showing samples in white. On the train after leaving there, I opened my case to put my garments in order, and a veteran traveling man accurately sized me up. "Pretty green, aren't you?" he said. He then took over and demonstrated the proper way to fold each sweater and lay out each skirt. In Chicago, overbooked by conventions, the Palmer House had to put me up on a cot in a display room.

But these incidents melted away when the Marshall Field buyer caught sight of the matching outfits and her eyes lit up. Pandora Partners helped me sell the separates I showed her as well. She, and others, placed good-sized orders.

One last obstacle threatened Pandora on my return. Like a watchdog, my father guarded the stream of orders for his jobbers and would shunt aside our skirts and sweaters.

"What you've sold, I'll ship," promised Sol.

Grimly, he by-passed Pa and co-ordinated our outfits. What I booked was delivered, together and on time.

Pandora had emerged from the incubator!

A flesh-and-blood baby incubated along with Pandora. A few months before it was due, I took a furlough from the knitting business. Sol and I moved to three and a half rooms off Fordham Road. Our apartment lay midway between and within walking distance of both our families. I ordered living-room furniture, a dinette set and baby furniture, and devoted myself to learning the skills of a housewife—though not completely.

I still went to the mill part-time, to break in a German refugee, Johanna. In Stuttgart, she had informed me, she ran seven floors of a sportswear and sweater operation single-handed. In America, resisting some of our unfamiliar ways, she needed a little boost from me to get started. I also met regularly with Jane to help shape Pandora's lines for the following season, and helped select a salesman to work with accounts I had already opened.

Each evening, Sol would report all the factory happenings to me. Each month, we analyzed the accountant's statement together. Continually, he fed me the latest developments in his tussle with my father for our stock. Pa persisted with the same tired excuses. "When I try to squeeze more money out of a banker or a bigger order from a jobber, I can't walk in, hat in hand, like a beggar. You can only deal from strength." With an impatient shake of his head, he would end with *Zwei gringe kep* [two nitwits]."

Sol refused to be brushed off by name-calling. "I've got to hand it to your ole man," he remarked to me. "Do you realize he never put one cent of his own money into this business? Who paid back his $3,000 loan on his insurance policy? The company did. Who put in the only real cash? We did, with our $1,642."

Sol kept hoping that Pa, on his own, would officially recognize our partnership. My father made no such move.

I had been doing my own wishful thinking. I had fancied that my sneezing might wane as my pregnancy waxed. But I was sneezing harder than ever. At the same time, I kept wavering between trust in my father— "Maybe he's right; he'd never go back on his word" —and support for Sol— "We may have to start from scratch all over again; let's figure out some alternative."

After a powwow with Sam, Sol came to a decision. "I'll wait a year; I'll even wait until the end of 1937. If your ole man hasn't come through by then, I'm getting out."

Sol and I agreed on most decisions. He did not share one, however, that I made the night Sara Mae was born. That evening, he was taking his final in integral calculus. I was waiting at home for the upholsterer to custom-fit some slipcovers.

The doorbell and the phone rang at the same moment. As they did, I felt my first labor pain. I let the upholsterer in and ran to the phone.

Sol was calling. "How do you feel?"

"Just fine," I said.

Labor with a first child usually drags on for hours, I reasoned. I would stick it out until Sol got home from school and could take me to the hospital. I would not interfere with his exam.

No sooner had I shown the workman the couch and chairs to be covered than the phone rang again.

"How do you feel?" Sol's mother was asking.

"Just fine," I told her.

The labor pains did not go away; I took refuge in the bedroom. Twenty minutes later the doorbell rang. I passed

the man cutting striped linen, pins sticking from his mouth,
and opened the door. There stood Fatso.

"What are you doing here?" I asked.

"You didn't sound right to me," she answered.

"You guessed it," I admitted. "The pains are getting
sharper, but I have to wait for Sol to come home."

Instantly, Captain Fatso took over.

"Call your father to take you to the hospital. Make him
come right away," she commanded. "Tell the doctor you're
going. I'll wait here for the man to finish and Solly to come."

I obeyed orders. My father drove me, my doctor met me
and, after a fuzzy interval, my beaming husband kissed me.

"I saw her. A perfect cherub!" he exclaimed.

Never again, though, was Sol to register for college
courses.

This year of our first-born, 1936, also marked twenty-five
years of my parents' marriage. Sara Mae arrived on May 14;
Morris had wed Bertha on June 10. Fresh from the hospital, I
plunged into arrangements for a fitting silver-anniversary
celebration for my parents.

I settled on the date (a Sunday, so that my orthodox
grandparents need not travel on the Sabbath), chose the place
(the Concourse Plaza Hotel), selected the menu (a chicken
dinner), and invited the guests. This took some forty telephone calls and letters. I even contacted the *Bronx Home
News*. One detail, however, had escaped me: I had not
specified a kosher meal!

With horror I realized this too late, and with dread I
watched a waiter set a plate of *trafe*, unholy, chicken in front
of Grandma, then Grandpa. Luckily, the guests included a
rabbi. He was a true cynic, asked no questions, but dug in
and ate with appetite. My *bobbe* and *zadeh* watched him; after
a moment's hesitation they ate, too.

"Not only kosher, but how tender the meat!" remarked
Grandma Leah to me.

The incident tickled my mother. "Yours is the sin," she pulled me aside and informed me. "You, not they, will have to answer to God for their eating *trafe* food."

Gladly I assumed the guilt, and both of us began to giggle like conspirators.

The anniversary couple departed to tour the Midwest on a second honeymoon. From a St. Louis fair my mother brought back for Sara Mae an infant's dress, white with red smocking and colorful Hungarian peasant embroidery. It was the sixty-second dress in our daughter's wardrobe.

To me, that baby seemed miraculous. Each day she revealed another trick, another surprise. Nagging doubt, however, dulled my rapture. How would I know whether I was doing justice to this child? No accountant would render a statement on my success as a mother.

"Millions of women have done it before you," I told myself, intimidated by a squealing, wriggling seven-pound infant. "You'll make it, too."

I sought the advice of the starched Swedish practical nurse who tended our daughter during my first two weeks at home. Could Olga Johnson tell me how to increase my milk supply?

"You must rest all you can when I'm around," Johnny said. "Drink lots of liquids and eat vegetables and fruits rich in vitamins."

I quit when, after eating a full pound of cherries, I nursed Sara Mae with pink milk.

Once Johnny left, Sol taught me how to diaper a baby, burp her and figure out why she cried. He moved with confidence; I, awkwardly. I sterilized practically everything in sight, made formula and, with red-hot needle tips, struggled to enlarge holes in forever-clogged rubber nipples.

I assigned myself another task: this daughter had to have every breath of fresh air she could possibly inhale. Early in the morning I would take the English pram down in the narrow self-service elevator. Twice a day I would wheel it for goodly distances, and I soon knew every bench in three different parks by heart.

One sultry August day, I was walking my eleven-week-old child when, suddenly, she threw up. Vomit oozed over her dainty pink dress and delicate pink silk cover. In distress I watched.

"Why did I ever wish this on myself?" I asked her. "Your daddy and I were getting along fine without you, kid."

During her first year I often pushed Sara's pram the mile and a half to my mother's house. One autumn morning, I parked sleeping baby and carriage in the back yard and ran upstairs to say hello.

"You've got to help me out," my mother greeted me.

From DeWitt Clinton High School, Ted's homeroom teacher had telephoned. He wanted to see her.

"So go," I told her. "Let him see you."

"You go, May. You have the college education. You know how to talk to those teachers," she pleaded. "I'll watch Sara Mae. You go."

I thought of a story from Ted's younger years. He had come running into the house one day after punching a neighbor's boy in the jaw.

"Don't let Mrs. Runkel know I'm here," he yelled out to my mother.

"Did you get into a fight with Eddie Runkel?" she asked.

"I only hit him back first," said Ted, running to hide in his bedroom closet.

Now I joked with my mother. "Maybe he hit his teacher back first." My mother looked so harried that I relented. "Okay, okay, I'll go."

On my return, I said, "You should never have sent me. You should have gone yourself. Ted's flunking three subjects out of four. He's goofing off on his homework. You have to keep after him each night to do every assignment. Otherwise he may not graduate."

"My Teddy is a good boy," she answered. "Maybe he doesn't understand how serious it is."

"He's good, he's handsome, he has personality," I conceded, "but he has to do homework."

For the rest of the term, though, when I could, I checked on Ted myself. Each time I did, I felt like a policeman.

On a wintry day a year later, my mother and I went for a stroll on the Grand Concourse. Sara Mae was taking her afternoon nap in the carriage. My mother was striding beside me, stern, flushed, staring straight ahead.

"When I married him, I never thought it would last this long," she said. "Once it did, I didn't dream I'd have to go through such a thing at this stage of my life.

"I said to Pa, I told him, 'You don't get rid of a wife like you did May's dog in New Rochelle! You don't divorce a wife for a twenty-three-year-old girl!'"

I stayed quiet, not knowing how to ease her hurt.

"What does she want with an old man like him, anyway," asked my mother, "a beautiful girl like Emma?"

"They just park in the car and do a little necking," I said, quoting a detective's report. "Emma's a decent girl. She won't let him go any further. She's only doing it because he's her boss and she needs her job."

My words made no impact on my mother.

"Those first few years, each day I expected he would pick himself up and take off," she went on. "My family, they warned me against a *Poilische*. They didn't like him; they didn't trust him. They never thought we would stay together."

"They didn't act that way when they came to your silver wedding last year."

Her face softened. "That party—you don't know what that party meant to me. I never believed I would have the joy of such a day. And when the picture came out in the *Bronx Home News!* I photograph terrible, but to see it in the paper!"

"I thought everyone looked fine," I said. "I read and

explained each word to Grandma, and she seemed so proud."

"Twenty-five years ago you couldn't have explained anything to her," my mother said. "They thought Pa too good-looking, a *luftmensch* [air person]. Every time he and Schwer argued, he was ready to fly. One day he talked of a mill that wanted him in Cleveland; the next day Rosie's brother was begging him to come back to Detroit.

"He seemed to settle down right after we were married. He was always very ambitious and always worked hard. I could talk to him," she recalled, "and he would listen to me. After a few years I began to feel easier, though I never thought we would have any more children.

"Then came the war and the draft. You remember how we took you to the draft board when Pa was called?" She stopped to figure out the date. "It must have been August 1917.

"We were getting along well with each other. Pa was doing good in business. We were badly scared when he was almost drafted. That's when we wanted another baby. If they didn't take him with one, surely they wouldn't draft him with two."

Ma had slowed her walking and her talking at the same time. "You can't push a button and have it happen just like that. I didn't get pregnant until the next year."

My brother's birth was her proudest achievement. She had produced a big baby, a beautiful boy, and, most important, she had presented a son to Morris.

"After Teddy came, I didn't think I'd ever have to worry again."

"If you had any doubts," I said, "I wonder why you married Pa in the first place. Aunt Jennie," I added, "once told me something about you as a girl."

"What did Aunt Jennie tell you?" she demanded, her eyes narrowing.

"She told me that you were so beautiful people would turn to look at you. She remembered one time—you were married already—when she was watching you wheel my carriage through Thompson Park. You didn't even notice, she said, but she did, the way the men stared after you. She said you dressed with taste and you dressed me with taste, too. You sewed every stitch yourself, yet you looked as if you had stepped out of a Paris fashion book."

My mother continued to look at me suspiciously.

"She told me that her brother-in-law, Sam, wanted to marry you, that many others wanted you—good substantial men, whose families your people knew from the old country. But once you met Pa, you had eyes only for him."

"Is that all Aunt Jennie told you?" my mother snapped at me.

"What else is there to tell?" I asked.

For a moment she did not answer. "Nobody ever spoke of it in all those years," she burst out. "Only once, Jennie threw it up to me. You know the piano teacher, the one you and her Ruthie both took lessons from? He told me how quick you learned and what hard pieces he gave you. I told this to Jennie. All of a sudden she let me have it. 'May has reason to be smart,' she said."

"I don't get it," I murmured. We had left the row of tenements lining the first block and reached the corner before Poe Park. Gently, I maneuvered sleeping baby and carriage down the curb.

"May has reason to be smart," she repeated. "I froze. I couldn't say another word. That was enough." She fell silent, her eyes brooding. "I always told you, May, that I was married on June 10," she blurted out. "I wasn't."

About to lift the carriage up the far curb, I stopped short with the wheels spinning in midair.

"We married July 9," she finished "I picked June 10 because your Cousin Ettie had her birtthday then and that helped me remember the date."

My mouth hung open. By "reason to be smart" my aunt must have meant that I had advanced as rapidly with the piano as I had through my mother's pregnancy, that I had appeared much too soon after the wedding. Mechanically, I motioned my mother to the first vacant park bench.

"I don't know why I can't keep it inside any longer—after all those years that I never talked about it," my mother began. "I feel so upset that I don't know where to turn.

"Your father and I went together for quite a few months. All of a sudden I found out I was going to have a baby. When I told him, he was a perfect gentleman. He said we would get married right away.

"What could my people say? In those days many girls in trouble couldn't even find the fellow. My mother and father swallowed it; they had to. Quick, they made arrangements for a little wedding. We were so poor—it was in the house— just the family.

"But up to the last minute I wasn't sure he would go through with it. I pictured myself standing alone under the *chupa* while he skipped off to Rosie in Detroit. He used to tease me about her."

But they did marry. Morris sent Bertha off for a week in Long Branch, New Jersey. "He came out for the weekend to bring me home. That was our honeymoon."

For years afterward, she doubted whether they would stay together.

"I didn't want any more children. If we broke up, I figured I could manage to earn my own living with just one. And then, we had so little money. I wanted you to have all we could afford. I almost had one thirteen months younger than you. I went to a doctor; he gave me a pill; the next morning I was rid of it."

As we sat on the park bench, my mother turned back the clock.

"He was a good father and, in his own way, a good husband and always a good provider. When we married he told me, 'We may not have much money now but some-day...' and I knew that someday we would. For the first twenty-five years of our marriage I could guarantee that he was a faithful husband. He has it too good now. He doesn't know how to take it easy and enjoy."

She sighed and shook her head. In sympathy I shook mine, too, but I could offer her no comfort. After a while I noticed Sara Mae stirring. We rose to go our separate ways. I pushed the carriage south, then west; she headed a dozen blocks north. I would feed and bathe my daughter and wait eagerly to greet and embrace Sol. She would cook for my brother and set aside a cold platter for my father to eat at whatever time he came. She might slip out to a movie to avoid being home and having to listen to him offer some lame excuse, if he offered one at all.

My insides churned as I walked home. "You were an accident," a small voice whispered.

It had never dawned on me that my parents had not welcomed me as much as they had welcomed my brother—maybe even passionately longed for me. I had sensed that they would have preferred a son, especially after my brother came. But surely you held your rightful place, I had thought.

"No such thing," said the small voice, growing in volume. "You were an accident, an accident. How hard you struggled to prove yourself the equal of any boy! A competition you were bound to lose."

I had almost reached home when I thought, lucky me; if not for the accident of my birth, I wouldn't even be alive.

I looked with double vision at a familiar world turned askew. The script had a new introduction, each character a strange dimension, each act a hidden meaning.

In response to a tearful appeal from my mother, Sol had already taken some action about my father. He had hired a detective for a few days to discover the extent of his partner's straying. My mother had read this report. After I told Sol of our conversation in the park, he took the next step. He spoke to my father.

"Aren't you the one, Mr. B.," he asked, "who lectured that you never shit where you eat?"

My father made short shrift of such logic. "What are you talking? The girl has a sick mother. I go out of my way to give her a lift home to Brooklyn each night. Big deal!"

Sol took one further step. He spoke directly with Emma.

"She didn't know how to say no to him," he told me afterward. "She'd love to stay on in a swell place like ours, but she's going to look for another job."

When Emma left the scene, Pa's symptoms seemed to subside. He must have made his peace with my mother, for once more he seemed like the husband and father I had known.

"Could we have triggered his fear of growing old when we presented him with his first grandchild?" I wondered out loud to Sol. "He's worked hard all his life, with no time for play. Maybe he wants to make up for the lost years."

"How will he react next June," asked Sol, "when we present him with his second grandchild? Right now, while he and Skinny seem back to normal, I have some unfinished business of my own to discuss with her."

I sat beside him while he did.

"The ole man and I are heading for trouble, Skinny," he told her. "Unless we have the partnership in writing, he can always renege."

"I've had to have patience with him," she said. "You must have patience, too."

"I've had all the patience I intend having," Sol replied. "It's going on for the seventh year. In one month, I'm getting out. By New Year's I'm going into the construction business."

My mother looked at me. "How will you manage, with two children?"

"If we could live through the Depression," I answered, "we can live through this."

She looked troubled.

Sol delivered his ultimatum to my father. I added a few comments of my own. Sam tried to reason with him. But it was neither Sam, nor Sol, nor I who turned the trick. My mother did.

"In those days he was still listening to me," she was to reminisce long after. "You should never stay in business alone," she warned him. "When you had Schwer for a partner, together you made out fine. By yourself you lost every cent." She went on to remind him, "Not every partner suits you. One you call a fourflusher; another, a piker. In Sol you have a willing horse.

"You need Sol and May, and it's time you kept your promise to them."

My father yielded. Early in 1938 Sam drew up formal agreements. The four of us signed them. Sol and I legally owned fifty percent of the Brookshire Knitting Mills stock.

When our curly-haired son arrived in June, the demands I made on myself multiplied. I had hardly gotten used to one child. With two I jumped around like a drop of water on a hot griddle.

Gene, I soon found out, had lustier lungs than Sara had and objected more strenuously to waiting for food. The pediatrician still mandated the four-hour schedule. I could not adhere to it and satisfy that hungry child. For weeks I stood by in agony while he howled and I waited for the exact moment to feed him.

Should Sara Mae see the infant suck at my breast? Very bad psychology, I thought. So, away for the summer, at a cottage hidden in the woods at Harmon, New York, I put her outdoors to play for the twenty minutes I nursed him. Once, when I went to find her, she had disappeared. I propelled Gene and his stroller to the road and ran like a madwoman, until I spied Sara Mae's small, crisp silhouette in a blue organdy sundress skipping up a distant hill.

When we returned from our vacation, we discovered that our expanded family had overflowed our apartment. Sara Mae slept in her crib in our bedroom; Gene, in his carriage in our foyer. Sol and I toyed with plans for transforming the dining area into a nursery. Meanwhile, we spent every Sunday searching for a larger apartment.

We had a tough time. Landlords seemed to love only childless, dogless couples.

"We'll have to buy," Sol informed me.

We had put aside funds to use in case Sol left knitting to look for construction work. These we now invested in a red-brick, single-family row house in lower Riverdale. Barely

completed, it boasted three bedrooms and a finished basement. We engaged a decorator with the odd name Albert
Albert. He had even odder ideas on how to make the house
livable, but Sol approved his fluted white dado board against
the blue walls of the dining room, and I liked the elegant,
though offbeat, drapes he designed for each room.

With our new home taking agreeable shape, and our
business status resolved, I now had time to enjoy husband,
son and daughter.

Even though Sol was leaving the house earlier and coming
home later each day, our annual statement showed we had
hit a plateau. Until the last year, our profits and volume had
gone steadily up. We had bought more machinery, rented the
loft upstairs when the hat man vacated, cleaned his feathers
out of every crevice, hired more people and borrowed more
money to finance our expansion. Thus our overhead and
labor costs had kept creeping upward while our income was
slipping. Jobbers, to fill orders quickly, had encouraged new
firms to enter the field. Some older contractors, our serious
competition, had moved out of town and could now offer
very low prices. The vogue for our most profitable item, two-
piece knit dresses, had passed its peak.

"A plateau spells danger," Sol summed up. "We'll never
get ahead by running in place."

"What can I do to help?" I asked. "Maybe I should come to
the factory part-time for a few months."

"I'd like that," said Sol. My fresh perspective, he felt,
might catch something obvious that he had missed. "Maybe
you can help me turn things around."

We agreed to try it for three months. I hired a German
refugee, Margo, as a housekeeper and went back to work
afternoons. It distressed me to leave the two children, Sara
Mae two years old, the baby seven months, with a stranger.
It distressed me still more as the three months stretched out
with no end in sight.

We searched for substitutes to supplement our regular
production. We experimented with cashmere; our samples

did not compare with the Scottish imports from Hawick. We edged into bathing suits; our quality fell far short of that of swimwear specialists. My answer, Pandora, languished as one salesman after another tried out and fizzled. The costs of these dry runs mounted. Even worse, we had failed to turn things around.

On Wednesday nights Sol and I usually ate dinner downtown together. Afterward he attended his weekly Mantle Club meeting while I went to a business English course at N.Y.U. I would get home after ten; Sol would follow within the hour.

One memorable Wednesday I left a peaceful scene after lunch. Sara Mae was riding her tricycle in the back yard. Gene had been tucked in for his nap. On the back porch Margo was dismantling cords she had tacked up for her string-bean plants.

That night, I left the subway at my station in Riverdale and started briskly up the long hill as usual. Then I slowed down. On the opposite side of the street, a ragtag gang of teenagers, many snub-nosed, many freckled and red-haired, was also climbing the hill. Some were yelling, others brandishing sticks, still others carrying rocks. A big crowd was massed at the corner. There, men were yelling, and I could see fists upraised. I heard the crash of breaking glass.

Men were throwing rocks. They had aimed at a fixture of three brightly lit electric globes inside a dentist's office one flight up in an apartment house across the way. Someone inside switched the lights off. Meanwhile, they were chanting, "Dirty Jew! Christ Killer!" I shrank against the wall of the apartment house and turned the corner. My heart was thumping, my knees wobbling.

Above the mob, standing in a covered wagon and framed in its arched doorway, stood a handsome young Irishman. His black cape was flung back to reveal a slash of red lining. A black tricorne fitted rakishly on his head. In his left hand he held the reins of two pawing white horses; his right hand was upraised to command silence. When he spoke—not reviling Jews, but simply reminding his hearers of their duties as Christians—I could almost see sparks shooting from him and firing the rabble.

I had heard the radio voice of Father Coughlin and had switched off his anti-Semitic rantings. From Margo and Johanna I had heard about the horrors of Hitler's Germany. But here in the flesh, not three blocks from my home, stood Mr. McNazi himself! Joe McWilliams, his covered wagon, his horde of hoodlums, ready to carry out his every bidding, were no phantoms: they all looked bigger than life.

I reached our house, fumbled clumsily for my key and turned it in the lock. Once inside, I leaned for a while against the door, shaking and listening. At the head of the cellar stairs, I heard Margo's deep, regular breathing downstairs. Upstairs, my son lay peacefully in his crib, my little girl in her bed. Still in darkness, I opened the front-bedroom window. Could I hear the rumble of the approaching mob?

I imagined Joe McWilliams egging on those men until their waving sticks and rocks turned into flaming torches and fire bombs and they fanned out into the neighborhood, singling out Jewish homes to burn. Paralyzed I sat by that open window in the dark, waiting for I knew not what, until Sol got home.

"Did you see anything?" I asked him the second he let himself in.

"No," he said, "nothing out of the way."

He had walked through deserted streets. When I described what I had seen, he tried to comfort me. Tomorrow, he felt sure, we would see some neighborhood action. The police would not permit such riots.

"I never saw one policeman," I told him. "Where did they hide themselves?"

He had no answer.

"How dare we bring innocent children into such a world?" I went on.

"Let's see what happens," he said, stroking my shoulders gently. "Whatever steps have to be taken, we'll do our part."

The next evening, at a synagogue around the corner from where Joe McWilliams had held forth, storekeepers and community people gathered. Sol and I were part of the overflow crowd. The house of worship occupied two stores, their front windows papered over. We sat on camp chairs under a patterned metal ceiling. Years later I recognized that very setting, duplicated, in Paddy Chayefsky's play *The Tenth Man*. Paddy, a Bar Mitzvah student at that synogogue, may have attended that night.

A rabbi introduced a police officer, who assured us that in future his men would break up any such rallies. These roughnecks, it seemed, called themselves the Christian Mobilizers and formed an entourage that followed McWilliams around. After questions from the floor, the rabbi offered the synagogue facilities for future meetings.

Sol and I made a vow that night. Neither of us had ever professed any religion; we shunned religious rituals. Panicked, however, we had run to the synagogue. We had better make sure that if, when, and where we needed one a synagogue existed. As for our children, they had a religion whether they chose it or not. We had better teach them the history and meaning of that religion.

We became templegoers and, in the following year, temple builders. We raised money to replace those two scrubby stores with a suitable house of worship.

Joe McWilliams had made Jews out of us.

Margo left me shortly after. This time, the change in housekeepers was a lucky one. Catherine, a Jamaican, doted on both our children. She had lost two infant sons, and developed a special soft spot for Gene, with his halo of ringlets and his father's hazel eyes. I could work my half-days downtown now with an easier mind.

In the factory I stayed on the knitting floor; Sol kept to the shipping floor. Occasionally I went down to talk with the shipping clerk. This bright young man was selling Pandora in his spare time, albeit with spotty results. Occasionally Sol went up; usually this signaled some emergency. Dulie, nephew of Julius, precipitated one such emergency.

Dulie wheeled baskets of knit goods to the brushing machine, on each side of which stood a girl who continuously straightened out the goods' curled edges. They fed a machine that relentlessly pulled the goods between rollers of steadily revolving wire teasels, making sure that the goods received an even nap.

One day, Dulie sauntered up with his load and, with a quick-as-lightning jerk, threw a startled, clawing mouse onto the moving goods. As the mouse was sucked into the rollers, it splattered the two screeching girls with blood and gore. It ruined the knit bodies, of course, and also disabled the machine for a week. But it won lasting fame in Pandora history for Dulie.

Mischief such as this furnished comic relief to a gloomy picture. I was still sneezing and no closer to understanding why. Each day my father was growing moodier and more unpredictable. In addition, after a few months' respite, he had resumed his chippy-chasing—a bit more discreetly and away from the mill. Sol grieved for my mother. "A gallant lady, but I pity her," he told me. He mourned that my father, whom he had longed to substitute for his own, could cause her such heartache.

Our business health was still suffering, too. A slight economic downturn accelerated our difficulties. My father kept hounding jobbers for orders large enough to pay profitable or, at least, break-even prices. He kept scouring the yarn market to take advantage of the slightest shift in quotations. He saw to it that the mill operated at capacity, but we had far less leeway than before.

We dared not deliver orders a day late, lest we risk a cancellation. We tightened our quality standards, so as not to give a customer the slightest pretext for returning merchandise. We ourselves could not maintain our usual relaxed pace, and people working in the factory could feel the stepped-up pressure.

Sol also felt uneasy about—he knew not what. "Something is going on," he told me, "some undercurrent. I can feel it." "Why do you say that?" I asked, and made light of it. "We've always been close to our people. They know you love them, Sol, and they love you in return. In the spring we went to Lucy's wedding; you just loaned twenty-five dollars to Pat when he had his pocket picked; the day before Labor Day we're invited to Mary's daughter's wedding. Maybe you're looking for trouble."

"Just a hunch," he said. "According to Emily, Pat may not have had his pocket picked. She took me aside to tell me she thinks he's mixed up in some racket." He paused. "I'll trust any man until he proves me wrong, but it takes only one rotten egg to spoil the whole batter."

Sol grew even more uneasy about the next round of industrywide wage increases slated for fall 1940. We prided ourselves on paying top scale to our employees. Could we absorb this next advance?

Seldom that summer did I hear Sol's hearty belly laugh. Instead, from that belly issued loud and long rumbles. His sallow complexion, poor appetite and restless sleep troubled me. He seemed entirely too tired. I insisted that he slow down, and over his protests, made him go for a medical checkup.

"You're heading for a nervous breakdown," our family doctor told him. "Rest and diet," he prescribed. "The main thing you must do is to get away for a week or two. Do it right away."

"How can I leave now?" Sol asked me afterward. "We're at the height of the season."

I proposed that he go to the resort-farm where we had spent our honeymoon. "Take Catherine and the two children with you. She'll keep them out of your hair, and it will free me."

I would work in the factory full-time. If I found my days too short, I would go to a hotel on 23rd Street.

"I can ask Doris" —she was our office girl— "to stay over with me," I said. "I'll fill in for you as best I can. You had better go."

The next morning Sol took off with his three passengers. "I'll come back a new man, Mug," he promised.

I hurried downtown. Sol had asked me to expedite certain shipments from knitting through shipping. I was to concentrate especially on one slow-moving intricately cut number. I worked on both floors, alerting my father when he had to help Emily cut missing sizes or colors and notifying Johanna when they had to be rushed through Merrow and finishing.

A few minutes before the first lunch break, I was waiting at the pressing iron for Pat to finish a load of goods that would complete an order. Suddenly I heard a terrible racket from near the elevator. Three men in rough clothes had bulled their way into the factory and were fanning out over the floor, throwing goods in the air and terrorizing the stitchers.

My father was standing at the cutting table, the heavy shears in his hand. He raised those shears on high and started after the first of the invaders. The men glimpsed the fury in his face and, not waiting for any elevator, scrambled down the stairway. As suddenly as they had appeared, they vanished.

I stood petrified. "What was that about?" I asked my father when I could talk again. "What did they want?"

"Mafia," he answered. "Do you want to pay protection money? This time it's just a scare; the next time they'll throw acid. They were sent to get the lay of the land."

"To get it, or did they know it?" I questioned. "I was standing next to Pat. I swear that first man knew him—I saw a look pass between them." Then I remembered Sol's hunch. "Sol suspected something funny was going on. I bet this is it."

"*Oy, schlecht*," my father said, shaking his head. "We're really in hot water if they have a cookie planted inside."

No one in the plant could get much work done that afternoon. The shakiness lingered. Before she left for home,

Doris agreed to stay with me at the hotel on 23rd Street from Sunday evening until the following Saturday. I could get to work as early as Sol and I would leave as late. No gangster would take over in Sol's absence!

Sometime that week I noticed our friend the yarn salesman calling on Pa. He came once, twice, then several more times. The two men seemed buried in serious talk.

"What does he want?" I asked Pa.

"He's talking about miles of empty buildings and plenty of willing workers in a mill town called Manchester, New Hampshire," he said. "Sounds interesting."

I paid little heed. We had chased many of these tips. Few of them panned out. Pa, though, had loosened many a tight-knotted problem by following up unlikely leads.

Over the Labor Day weekend he traveled to Manchester. That same weekend my husband returned, looking more like himself again. Catherine and the children couldn't stop talking about their holiday.

On Tuesday morning I had barely shown Sol the orders to be completed when my father summoned us into the office. Excitedly he described a strange world I could hardly visualize.

The Amoskeag Textile Mills had dominated Manchester for almost a hundred years. Red-brick factories, interconnected, stretched great distances along the banks of the Merrimack River. At one time it was the largest of its kind in the world and had recruited everywhere. French-Canadian, Irish, Scottish, German, Polish, Greek and Chinese men and women had funneled into its employ.

Males and females had boarded in separate corporation dormitories; families had rented corporation houses. They had gone to schools, churches and hospitals and had been buried in cemeteries built or subsidized by Amoskeag.

In the mid-1930s this giant toppled. Strikes, two floods and misunderstandings between workers and management had delivered fatal blows. Some 25,000 mill hands, many on relief, now marked time. Floor space aplenty lay fallow in what one magazine article later called "The City That Nearly Died."

"The mucky-mucks in Manchester took me around like a long-lost brother," my father said. "Their tongues are hanging out for small businesses like ours to move in. They'll do everything they can to help us get started."

Pa laid out a program that flabbergasted me. Sol and I were to tear up our roots and move mill and family to New England? "Go up," he urged Sol. "Go up and see for yourself."

Sol and I weighed the pros and cons. The potential for growth and for savings in overhead had to be balanced against the difficulties of meshing sweaters and customers across 250 miles, transforming textile hands into sweater people, and raising the money this move would take.

I resisted, unwilling to abandon our cheerful home, our circle of friends and our familiar routines.

"Would you consider calling it quits in knitting?" I ventured. "Suppose we sold the company. You could go back to construction."

Sol did not answer right away. "A few years ago," he admitted, "I considered it seriously. You know that. I had fantasies that someday I would direct a major construction job.

"I once had the chance to go to Russia," he added, "to help supervise the building of a huge hydroelectric dam. But we were keeping company. I never even mentioned it, just turned it down."

Sol could still surprise me.

"I've put too much of myself into this business," he continued, "and you have, too. Suppose I drive up to New Hampshire and look it over."

The next weekend, he did look it over, and came back fully convinced. He saw space on one floor equal to that on the two we were occupying, and at a fraction of the rent. At a WPA project, he saw rows and rows of Singer machines manned by young people with bright faces, craving the chance to prove their skills. He spoke to townsmen, including Arthur L. Franks, an electrical contractor, eager to extend credit and guide him in getting settled.

"A tall, slender Yankee, straight as a ramrod" was how he described Franks. "He talked like a father to me. I know I can trust each word he says."

"How about me and the children?" I asked. "How will we fit into small-town life?"

"I've never liked living in New York," confessed Sol. "I loved Albany when I worked there—just didn't like being separated from you. I've always hankered for the chance to get out of town."

Another surprise. Imagine being married to a guy for nine years, I thought, before I find out he doesn't like city living!

Quietly, I weighed my choices. From earliest childhood I had learned from my mother that "the man leads; his woman follows." My father taught, "Never waste your energy and *no pishing mit die oigelech* [no pissing with your precious little eyes]. If you'll have to say yes at the end, why bother to say no at the beginning?"

"All right," I said. "If that's the way you feel, we'll try Manchester."

SIX

The Big Move

TWO WEEKS ELAPSED between the pact and the act, two hectic weeks. Sol crated machinery, hired movers, finished out our season's commitments and canvassed our people to learn who would make the move with us. My father sold off outdated equipment, cashed in odd lots of yarn and surplus fabrics, and got commitments, conditional ones, from jobbers and bankers. I toured manufacturing plants to pick the brains of our competitors. What could they teach us about setting up a more efficient mill? These tours were interrupted for two days by a project Sol and I undertook together. We traveled to Manchester to seek our future home.

For seven hours one sunny Friday we drove northeast. The streets of the Bronx, loaded with heavy traffic and lined with towering tenements, yielded to grassy parkways in Westchester and Connecticut, then, in Massachusetts, to two-lane roads growing ever narrower and more winding as we approached New Hampshire. By afternoon, we were passing through long stretches of woods. Purple, yellow and scarlet patches against the evergreen hinted of autumn. These cool, shadowy runs were interspersed with bright sunlit towns. Each centered about a village green punctuated by a white gazebo bandstand. Shops and picket-fenced houses nestled between red-brick or white-wooden churches, each crowned by a sky-piercing steeple, a generous cross or both.

"So many churches!" I murmured to Sol.

Darkness was pressing in when we came to the marker that read "Manchester—City Limits." I noticed two-family and private homes overshadowed by tenements with triple-layers of corner porches. On them, sheets, shirts, and diapers flapped briskly in the breeze.

On Sol's previous trip a used-machinery dealer had offered to show us around. When we reached the leading hotel, Sol called him, while I, curious yet fearful, surveyed the long rows of red-brick corporation long houses (formerly dormitories) that swept all the way down to endless factory buildings stretching on both banks of the Merrimack. The river was full of whitecapped eddies and foamy ripples. How neatly it bisected Manchester!

"He's treating us to dinner," Sol said. "We have to meet him downstairs in twenty minutes."

As we stepped from the elevator, Sol saw the man waiting.

"No 'Mr.' stuff—just call me Ben," our host warned. "I'm taking you to the Manchester Country Club."

As he drove, he mentioned what a rare privilege it was for him to belong to it. "Only two Jews have ever been admitted," he explained. The other Jew had made Kiwanis as well. "I'm still trying for Rotary."

At the club, a thin, elderly, long-skirted hostess greeted Ben and led the way into a two-story-high dining room. She seated us in a distant corner.

Ben showered loud "hellos" on some of the people we passed. The cordiality seemed all on his side; the "hellos" he got in return sounded skimpy and strained.

While we ate, we pumped Ben with questions. He gave us tips about apartments, schools, shopping and religion. The best public schools, the choicest food stores and the wealthiest homes were clustered in the North End. French-Canadians, almost exclusively, occupied the West Side.

At least sixty percent of Manchester's children attended parochial school. Jews? Not more than four or five hundred lived here. He made a wry face about our black housekeeper. "In this city of eighty thousand, I know of only one black, an auto mechanic named Ernie," he told us.

New Hampshire voted almost solidly Republican, he went on. People traveled to Boston for "culture," like the "Pops" or the Boston Symphony. He raised an eyebrow about renting, rather than buying.

"He sent out two messages," I told Sol after we got back to the hotel. "One says, 'Jump in and enjoy; the water's fine.' The other warns of bigotry, of prejudice against Jews and Negroes."

"Horsefeathers," said Sol. "Don't react to one man. You'll see—we'll do fine."

The next morning we walked to the tall iron entrance gates of the millyard. Sol steered me down a hill to the building where we had rented space. Once inside, Sol tugged on a heavy rope beside an ancient elevator shaft. From the bowels of the shaft a mechanism approached. The floor gaped to admit a lift with open sides. Sol gave an upward tug to a short belt, and top and bottom gates parted. After we got on, he pulled the same belt downward, and the gates clanked shut. For our ascent to the top floor he pulled once more on the side rope.

"Wow!" I marveled, looking at a vast length of unencumbered space. Daylight was streaming in windows that faced both east and west. "You claimed we could put both lofts we now have in this one," I remarked. "We'd still have space left over."

"We have a big job to adapt this to a knitting mill," Sol said. "But wait till you meet the fellows—plumbers, carpenters, and, especially, Arthur Franks—all swell guys and all hell-bent on helping us."

Like a magnet, the pull of blueprints, contractors and construction was drawing Sol; I could feel his impatience to get started.

Back in our car, we cruised the North End block by block, noting the location of the Webster School. At last we spied a sign outside a duplex house that read TENEMENT FOR RENT. Sol called the phone number given and soon obtained a key that admitted us to the upstairs of the house with the sign.

Though the pleasant apartment had only two bedrooms, it boasted a large sun parlor, and the tenant would have exclusive use of the attic. Sara Mae and Gene would have to share a bedroom; Catherine could be made comfortable in the attic; an occasional guest could be put up in the sun parlor. In the kitchen I confronted a black gas range with a galvanized-iron flue. Beside it stood a brown oak icebox.

"These don't faze me," I told Sol. "We can replace them later on."

We agreed to rent the tenement. When we took the key back, its owner invited us in. A stubby man with shrewd, dancing eyes, he presented us to his wife, a head taller, graceful, flushed, and a young daughter, who had red-gold hair and freckles. Over tea and homemade cookies, the man quoted the price for the tenement; Sol wrote out a check, and we received the key in return.

On the way downtown I stopped off at a grocery store to check prices. Each item was a few cents cheaper than in New York. Sol and I made the rounds of rooming and boarding houses. We walked through two department stores and sampled a meal at a restaurant. After all, a dozen or more people would be moving with us. Where would they be housed? Where would they eat? Where would they shop? We had committed ourselves, our family, our future; others, too, depended on us. Only one week separated us all from the leap into the unknown.

On the first day of September 1940, our knitting mill was dismantled in twentieth-century Manhattan, to be reassembled in Victorian Manchester. Simultaneously, Sol transported me, Sara Mae, Gene and Catherine from New York to New Hampshire. After unloading us, he went to the mill-yard, grappled with the elevator ropes, set foot in our loft— and stood horrified.

The space echoed as if with thunderclaps; far worse, its whole floor shook.

Sol ran down a double flight of stairs to the floor directly below. There, he discovered the huge spinning frames of a textile mill clamoring away, ceiling and walls shuddering with each rotation of the gears.

Sol shuddered, too. On weekends, the mill below lay quiet. No wonder he, my father and I had felt nothing, heard nothing. Now we must live with a floor that shimmied to a staccato rumble five days a week, twenty-four hours a day.

Sol spilled out his woes that evening. "I didn't have time to haul out my layout. I had no chance to identify supporting beams, to see what structural changes we could make. I could do nothing, because just then the first truckload of knitting machines arrived."

And at that precise moment, Julius had poked his head in the doorway. One son and three nephews, all big and blond, our knitter-apprentices, flanked him.

"I didn't even have a second to welcome them," Sol went on.

A crane and its team had waited all afternoon to hoist the flat machines into place. In no time, the first one came off the truck, went soaring upward in jerky stages, was hauled through a double window with casement removed, and uncrated on our floor. The other machines were hauled through the windows before dusk.

Julius had stood quietly by, pursing his lips and shaking his head. "These floors shake like Jell-O," he had declared in his rasping voice. "The flats won't run one course without a dropout."

"I had to agree with him," Sol told me. "Mug, you can get seasick from the vibrations, and those sensitive carriages, as you know, can't knit back and forth smoothly except on a level surface. Tomorrow we brace the floor."

Julius and his entourage reported early the next day in work clothes. Under his supervision, his four helpers (including a far more serious Dulie, no longer experimenting with mice) began putting the machinery into operating order. When I came in I found the movers reinstalling the windows, two electricians working on overhead wiring and some carpenters reinforcing beams.

Julius stood on a tall ladder, connecting the stop motion,

the safety mechanism of the knitting machine, to the power line. As a carpenter below fitted two beams clumsily, he began to yell at him, gesticulating with long, bony arms. Suddenly his ladder teetered, then toppled, and Julius crashed to the floor.

Sol and I rushed over to help him.

"I don't need your help," he said. Gingerly, he picked himself up, brushed off his clothes, and righted the ladder. As he started to climb up once more, he halted for a second to explain. "You have to know how to fall."

I searched for a nursery school for our four-year-old daughter. Those I saw seemed overly disciplined and joyless; none remotely resembled the progressive one in Riverdale. I settled for a small school with a relaxed, if not fully-accredited, teacher, enrolled Sara Mae, and then, more freely, immersed myself in mill routine.

Serious George, our bald, English circular-machine mechanic, had arrived with his dark-maned wife, Lee, our finishing forelady, and their teen-age daughter. Sol located an apartment for them. He then asked me to hire some trainees, so George could set up and run his stand of Jacquards.

The state employment office sent over one young man after another.

"How much is two-thirds of twenty-four?" I would ask, alternating the last number with 72 or 144.

If a circular machine knit a body and a half (or two and a half pairs of sleeves) in one stripe, the knitter had to know how many stripes to knit for an order of two, six or twelve dozen bodies or sleeves.

I interviewed a half-dozen applicants, with sad results. They would reach for pencil and pad, then stare helplessly at me or make some wild guess. The sixth young man, a homely fellow, revealed two front teeth missing when he grinned and had a broken, beaklike nose. With pain I watched him multiply twenty-four by two, then divide it by three, the long way, with many scratches of his head and bites on the end of the pencil. When he came up with sixteen, I rushed him over to George. It took two more days before I could hire two more learners.

I wondered about public and parochial school standards.

Beginning with a payroll of perhaps twenty, we began to break in local hands. Young people trained in the slow-motion routines of a WPA factory proved hard to adapt.

I watched Johanna show two learners how to operate a Merrow. With one clean sweep she had stitched together the twenty-four-inch seam of an open sleeve. Copying her teacher, a sturdy Polish girl fed backs and fronts into the machine, but with butterfingers, forever dropping back or front and fumbling to fit them together again. Beside her, an attractive Greek woman halted her treadle after each inch to make sure she followed a straight line.

If these younger people seemed clumsy, how much so did seasoned mill hands ossified by generations of traditional Amoskeag textile-weaving habits. Neither Sol nor I nor our instructors could invent any scheme to speed these people into the brisk tempo demanded from piece workers. Some of the New Yorkers persevered; others grew discouraged or homesick and left.

Johanna played a crucial part as instructor and technician. She knew and could teach every operation, whether hand or machine. Patient with novices, she could simplify and streamline procedures without sacrificing quality. She seemed indefatigable.

Her performance was offset by that of her unexpected new husband, Viktor. We had to find a slot for a haughty, fault-finding man with a harsh, guttural accent and illegible handwriting. Sol made him a shipping clerk, but personally checked each package he sent out.

Viktor griped long and loud to Johanna; Johanna, in turn, passed the griping along to me. But we put up with her and the lordly Viktor.

Social customs as well as business customs in Manchester differed markedly from the ones we knew. Soon after we moved in, our next-door neighbors invited us to a dinner party. We appreciated their thoughtfulness. Our hostess served a gourmet buffet to a half-dozen couples. As if by ritual, when the meal ended, the women remained around the table, while the men trooped off to the living room. I'm back in the Middle Ages, I thought.

With birdlike motions of her head a small, perky woman divulged a secret to the other ladies. "If you return a dozen wire hangers to the Spotless Cleaners, they pay five cents for the dozen."

The other women pecked at this morsel of information; I yearned to join the men around the fireplace in the living room. "Sit still," an inner voice counseled me. I kept quiet and sat still.

On the High Holidays we attended a service at the synagogue. Males sat downstairs; females were relegated to the gallery. The prayers droned on and on. With his fingers thoughtfully stroking his wiry, tufted beard, the rabbi delivered a sermon. No details of Hitler's treatment of Jews or his total curb on Jewish emigration; no current events for him! Instead, he analyzed the ten sayings of the Lord when he created the world. By the time he had dissected the tenth one, I sat tortured and squirming on the unyielding wooden pew.

"Not my kind of religion," I told Sol as we left.

Catherine, an observing Catholic, was finding her adjustment even tougher. On the first Sunday after we came, she put on a neat white-collared dress and took a bus to High Mass at the cathedral. She found herself one black blob in a sea of icy white French-Canadian faces. Many stared, but no one spoke to her. Not a single parishioner even smiled at her. In the central doors, as the congregation departed, the priest passed her by quickly. The sea stayed frozen.

She tried again on the next Sunday—and once again. Then she gave up. Not her kind of religion either.

My father had sublet space in the showrooms of a children's underwear firm on Broadway off Herald Square. At first, he appeared frequently at the mill, often bringing my mother along. Gradually, he stayed more and more in New York, soothing customers, stalling creditors, or shopping yarn and machinery markets. When not making his rounds, he often played gin rummy with his friend the yarn salesman.

At the Christmas holidays a new face showed up. It belonged to my brother, now a college senior.

Sol had always treated Ted with great affection, like the younger brother he never had. Ted had returned the affection. With me, his relationship has seesawed. Because of my role as assistant mother, we often had spats. After one, he had refused to speak to me for several years.

In Manchester, I realized I no longer had a little brother. As tall as Sol, well built, personable, he had come to offer his willing hands.

"I'm staying," he told Sol. "You're not sending me back."

"You're in your last year," I said. "How will you get your degree?"

"Jean will sit in for me," he explained.

For the past year he had been dating a pretty, fair-haired, blue-eyed coed.

"In those large classes," he said, "as long as a warm body fills a seat, you are marked present. Next semester I need only two more credits in a religion course. I'm talking the teacher into letting me research the Shakers. They have a colony here in New Hampshire—at Canterbury."

"You've got it all figured out," said Sol admiringly. "I sure can use you. You remember Al, the yarn man? He and Claudia used to work at your father's old S & B, then they worked on and off for us at 20th Street."

Ted nodded.

"He's driving up to get the lay of the land. Until he moves his family up and gets set, you can do production control and yarn inventory. At the same time, you'll cover the night shift."

Ted looked pleased.

"You're living right here with us," Sol continued. "Take a look at the sun parlor. From now on, that's your hangout."

Ted hauled his suitcases into that room and unpacked. But he occupied his quarters for only six weeks. During one supper before the New Year he confided that he was asking Jean to marry him.

"I hope she says yes," I commented, "but she's only a sophomore. Will her people let her quit college?"

"It's like this," Ted told us. "The family, even Jean's aunt, live with the grandmother in the grandmother's house. Grandma calls the tunes and they dance to her music. I'm in good with Grandma. I think she'll swing it."

After Ted left to check on the night knitters, Sol spoke up. "I wonder how Jean will feel about his working on the second shift."

"When you did, I put up with it," I said.

With thirteen of us present, Ted married Jean on February 1. The ceremony took place in a private room at the Hotel Carpenter in Manchester. The flushed and girlish bride wore blue, and Sara Mae sprinkled rose petals before her. The rabbi with the tufted beard performed the ceremony, but Pa paid him and he disappeared before the rest of us celebrated with a roast beef dinner.

Ted and Jean, after a one-week honeymoon in nearby Chester, moved into one and a half furnished rooms facing a downtown park, the Victory Common. We made a job for Jean in the office. She and Ted walked to work, although at different hours, and subsisted on his salary of twenty dollars and hers of fourteen dollars.

Every Thursday Ted would hand Jean his pay envelope. Scrupulously she stowed money away in envelopes marked Food, Rent, Clothing, Medical, and Sundries. Sometimes on Wednesdays, they ate cornflakes. They did not protest.

The blows never let up that first year. We reeled back from one only to get socked with the next.

"Seckler bawled the shit out of me last week," my father reported. Seckler headed Shepherd, still our most profitable jobbing account; his complaints carried great weight. "He claims he can get his cashmeres from Hawick in Scotland quicker than his shetlands from us."

"He's talking about that shipment that got lost on the road," Sol said. He had traced its course first to Providence, then to Newark, where it lay shunted aside in the depot for days before being rerouted to Manhattan.

"Till we get the yarn delivered and then dyed..." I began.

"I know, I know," my father interrupted. "I know all the alibis by heart. When it comes to alibis, you don't have to give me lessons."

"He's not griping about the quality," I offered.

"Yeah, but how long does it take to get one sweater through the mill?"

Only constant practice would speed up our green help. Until they gained experience, we could not be sure of hanging on to our wholesale customers. Sol and I were also trying to hang on to our Pandora customers.

To appease us, Pa had hired a retired army major with long-ago retail contacts who maintained that he still had an "in" with important buyers. Tall, erect, speaking with the voice of authority, he must have bedazzled my father. Before we could investigate his references, or even meet him, we found his name on the payroll, and next to it a hefty drawing account. We waited for results.

Red tartan yard goods ordered before our move, goods we could not cancel, had been delivered to Manchester. By coincidence, Jane had relocated in Boston and now came to Manchester and designed a simple plaid dirndl skirt and matching vest for our young customers. With it we showed classic crew-neck sweaters in colors that matched the red, green or navy of the plaid and used the same colors in knit trim that bordered the vest.

Three hundred skirts and vests soon hung on movable racks, waiting for our star salesman to come through with orders. He never brought in one piece of paper. Eventually, an odd-goods "undertaker" came to close out—at a dollar apiece—the fragments of our shattered hopes. By then we had parted company with the major. Only his sadly over-drawn account stayed behind. We had used up labor and capital, a luxury we could ill afford.

One day in midwinter, Al drove up from New York. On an icy road a few miles short of the New Hampshire border, his Chevrolet skidded and crashed into a tree. Al suffered a triple fracture of the hip and a smashed nose.

Pa called his wife, broke the news, and offered her immediate employment in Manchester as a winder. Leaving their two daughters with her sister in Brooklyn, Claudia came by bus and started to work. For many weeks thereafter, Sol, our children and I spent Sundays visiting Al in the Fitchburg hospital. Sometimes Claudia came with us; other times she shuttled to Brooklyn to check on her girls. Always, Al gave us his free and easy smile and had a snappy comeback for any questions. He would mend, we were told, probably walk with a slight limp, but could not work for months.

On the home front a different worry occupied us. Catherine's loneliness was getting her down.

During the first weeks, she would call me at work to share some of the children's doings with me. A few months later she would call, but only to give me a shopping list. Then she stopped calling.

"I think we have a partner to our liquor," Sol informed me one night as he held a bottle of Chivas Regal up to the light before he poured some for my father.

Lately I had found Catherine's quick, sharp tongue a bit slower and her answers slurred. With Sol's comment, a vague suspicion took firmer shape. By the next afternoon it gave me no peace.

"This lot of four dozen size forty in blue completes a shipment," I told Johanna at the cutting table. "Push the ticket through the mill, will you?"

Then I left for home. I looked for Gene in the back yard. A forlorn tricycle stood there in the sunshine with no rider. I went upstairs. No Catherine, no Gene. But overhead I heard a creaking and a soft, wailing noise. Although I seldom invaded Catherine's domain, I ran up to the shadowy attic. It had a stale, sour smell.

Rocking back and forth, cuddling my two-year-old, who lay half asleep in her lap, Catherine was singing in a shrill falsetto: "Hush, little baby, don't say a word, Mommy's gonna buy you a mocking bird..." Bleary-eyed, she smiled at me. "He just puts me in mind of my own two-year-old that I lost. Some children are too good for this world, entirely too good." Tears started to slither down her cheeks. Disengaging my young one from her arms, I stumbled on a gallon jug of wine lying on its side at her feet.

When Catherine came downstairs much later, she still seemed befuddled. Sol gently announced we were parting company with her. The next morning he drove her to the terminal, and she took the express bus back to Harlem.

Frantically, I tried a stream of other housekeepers. Prim, righteous Edna, after several months, asked if her illegimate daughter could live with us. Mary had a hoard of pornographic pictures. Returning unexpectedly one evening, we surprised her with a lusty-looking boy friend. B. G., from the reform school, worked hard and well; one day she simply vanished, leaving her meager wardrobe and brass jewelry behind.

In emergencies, sometimes my mother, but more often my vigorous, take-charge mother-in-law spelled me. She welcomed the chance to visit with her grandchildren. When she left, however, our troubles remained.

"How much more can we take?" I asked Sol at one juncture.

"We've bottomed out," he reassured me. "Things can only get better. I hear Al will soon be back."

Discharged at last from the hospital, Al made his appearance at the mill. He and his family moved into an apartment not far from us. Their hearts bigger than their pocketbook, they held court on Thursday nights. Claudia served pasta with a meat sauce that she had simmered for hours; Al limped around dispensing cans of beer and cracking jokes. We and others made a practice of dropping in.

While our people were finally getting their bearings in

town, they were also establishing better teamwork in the factory. Sol and my father, each now firmly established in his own sphere, were co-ordinating well. Temporarily, Pandora had been pigeonholed. Our jobbers, grabbing at our prices, were now coming through with hefty orders. The worst kinks of the transition seemed to be getting smoothed out. From this point on, as Sol had prophesied, would things only get better? I dared to hope.

Swiftly and crushingly my hopes were dashed. Before the end of the year the mightiest blow of all clobbered us.

On December 7, 1941, Pearl Harbor stunned our nation and paralyzed Brookshire. The bombs that exploded in the Pacific reverberated through our shaky floor in the Amoskeag millyard. The government had to gear up every facility for the war effort. Until Uncle Sam had reordered his priorities, he suspended all civilian production.

Days, let alone weeks, without work would deal us a death blow. The changeover had consumed all our cash reserves; bills were coming due. Without shipments, we could get no money from customers. When and how could we get our machines humming again? If we did, when and how could we get more yarn?

"Can you get up here right away?" Sol asked my father on the phone, as our factory ground to a standstill.

At once, he and my mother drove up. Somehow, from somewhere, Pa had captured two dozen bundles of khaki and navy yarn. He had them tied in brown paper rather than unwieldy cartons. Bulky but resilient, these had been crammed into the back seat and, secured with ropes, into the open trunk and on the roof of the car.

That evening the four of us got together in their hotel room and came up with a triple strategy. Sol was to apply for government contracts, making low, low competitive bids for two items: olive drab mufflers, heavily brushed, and navy knit shirts with collar, placket and breast pocket. Thanks to Pa, we had wool for samples.

We would delay paying our debts. Sol would ask Arthur

Franks, who had never billed us, to hold off. My father would return to New York to stall the bank on our loan and to plead with our yarn suppliers for more time.

We had to raise new money. Neither my father nor my mother had any reserves left. Sol would borrow money on his life insurance. I would strip our children's bank accounts. My mother would baby-sit with our children while I returned to New York with my father. I would approach Uncle Schwer for a loan, hoping he still had a soft spot for me.

"What will happen to us," I asked my father, on the drive to New York, "if we don't land any government contracts? Or if the bankers tell you 'no dice' or Uncle Schwer turns me down?"

"Never let bankers see you *tsitter* [shiver]," he pontificated. "With them, you must always talk from strength. When I went to that banker in the Amoskeag, I told him, 'When I visit a banker, I take my shoes off, not my hat.' Let him smell my stinking feet. When he knows how hard I sweat to make a buck, then he knows what good security he has."

"But," I retorted, "he didn't rush forward to lend you any money."

"I didn't ask," he said. "Here in New York I know how to handle the *chevra*, the kinsmen. With me, they're not stiff, they'll bend a little. Not like those Yankee horse traders."

His air of confidence did not rub off on me. All night I tossed, and barely slept.

Uncle Schwer had invited me to come to his apartment in Washington Heights. Promptly at nine, I presented myself. We sat at a massive mahogany table in his dining room and sipped tea.

"I came for a loan," I told him.

"Will $5,000 help you out?" he asked.

I sat there, my mouth open with relief. He wrote out the check.

"Now tell me about Pandora," he said.

Sadly, I related the history of the red-tartan closeout, and the set-back the major had dealt Pandora.

"When we get out of this squeeze," I finished, "I can't see us making skirts or sportswear for Pandora Partners; we can't afford the risk. And I don't want to settle for second best—sweaters alone.

"How excited the buyers got when I showed them bottoms that co-ordinated with the tops! No one else had ever shown them anything like that."

Uncle Schwer heard me out, twisting the end of his trim mustache between thumb and forefinger. Then he clasped his chin, peered at me out of heavy prism eyeglasses and shook his head.

"No one goes through life getting a hundred percent. When the time comes for you to start Pandora again, don't get greedy. If you can show only sweaters, settle for fifty percent. Just sweaters can work out fine, too."

I kissed his gentle face good-bye, and returned to Pa, waiting in our tiny office. Matter-of-factly, he accepted Schwer's check, then gave me his own good news. Our bankers had granted him the extension. He had had a knock-down, drag-out battle with the spinner who supplied most of our yarn. His sales representative, supposedly my father's dear friend, had leaked news to his boss of our sportswear fiasco.

"You sidetracked my yarn money to pay for yard goods?" the angry spinner had accused my father.

"You'll get your money," said Pa, toughing it out. "Is my word good?"

He had finally bludgeoned the spinner into giving us the sixty days extra we needed.

Back in Manchester, Sol had secured specifications for the G.I. materiel and figured out our costs. He and my father sat late into the night figuring out how sharp a bid they dared make on each item.

In the all-but-deserted factory the next day, my father ran down samples of the muffler on the dinky. He brushed them many times over; Sol weighed a dozen of them on a table scale. Julius, meanwhile, knit cloth and trimming for the shirts. Again Sol weighed them. Johanna made a pattern, cut the cloth, measured out collars and three-button plackets from the trim, marked the breast pockets and stitched the parts together. My mother pulled in Merrow ends and cut dangling threads. Then the two men checked their costs once more and were able to revise their bids slightly downward.

Our mill stayed closed for seven weeks. When we re-opened, we had been assigned yarn for the substantial contracts we had won. Of this, the government was allowing us to divert a small percentage to civilian production.

One other benefit derived from those contracts.

"On those forms, Mr. B.," Sol told my father, "I listed Ted as my key man. That should save him from the draft, at least for the length of these contracts."

Several weeks passed until the mill geared up, until waves of olive drab and navy blue started pouring down from the machines. Each of those weeks a razor-thin, unsmiling woman inspector from Army Procurement checked to make sure we observed every word and figure in the printed federal form. She weighed random garments on a scale; with a magnifying glass she checked the number of needles and rounds to the inch.

"Poor girl!" Sol commented after one such visit. "She had so little to pick on this time."

"What a revolution in this plant!" I said. "Yet how quickly we adapt to strange people like her wandering around and laying down strange rules."

"We've adapted, but I still can't get used to all this khaki flooding the factory," said Sol.

"Let's take advantage of our civilian yarn quota," I suggested. "Even with Snoopy Sue weighing each garment, we do have some surplus. Instead of wasting it on Pa's jobbers, we should knit Pandora sweaters out of every ounce of it. Maybe I should go on the road with samples."

Sol looked thoughtful. "You could show classics, easy-to-make sweaters. You should also take children's sweaters with you. A baby boom is coming. We should get in on it."

"Money's tight. How about travel expenses?"

Sol emptied the factory's petty-cash box and his billfold; I came up with savings from my household money.

"What about the kids?" I asked. One housekeeper had gone; the next had not yet appeared.

Sol's mother agreed to come, and our children clapped their hands for joy. Fatso flew up on the same plane on which I was to leave. In their excitement, the children almost forgot to say good-bye to me.

Once more I felt the familiar strain of sample cases pulling on arm sockets. The logistics of arranging flights to ten cities in eleven days and keeping track of three cases flustered me. I sometimes couldn't reserve a plane seat. When I did, I often got bumped for army brass. Twice I got rerouted.

Never had I expected such a welcome as those retailers gave me! In Philadelphia, Cleveland, Detroit and Chicago they longed to stock their empty shelves; like scavengers they were scouring for goods. Bookings came easy; stores would take all we could spare.

In Chicago I had an early appointment with Eunice Craig, children's buyer for Marshall Field. However, I had left without children's swatches. Sol had put together and mailed every conceivable shade, and just in time this special-delivery package reached me. That rainbow of colors made a big hit with Miss Craig. It broke ground for a huge initial order.

In this seller's market, Pandora really mushroomed. Word spread from one branch to the next in a chain, from one store to another. Reports from Marshall Field launched us nationally in all children's departments.

In our modest New York quarters, with no high-priced sales force to add to our overhead, my father sat alone. Buyers found their way to him. His only dilemma: How much could he allocate to each one?

Eunice Craig met Morris Blum; they became staunch friends. She would drop in on him and greet him with a twist of the strawberry curl on his forehead.

"How many dozen can you ship me, Morris?" she would ask while they drained glasses of Drambuie.

As if the word had descended from Moses (Pa's name in Hebrew), whatever he said she accepted as law.

Pa reveled in his new role. From extolling those sacred cows his jobbers, he switched 180 degrees to glorifying Pandora's retailers. Two saleswomen who carried the children's underwear line in the adjoining showroom persuaded him to let them carry Pandora as a sideline. Elizabeth covered the West Coast; Carrie traveled the Deep South. Both had loyal followings; both brought in substantial business. Their orders and enthusiasm speeded his conversion.

After a while, as our roster of the nation's top retailers expanded, Pa forgot how Pandora came into existence. Gradually he came to believe that he himself had conceived her. We did not undeceive him, or remind him of the roadblocks he had thrown in our way for seven years. Instead, we welcomed Pa to our team.

In the spring of 1943, during an overnight stay in New York, I met my mother downtown at Schrafft's for lunch. She had recently returned from a Miami vacation with my father.

"Night after night I sat alone in that hotel room, all the lights out," she told me. "Aunt Dora and Uncle Motl go for a walk on Collins Avenue in the evening. I didn't want, if they should look up at our windows, they should find out that Pa had left me behind while he went *spatzering* [sporting]. I didn't dare leave the room to cross the lobby. Someone might ask, 'Where's your husband?' I was even afraid to pick up the phone. So behind the curtains I sat by myself, alone in the dark, waiting, waiting—until around four o'clock in the morning. In would come *der grosse Held* [the big achiever] and I would make believe I was fast asleep."

Since their return his hours had grown more and more irregular, she went on. Would he show up? When? She could not endure the guessing game.

"So I'll prepare him a plate of salmon and scallions, and I'll go into a movie or window-shopping on Fordham Road."

He retaliated. He mortified her by making her ask once, twice and then again for her weekly household money. He sometimes ended up by throwing it in her direction. I never saw this. Sara Mae told me about it, after she had slept at my parents'. She had watched "Peep" throw a pay envelope at my mother in the living room. It landed on the couch and opened up. Some bills spilled out of the envelope and were strewn over the floor. Grandma stared, then fled into the bedroom. After a while, slowly and with red eyes, she came back. One by one she picked up the bills and straightened them out.

My mother never mentioned this incident, nor did I bring it up. Wishfully she was still singing the same song: "Someday he'll snap out of it; you'll see." I did not try to reason with her.

After our lunch, Ma headed for her too-quiet apartment in the Bronx; I headed for a far-from-quiet apartment also in the Bronx. I was meeting Sol for supper at his mother's.

Sol's two sisters, each married to a soldier, had come home to Mother. Tootsie had a year-old infant; Ruth was expecting. Each of them, as well as Fatso, was entertaining a guest. Sol's brother, Lou, his wife and son also milled about. Now installed in their own apartment, they ate many meals at Fatso's.

Sol came in late, made his hellos and warned his mother that he had to eat and dash. Precisely at eight o'clock he had to answer roll call at the Mantle Club in mid-Manhattan. His schedule fitted in with Fatso's. She decreed that she and I would visit Auntie Annie, who lay ill in a Brooklyn hospital and wasn't getting better.

"The trouble is the food," explained my mother-in-law. "She needs some homemade chicken soup."

When we emerged from the subway in Brooklyn, she had been toting a shopping bag. From it she extricated a jar, stripped it of many insulating layers of brown paper bags and plunked it into the deep valley between her breasts. We sailed past the guards, past the head floor nurse at her station and reached the patient's bedside. There, Fatso sat and patiently spooned out precious soup to an emaciated Auntie Annie.

Fatso and Skinny shared their doings with us; not so my father. Only by chance did I back into his private affairs. When I did, I regretted it.

A chain of events began in Manchester when my father had dinner with us one evening, after visiting my brother.

Ted no longer worked nights. He had become an excellent sweater maker. He loved the research behind each sample and turned out garments of quality. Jean no longer worked. She had given birth to their first child, and she and Ted had bought their first home.

"You don't have to list Teddy as a key man any more," Pa announced. "He's manufactured his own exemption. What a baby! What a boy!" I could almost hear the flourish of trumpets.

"They did a good job," said Sol. "They've got quite a buster there."

"Say hello to the children," I put in. "I think Sara Mae's still up."

Peep, as the children called him, tiptoed into the bedroom, grotesquely exaggerating each step. I heard him teasing Sara Mae with a familiar refrain.

"Do you know what you did to me?" he asked. "You made me into a grandpa. Who needed you? Are you trying to make an old man out of me?"

After more of the same, she came running out in her nightgown to bury her sobs in my lap. I held her close, tucked her back in bed, and stormed out to confront my father.

"You bully," I raged, "why don't you pick on me and let her alone?"

"That's easy. Why do you forever wear black? You look like my Mimeh Fageh." This decrepit, aged aunt, mother of the Tzudikers, was the butt of much family ridicule.

To my dismay, Sol agreed. "He has a point, May. You're trying to look slim, but you also want to look hep."

Suddenly I thought of a red-letter day some twenty years before. My father had been delegated to buy me a winter coat. At Franklin Simon's he had chosen a navy coat with a squirrel collar and paid $79.50, an outrageous price at that time.

"I knew if I sent him," my mother had confided to Aunt Jennie, "he would pick only the best—more than I would ever dare to spend."

Now, I asked, "How about shopping with me for a new winter coat? I'd love to have you along."

Flattered, he readily agreed. When Sol and I next went to New York, I met my father in Altman's. At his urging, I bought a bright-red coat with black Persian-lamb collar and lining and a hat to go with it. I modeled them for Sol at the office.

"Smash!" he exclaimed. "We'll have to step out and celebrate."

Very pleased with myself and my father, I hung the coat in the wardrobe, where I noticed another handsome coat, a soft beige plush with a wide fox shawl collar. Elsie, our girl Friday, about to leave for lunch, came over, reached for it and slipped it on. It fitted her most becomingly.

"New?" I asked. "Where did you get it?"

She reached back to hoist up and show me the label. At the same time a wave of crimson mounted from her neck and suffused her face. Not only could I read "Lord & Taylor," but also I could recognize the invisible signature that had paid for it.

Sol and I had seriously discussed the advantages of a vertical setup, where we controlled every stage of sweater making, from buying tow, or raw wool, to the finished product on our customers' counters. We lacked the first two processes: spinning and dyeing.

Sol enlisted my father's help. Together they found a master

spinner willing to invest as a partner in a mill. Before the year-end we had opened a spinning facility in Lowell, Massachusetts. Once we controlled our raw materials, we could channel ever-greater quantities of yarn into civilian production.

Gradually the long, hard pull was easing. From twenty employees, our payroll had grown to over over one hundred. Our business had rooted and was bearing fruit.Now I had to accept Manchester, to take root and likewise to bear fruit. The timetable Sol and I had laid out on our honeymoon for our family of six children had been badly disrupted. Before the end of 1943 I was pregnant again.

I lingered over making my exit from the factory. Johanna—and Viktor—had long since departed. Lean, stoop-shouldered Oscar supervised the stitching floor.

"It's time you stayed home already," he lectured me one spring day, wagging his bony forefinger at me. "We can manage fine without you. Stay home and enjoy, enjoy."

"How about it, Runt?" Sol said. "Whether you work in or out of the factory, you'll always pull your oar. And remember, Ted will be sticking around."

The army had sent Ted its greetings. Both he and his wife had assumed that so splendid a specimen of manhood would be thrust into uniform immediately. They had placed their house on the market; Jean and their small son would live with her parents for the duration.

But Ted had been rated 4-F. He had been rejected for astigmatism and flat feet. Crestfallen, the young couple had taken their house off the market and canceled their hasty plans.

"The starch seems to have left Ted," my husband said later. "I've got to get him going again. I'll have to give him more time, let him have his head, even let him make some mistakes. Nothing seasons a businessman like trial and error."

"If it doesn't cost too much," I added.

But Sol seemed to have the situation under control. By Easter, big with a lively, kicking baby, I bowed out.

SEVEN

Tangled Yarn

IN LATE SPRING we registered Sara Mae for an entire season at a camp. At the same time, we rented a vacation cottage on the shore of Paugus Bay, off Lake Winnipesaukee. During July and August, Sol would spend weekends and one night midweek there. A high-schooler, who worked for me during the year, would come to the cottage as my helper. Gene, my only child for the summer, would have me all to himself.

At the lake I could look ahead to idle hours, sweet, unhurried leisure. Mornings I would take Gene on jaunts; afternoons I would loll on the rocks at the water's edge, my back propped against the trunk of a lofty tree.

I would bring along a book, *The Bible as Designed for Living Literature.* I would read a few pages, enjoy the starkness of the writing, raise my eyes to the sun descending over majestic trees on the opposite shore, then go back to the Bible until I had read it from cover to cover.

Two events, one in July and one in early August, disrupted this midsummer dream. One fine day in July, Gene and I took a walk in the woods to pick blueberries. I emerged from that excursion with the most virulent case of poison ivy I had ever suffered. Thickest around my eyes, forehead and cheeks and along my neck, shoulders and forearms, the rash also encrusted my legs and thighs. None of the old sure-fire remedies relieved me. Desperate with itching, I painted the oozing sores with potassium permanganate, an indelibly purple liquid. Lurid splotches covered me from head to toe and framed my belly in its ninth month of pregnancy.

Early in August, my father came to visit us. His eyes goggled when he beheld me. Recovering from the initial shock, he passed feisty comments on the state of my beauty and another few on the dimensions of my stomach.

"What are you trying to do?" he asked. "Be one of those *Italianeh* with a long string of children trailing after you?"

Not even bothering to fence with him on his familiar theme, I prepared to serve lunch. When I ignored him, he began to taunt Gene on the doubtful glories of blueberrying. Gene's hazel eyes, ringed with heavy lashes, began to well up.

"Come, son," said Sol. "We'll set the table on the porch."

We enjoyed a comparatively peaceful meal.

"How about a row on the lake?" Pa asked over coffee. "You have her here." He shoved his shoulder in my helper's direction. "Let her stay with the kid and we'll have a little quiet."

Sol led the way to an aged rowboat, helped us in and took the oars. My eyes drank in the grandeur of distant mountains, sprawling fingers of lazy clouds and calmly lapping water. A little way out, my father broke the spell and came to the point. He proposed that my brother become a partner in Pandora.

"He's green yet, he doesn't know where he's going. But if we want him to stay, we must make him feel a real part of the business," he began.

"How do you propose we do that?" Sol asked.

"The old lady and I each have to give Teddy part of our share; you and May should do the same thing. That way you make a young buck feel he should dig in and produce."

"Why should we do that?" I protested. "Anything you and Ma want to do with your share is fine with us, but why should we give anything away? We've worked too hard for it."

"So stiff!" remarked my father.

"You know, ole man, I believe in the motto 'Reward worthy men,'" Sol said. "Ted has only worked in the factory three years. He's raw yet."

"Are you anxious to see the family stay together?" asked Pa.

"Are you?" countered Sol.

"Very much so," said my father. "Here's one way to keep the family together."

For a few minutes we sat silent, looking at the gently rippling water and letting the implications of his threat sink in.

"What do you propose?" Sol asked at last.

"Let's split it three ways," my father answered.

"Never!" Without thinking, I had spat the word out. Three ways meant Pa, Sol and Ted. Didn't I count? In one instant he had shoved me right out of the picture.

"Most unreasonable, Mr. B.," said my husband. "May and I have put in thirteen years of work, the hardest kind of work." He totaled it up, almost to himself. "Nine years before we moved here, then digging up our roots to make the move, and four of the toughest years since." Looking squarely at my father, he said, "Do you know what you're asking?"

"Don't build a federal case," my father singsonged. "You want to encourage young blood."

"You're not doing your son any favors, Pa," I put in. "Let him get his feet wet; let him earn it. You're fair neither to him nor to yourself, and surely not to us."

"Fair, not fair," my father mocked me, then addressed Sol. "What have we got if not our family?"

After a long pause Sol spoke. "We'll let you know, Mr. B. We need time to think this over."

We rowed back to the rocky shore. My father seemed impatient to be on his way. Sol and Gene drove him to the station.

On his return Sol phoned Sam.

"Don't be a fool," exploded Sam when he heard my father's proposal. "For seven years we sweated before we got your fifty percent down on paper. Give away one percent of that and you lose control of your business."

"But, Sam," answered Sol, "maybe he's tired of running around—grateful his son wasn't drafted—really wants to get back with the ole lady."

The conversation went on and on while I fumed. At last Sol hung up.

"Blackmail, pure blackmail! He plans to leave her anyway," I told him. "His word is his bond with any stranger. When it comes to his family, he'll use us any way he can."

"I couldn't live with myself," Sol spelled out slowly, "if there's even one chance in a hundred that these two might stay together."

I ranted about life being a game of give-and-take, with no medals going to those who give too much. To no avail. Like my father, Sol never heard me.

Eager to patch my mother's heartbreak, he insisted that this concession might sway my father. Distrustful and bucking, I gave in. Sometime that fall, I agreed, not to a three-way, but to a five-way split.

The four original partners added a fifth, my brother.

Our newborn arrived on schedule in September. Ralph proved an "easy" baby. He did nothing but gurgle, gain weight and grow.

Homemakers who punch no time clocks should, I thought, pace themselves in fairly unhurried fashion. A newborn might complicate the routine at first, but after a few months I would achieve a comfortable tempo. I never accomplished this. I kept juggling many balls in the air—and I kept sneezing without letup.

The pressure from our growing family taxed me. "These children need you, Sol," I said, "not just the baby, but the older ones."

"I can't slacken off right now," he explained. "I thought your father would simmer down. No such thing. I don't know what he'll do next, or where to lay my hands on him when I need him. And I'd better find the right doctors.

Those rumblings in my stomach are getting worse, and no one in town seems able to help me."

We made a date with a highly recommended internist at a Boston clinic. Dr. Thannhauser gave Sol extensive tests over a period of several weeks, then called him into his office before the year's end. I went along.

"Never before have I found this condition in one so young," said the portly physician. "You have diverticulitis."

He explained to Sol the formation of small pockets in the wall of the intestine. Certain foods would collect and stagnate in these pockets, causing discomfort. If the patient followed a restricted diet—no seeds, no roughage and no fried foods—he would feel better.

Driving home over roads glazed with snow, I started to think out loud.

"Aggravation could have brought on that diverticulitis. From each trip to New York you come back tied in knots. You don't recover for days. I'm going to start going with you again, even if I have to wean Ralph."

"Come along, Runt," Sol said. "I've missed you. And that pumpkin's doing fine. I'm also going to try something different. I'm coming home for lunch and for an early supper with the kids. If I leave work unfinished, I'll go back to the factory later in the evening."

"A switch, Sol, but a very welcome one," I told him. Then I continued: "I have a confession to make. It involves an even bigger switch."

My husband looked at me expectantly.

"You remember how, when we first moved here, you wanted to buy, not rent, and how I objected. Well, I'm ready now. Your precious pumpkin has crowded us out of our home. Each of our children should have his own bedroom, you need a study all your own, and I want a house nearer the school, with a good-size porch and a back yard full of trees."

Sol grabbed at my proposal. "I heard of one house that could be going on the market," he said thoughtfully. "It might need alterations. So what?"

With his yen for construction, the prospect of alterations

enhanced the project. By New Year's we had purchased the house.

During the next few months I prepared for the changeover. I decided to consult with Albert, our Bronx-based designer. He had advised us in Riverdale, with happy results. With Sol's house plans, I journeyed down to Albert's. He foresaw no problems and arranged one trip to Manchester to survey the scene and meet the contractors. I commented on a pair of end tables in his current display of furniture. A glass shelf rested on three bleached-wood acanthus leaves; these flared dramatically upward and outward from a narrow base. "A bit spectacular," I remarked.

"But just right for you," Albert returned, with a shrug and a laugh. "We'll show those yokels."

His word "yokels" grated on me, but I decided to withhold judgment.

After seeing Albert, I went down to our showroom; my father scarcely interrupted his game of gin rummy to grunt hello. Sol had left to inspect the latest knitting machine attachments at a foreign machinery agency.

"Let me treat you to lunch, honey," said Carrie, our Southern sales representative. A small, black-browed, white-haired woman, she could turn on the Dixie drawl and charm like turning on a spigot.

"A seller's market doesn't last forever," Carrie said as we ate. "Eventually, y'all will have to hire a sales manager. You must get the very best. Your pappy acts real jumpy, May, but you must make him wait for Carl."

She and Elizabeth had been singing Carl's praises; he had managed sales for the children's underwear firm the two women represented. While he served his stint in the navy, fewer and fewer customers had remained loyal, until the owners were on the verge of folding the operation.

"He'll be discharged early next year," Carrie concluded. "Y'all have been swamped with orders for children's goods. That's Carl's forte. Don't let Mr. B. jump the gun."

"We won't," I told her. "I'll remind my father of an army major he once hired."

I made the rounds of the stores to check on a new item, a long, long sweater called "Sloppy Joe."

"I've bought one," I told Sol by phone. "If it takes off the way the salesgirls say, we must change all our measurements for fall."

"Meet you at Fatso's," he said. "By the way, Sam told me that Ted had no part in that partnership deal. He and Jean questioned your father about whether they should accept it. They sensed our resentment."

"But they did accept it," I answered, "and now they're staying as far away from us as they can get."

We could talk no further about it at his mother's. Not one, but two small toddlers were playing tag underfoot and adding their shrieks to the commotion. When Sol took the subway down to his meeting, I rode uptown to my mother's.

"My troubles get bigger, not smaller," she said as we sipped tea together. "I thought it would make life easier if I stayed away from Florida this winter. Instead, I have a new improvement."

At odd hours of the night her phone rang. There was never an answer to her hello.

"I pick up the receiver, I talk, and all I hear is someone breathing, listening and breathing, heavy breathing." she said.

"Where is Pa when it rings?" I asked. "Is he out or has he 'it the 'ay?"

"Either way. If he answers, he says nothing afterward to me. Last night he didn't come home at all. I picked up the phone the first time it rang," she said, "but it rang twice more around midnight and I wouldn't answer."

"Scared?" I asked.

"I don't remember when I last had a decent night's sleep," she said. "But I'm more scared for him than for me. Maybe he got himself mixed up with gangsters, or maybe some husband don't like how he's carrying on with his wife. He can get himself killed."

"Let me talk to Sol about it," I told her.

Sol hired a detective to tail Pa. On a Sunday morning the

agent followed my father to a run-down section of Brooklyn. He was carrying two shopping bags, loaded with goodies from a gourmet store and from the bakery next door. He took them to a tall tenement house and rang the bell of a third-floor apartment. Later the detective rang the same bell. A flashily dressed woman with henna hair answered.

The private eye's report changed nothing. My mother's phone never ceased its mysterious midnight ringings, not while my father remained in the house.

On Washington's Birthday we moved into our new home. Soon after, we held open house for our friends. As guests entered, Sara and Gene took their coats upstairs, running on gray broadloom steps past wallpaper of silver, Kelly green and fuchsia.

In the living room, Sol served drinks from a portable white bar in front of a black Carrara fireplace. On each side was a love seat upholstered in black cotton that repeated the green and fuchsia of the wallpaper. They were flanked by glass-topped tables with dramatic acanthus-leaf bases. All was reflected in a mirrored window flower box.

From a silver bowl on a long black table in the dining room, I ladled champagne punch. I refilled the bowl and canapé trays in a kitchen with walls of washable beige and floor of large red and white squares. I walked past a huge custom-built, U-shaped breakfast table framed by a wrap-around seat of dark red leather.

Folks venturing upstairs glimpsed a practical nurse, her gray bobbed hair carefully marcelled, who was guarding our infant son. Occasionally she rinsed his diapers in a bathroom with maroon glass walls and mirrored ceiling.

I waited for comments. None seemed forthcoming.

Finally one person spoke up. "You have brought us a touch of New York," she said. I recognized how kindly she had phrased it.

The previous spring I had questioned some practices, such as corporal punishment, in the public schools. I had gone from teacher to principal to school superintendent seeking answers. I got none. One night, I observed a session of the Manchester School Board. Most committeemen, I learned, sent their children to parochial schools. One member could neither read nor write; he worked as a janitor at the *Manchester Union-Leader.*

I thought the local League of Women Voters could persuade qualified candidates to run for the school board. But Manchester had no unit. The state League helped me form a committee, and a prominent lady gave us her blessing and opened her home to forty prospective members at an afternoon tea. Before we left, we had organized. The first item on our agenda: working to improve Manchester's public schools.

As the member responsible for public relations, I began publishing a mini-newsletter, the *Voice of the Voter.* This tickled Sol. He proposed that I put out a company newspaper as well. Pandora people, he believed, should have all the information about the business that we could supply.

I recruited a group of reporters in the factory. Digging up material, writing copy, delivering it to the printer, getting proofs, proofreading, making the layout could all be compressed into convenient stretches of time over a few days, once a month.

Sol's proposal dovetailed with my resolve never to let the housewife blot out the businesswoman. As editor of a house organ, I would know from the inside what was happening throughout. My only question was "When do I start?"

The *Brookshire Yarn* made its debut in October 1945. The four small pages soon grew to six and, later, to eight full-size pages. Once a month I wrote the lead story. Executives contributed their news, reporters collected gossip items; Sol wrote a "Message from Management." Employees welcomed each issue and took it home to their families.

The first *Yarn* headlined a "School for Suggestions." Sol had employed a pair of time-and-motion experts to streamline our handling of goods. One, a backup man, filled in all the details for his associate, the idea man. To Sol they had suggested simple but significant changes to reduce the handling of goods and to cut down the waste motions of workers, and even suggested eliminating whole operations.

Straightway, Sol had hired the same consultants to teach a course for our top and middle management. Classes were held two nights a week for three weeks at the Chamber of Commerce building. The students reacted with such enthusiasm and came up with so many brainstorms that Sol decided to stage a suggestion contest. The School for Suggestions and the resulting contest were described on the front page of the *Yarn*.

A smaller item proclaimed "Pandora Goes National." After making the rounds of a half-dozen advertising agencies, Sol and I had hired a Boston firm. The *Yarn* reproduced our first ad, one for *Seventeen* magazine.

"Welcome Home, Veterans," said one *Yarn* headline early the next year. The article pictured four local servicemen, returned from the army. From the navy came one other serviceman, the man Carrie had recommended. Tall, handsome Carl, still in his officer's uniform, had been interviewed for sales manager.

"Carl Charisma," I had whispered to Sol.

He had accepted our offer, making three stipulations: a more suitable showroom, a New York advertising agency—too tough to work long distance with Boston—and a stay at the mill to learn how to knit and purl.

Willingly my father and Sol agreed to all three. A showroom, still a sublet but with twice the floor space, was leased at a more prestigious Broadway address. A Madison Avenue advertising agency produced a crackling maverick, Harriet, who materialized at Carl's side with prize-winning ads. Carl spent ten days at the mill to grasp the techniques of Stoll, Dubied and Jacquard machines.

Dulie had knit swatches for him from each type of machine, from a variety of yarns and in an endless parade of gauges and stitches. Carl, an apt pupil, developed a system of specifications for his sample requests.

"I'm asking any designer I hire to work here at the mill," he told Sol. "I find everyone so warm and co-operative, from the floor sweeper on up.

"Tell me," he asked, "can you manufacture everything I can sell? Remember, I plan to build a powerhouse of a sales force."

"You sell! We'll ship!" promised Sol, as he had once promised me. "We've been considering buying our own building in the millyard if we must expand. We'll keep you posted."

On this subject Carl heard nothing more for the next few months. Other matters—one concerning Skinny; one, Fatso—preoccupied Sol.

My father brought his "ten-year time of troubles" in his marriage to a head. He contrived an argument one evening that got my mother angry enough to yell, "Get out of this house."

On the following afternoon, a bleak one, he left the showroom and took the subway home. Before he got there, he stopped off at a nearby park; for many hours he sat there alone. Then he walked to the apartment, which was empty, packed his suitcases and left.

"Move to Manchester, Skinny," Sol begged.

"I can't. Any day I expect Pa to open the door, walk in and take up again where he left off. I wait for his key to turn in the lock."

She stayed there and waited.

That same spring, at six o'clock one morning, Sol's older sister phoned us. "Fatso has had a stroke. The doctor's on his way over. We don't know if she'll even make it until he gets here."

When Sol and I walked into Fatso's apartment, the family doctor and a renowned specialist were consulting at her bedside. Neither gave Sol's mother odds to last twenty-four hours.

Children and in-laws hovered around; doctors came and

went; a second-shift nurse relieved the earlier one. We left after the third-shift nurse went on duty, but resumed our vigil early the next day.

"A miracle," said her doctor that morning.

None of this dying nonsense for her! Within a month Fatso was forcing herself off the bed and learning to walk again, clinging to the wall for support.

One suffocating day in July she summoned us. All nurses had disappeared; her younger daughter was caring for her. Fatso caressed our cheeks with her good hand and asked after our children. Then she got off the bed and, holding on to a chair, the dresser and the wall, showed us how well she got around. Perspiring profusely, she completed a circuit of the room and fumbled her way back to bed. Sol plugged in a small electric fan he had brought her to circulate the oppressive air. She sat up high to catch its slight breeze.

Fatso had grown thin and strained. Her hair was drawn back in a skimpy knot; her right eye and the right corner of her mouth still sagged.

"There's something I really need," she mumbled, "and, Solly, I don't want you should say no."

"What is it, Mom? You know we'll do anything we can."

A stay at a beach resort to escape the dreadful heat? A different specialist? A physical therapist to work with her? A housekeeping service for a thorough cleanup of her littered apartment?

On that stifling, summer day, that crippled, back-from-the-dead woman told her son the one thing in the world she really had to have: "I want a Persian lamb coat!"

During a heat wave in August a neighborhood furrier fitted her. The next month, leaning heavily on Lou's arm, she wore it to the Bar Mitzvah of her first grandson. In October she wore it when she flew up to Manchester to share our fifteenth wedding anniversary.

"Wherever I go," she informed Sol, "my children don't have to feel ashamed of the way their mother looks."

These dramas starring our mothers never made the pages of the *Yarn*; nor did any small aside about my incessant sneezing. Other stories did. Under the subhead "Stork Club" were printed these two-liners: "Ted and Jeanette Blum announce the birth of their second child, a girl"; and, in the last issue of 1946, "The Sol Sidores are adding a new member to their family."

Some of the *Yarn* stories produced predictable sequels, but we had no inkling of the ripple effect that had been generated by the time-and-motion experts.

"Transport loaded," Sol would yell as one of the kids came down to breakfast and then raced upstairs for a forgotten schoolbook or homework paper. "Transport loaded" became our motto as any of us moved from one floor or area to another. Automatically we piled items up at the bottom or head of the stairs or on the window seat outside our bedroom.

In the mill, Sol painstakingly tracked the number of trips each supervisor and/or his floor help took during a day's work. With the persons involved, he devised shortcuts to halve the number of those trips. He instituted an exercise, that of rotating the arms at their fullest both vertically and horizontally. Had we taken advantage of every work space in this area? I designed a cutting table with a semicircle carved out of its center. A cutter in this keyhole could reach with her shears to the outer edges. Sol reviewed other work stations. He built more convenient holding baskets for the stitchers, larger side shelves for the pressers, and higher tables for the inspectors. He invented a brushing device that enabled certain types of knit goods to be brushed by a single girl, and had it patented.

Innovations came not only from management but from people on the line and in the office. A telephone squad applied early pressure on accounts behind in paying bills; the loopers used an ingenious attachment to loop, rather than stitch, grosgrain ribbon on cardigans.

The attack on wasted space permeated our home as well. In my kitchen I discovered areas suitable for mini-shelves. Sol constructed a back porch under our kitchen window. A pair of carpenters working under his direction stayed so many years on these and other improvements that our children considered the two men members of the family.

"Better Pandoras the Easier Way" was distributed to every employee in the plant. I wrote this booklet during my fourth pregnancy and had it illustrated with comic drawings by a high-schooler, the son of my cleaning woman. It showed the do's and don'ts of the most repeated operations of sweater-making. Sol took great pride in it.

"We need more than booklets, though," he said, looking around at the floor on which we had been rocking away for the seventh year. "We're too cramped."

He longed for enough space to lay out each department according to the principles of time and motion. He envisioned receiving raw wool (then processed in our Lowell, Massachusetts, plant) at one end, putting it through each stage in order, until he shipped finished sweaters out the door. As if in answer to his prayers, Arthur Franks gave him a tip: the building next to ours in the millyard was going on the market.

"I can't get hold of your father," said Sol. "Ted doesn't know where to reach him either." Pa had disappeared on his annual Florida vacation, leaving neither forwarding address nor phone number. "What if the building gets grabbed up before he gets back?"

Casually, one morning, the missing partner phoned from La Guardia. "Hello, *meine kinderlech* [my dear little children]," he squeaked in a falsetto. "I'm back."

Sol ignored Pa's so-called humor. "Grab the next plane. Come right up to Manchester," he said. "Don't even go into the city."

My father's return, his inspection of the property, and its purchase all took place on the same day. A picture of a building seven stories high and four-hundred feet long filled the front page of the February 1947 *Yarn*. "Our Future Home" read the headline.

Two years would pass before most tenants completed their leases in this Amoskeag mill, three years before the printing plant on the two floors below ground level would move. Sol used the interval to frame details of the changeover. He enlisted the help of all who worked at Pandora, by this time numbering 150 on the day shift alone.

He was accustomed to calling our employees together four times a year for a state-of-our-business meeting. Ted and Carl would usually sit in the front row; Pa rarely showed up. I would sit with the crowd, delighting in the warmth Sol sparked.

"I see before me the most beautiful girls in Manchester," he would begin. "Sorry, fellows, can't say you're the most beautiful."

A ripple of laughter would sweep through the audience. He would brief everyone on the prospects for the next few months. He sometimes threw in a plug for the latest time-and-motion seminar or announced the winners of a suggestion contest. He would then call for questions from the floor.

"Use your heads as well as your hands," he would say in closing. "We need new ideas."

"I have an idea," I told Sol after one of these quarterly meetings. "What if I met with groups of from ten to twenty in each department? I'll ask: 'What can we do smarter in the new building?' That should generate a lot of interest."

"You feel up to it?" asked Sol, and patted my blooming belly.

"I'll do one department a month when I go through collecting material for the *Yarn*. It might take two years," I calculated. "Even longer if I cover all shifts."

Sol nodded his agreement. "I have something I must get started myself," he said. "I want to put in profit-sharing. The people who share in making the money should share in the profits."

Sol had long cherished this dream; my father had scoffed at it.

"You figure you'll make profits all the time?" I could almost hear Pa's voice. "People'll gladly take your money when you give it away. Will they share in your losses when you have a bad year?"

"Follow your instinct," I advised Sol, and braced myself for innings with my father.

Sol carried the day. "Profit-Sharing for Employees," read the banner of the *Yarn's* March 1947 issue. Later issues contained news of a company foundation for annual gifts to community causes, college scholarships for employees' children, a pension system. Always, my father would mutter about immature adults with *gringe kep*, fluttery heads.

Carl arrived early to prepare for his March sales meeting.

"I can't get over everyone's co-operation," he told us one evening over dinner. "All the samples ready, and on time! I still have to find where Ted hides his desk. I don't believe he has one. As for his writing down sample requests, forget it. But the line looks great; he has knocked out some gorgeous stuff."

"Don't you sense an upbeat feeling everywhere?" I asked.

"We should take advantage of it," said Carl. "Long and loud, we should broadcast to the trade about our mill. I get compliments whenever I bring a buyer up here."

"When I worked as a salesgirl, I didn't pay much attention to the buyer," I said. "I would pick my favorite items in the stock and push those. Why not bring the key saleslady of each key account to the mill. What a boosters' club we would then have!"

"A Salesgirls' Convention here at the mill!" exclaimed Carl.

He and Sol decided it should be held just before Labor Day.

"Whoa there," I called. "I have a baby coming in June. How about next year?"

I was overruled. Before the meal ended, the two men had planned the details. Thirty of our leading accounts would be invited to send a favorite salesgirl. The invitation, an all-expenses-paid opportunity for in-service training, would come as a bonus after customers had made their fall commitments.

Advance notice of the Salesgirls' Convention appeared in a summer *Yarn*, not far from another brief entry: "Friday, June 13, brings luck to the Sol Sidores. It's a girl!"

"She looks just like a Dresden doll, Sol. Surely Rebecca is the most beautiful of all our babies," I said as her father sat holding my hand in the hospital.

"You say that about each one," he answered.

In early September, thirty salesgirls and heavy hitters among our sales representatives converged from all corners of the country at Boston's airport. That Thursday, our guests were driven by bus to Lowell to inspect our spinning mill, then on to Manchester. On Friday, in the factory, each department staged a demonstration for them. This ended at tag-and-box, where each visitor happily selected a garment of her choice as a souvenir. Everyone enjoyed a gourmet New England clambake on the hotel patio that evening.

Saturday, the program concluded with a fashion show. Among the models, Ralph and Dulie's daughter, Judy, both aged three, paraded in matching Argyle sweaters.

The salesgirls were enthusiastic, and, in summation, Carl said, "Bull's eye!"

Temporarily, I shared Carl's euphoria; by winter, I was experiencing deep dejection. Pa was returning to Florida, determined to go through with a divorce. Had matters really reached an irrevocable stage? One day in Manhattan I invited him for a walk in Bryant Park. I had a speech rehearsed for the occasion.

"It hardly seems fair," I began, "to gain your happiness at the expense of someone else's hurt. Some wounds, you know, never heal."

I reminded him how, as a little girl, Sara Mae had cried, saying to me that maybe she shouldn't have been born at all, because she had made a grandpa out of Peep. "Maybe I shouldn't have been born either," I said, "because I made a father out of you."

He stopped me short. "Never as long as I live could I go back to your mother," he declared, slowing his pace and looking directly at me. "If she had been willing to put up with me, she could still be living with me to this day."

Mutely I adjusted my steps to his. Could I tell him how often my mother spoke of the woman who had ended her troubles by jumping from the roof of their apartment house? Had my father committed himself to someone else? He seemed so set in his decision. We finished our walk in silence, broken by my occasional sneezes.

My mother received a registered letter from a Florida court sometime after Pa went south. Morris Blum, having established residence, was suing for divorce.

"I won't raise a finger to stop him," she declared when she showed me the official notice. She kept folding it, unfolding it, smoothing out the creases. "On what grounds can a judge give him a divorce? I run around? I drink too much? I don't keep a clean house? I didn't look after my children? What can he say about me bad enough for a judge to let him divorce me?"

"I wouldn't depend on any judge," I answered. "If I wanted my husband, I'd go to Florida and fight like hell."

"He could be a king on a throne," she said. "Let him roll in the gutter. I won't make a move to call him back, and I won't try to stop him."

She never did raise a finger. Pa got his divorce.

Shortly after the divorce became final, my father and I had a talk in Manchester. He had invited me to his hotel room.

"Why did it happen, Pa? When did you realize that you and Ma weren't making a go of it?"

"In New Rochelle."

Twenty-five years before! I winced to think of all the years he had suppressed his unhappiness.

"I moved to New Rochelle because I wanted the best for my family. I bought a fine house, and in the best neighborhood. I got a car; I joined the Elks. I made friends, all the friends I'd want." He paused. "Not her. She kept busy with the house. I said, 'Get someone to help you.' She wouldn't. 'Learn to drive.' She wouldn't. She made no friends, though we had nice neighbors. Money was no object—she knew that.

"All she wanted was the Bronx. Every Sunday we had the same two operas: one Sunday Aunt Jennie, the next Aunt Dora.

"I knew then that she'd never change. She couldn't keep step with me—too stubborn, too old-fashioned."

He told me what he had been thinking that afternoon when he sat in the park and decided to leave my mother.

"I would do nothing while you children were still in the house. You married young—you were hot in the pants. Then Teddy finished high school. Once he went to college, we hardly saw him. When he moved to Manchester, we two were left alone in the house.

"It's not for me to come home to an empty house and find a cold plate on the kitchen table. And when she was home we had nothing to talk about. The whole life got too empty."

"Don't make yourself such an angel," I protested. "You knew Ma wouldn't change. She wouldn't bleach her hair peroxide blond, or diet herself into a slick chick, or run with you to the race track, or take rhumba lessons. She claims you did plenty of mischief yourself."

"She'll claim this, she'll claim that," he mimicked me, "but I'm a young man yet. I've got plenty of good years in me. I still feel full of piss and vinegar." He hesitated. "I have no one now, but I'll find someone, someone more up-to-the-minute."

Pa had an expression, "Not interested." He had taken my mother's file and stamped "Not interested" across it.

My father had stepped out of character to defend his actions to me. Was he seeking our sympathy? Not according to his business conduct. Sol found his partner as ornery as ever.

Carl wanted Pandora to lease its own showroom in a skyscraper still under construction. The landlord would make many concessions to attract desirable tenants.

"Who needs extra overhead?" grumbled my father.

Sol had to chip away at his objections until he reasoned him into co-operation. Sol stewed, too, at his lack of availability at crucial times.

If such annoyances plagued Sol at work, others beclouded his off-work hours. We fretted over my mother—unhappy, alone and far away. We fretted over Sol's sick mother. After that first major stroke she had suffered a minor one. Whenever the phone rang too late at night or too early in the morning, we dreaded answering.

I still had my sneezing; Sol had taken to cracking his knuckles or, even worse, picking his cuticles until the skin was raw and bleeding. He had another problem: he was losing the hearing in his left ear. I had to repeat everything I said to him.

"I'm tired of chewing my onions twice," I told a speech professor I had sought out at Boston University. "Can you suggest any remedy so my husband will hear me the first time?"

He taught me to pitch my voice an octave higher. Shriller notes would register with Sol more clearly. At the same time, we went from one specialist to another for help with Sol's hearing.

In his spare moments, Sol was leading the search for a more modern rabbi. After he had persuaded a visionary with dark, flashing eyes to accept, he led a drive for a more attractive temple—an uphill fight. The tension of his community work soon matched that of his business.

I contributed my tensions as well. The League of Women Voters had suffered a setback. One of our speakers, Harlow Shapley, Harvard astronomer and member of UNESCO, was attacked in print by the new publisher of the *Union-Leader*, William Loeb. Lambasting us in a front-page editorial, he asked how we dared besmirch the fair name of the Queen City by sponsoring a known Communist.

Hastily we met in executive session with two of Manchester's foremost lawyers, men related to members. We fumed; we jabbered about libel suits; we looked to the lawyers. Do nothing, they advised; ignore Loeb. Powerless, we did nothing.

One of our members had been elected to the school board. We had grown steadily in influence and numbers. After Loeb's blast, we lost our momentum; our membership began dropping; our League unit never fully recovered.

While mulling over my frustrations, I heard a rumor: the Granite State was getting another newspaper. Blair Clark had come to town. He was going to publish the *New Hampshire Sunday News*. He was backed, we were told, by money from Coats and Clark, makers of cotton thread, and was surrounded by an impressive staff.

Scoops soon began to appear in this paper, scoops unmatched by the old competition. Some bore the by-line of a young reporter, Ben Bradlee. A state official, in collusion with a local contractor, had given out contracts without getting formal bids. Thanks to the *News* exposé, both men landed in jail. Years later, at the *Washington Post*, Ben Bradlee was still coming up with scoops.

Another *News* reporter, Norma, appeared at an evening study group of the League. Behind beetling black brows, pop eyes and irregular features, she had a lively brain. It was a relief to find someone tuned in to the world outside Manchester. We became friends.

"Loeb is putting blinders on Manchester people," I told her one day. To disclaim his Jewish ancestry, he had printed his baptismal certificate on the front page of his Vermont newspaper. What bigotry such a man could stir up, and how little we needed another Joe McCarthy! He featured stories about Communists and Russia on his front page, and he persisted with editorials like the one that had blasted Harlow Shapley. "How can we ever combat him?" I asked Norma.

"That's why many of us are working for peanuts and giving our all to Blair Clark," she answered.

"You can't compare the impact of a weekly with that of a daily," I protested.

Nevertheless, I took heart from her paper, as did many *News* readers. A dent, albeit a small one, was being made in the power of the *Union-Leader*.

During the July Fourth week of factory shutdown, Sol and I took a cross-country good-will trip. In six days we called on a dozen retailers who had sent salesgirls to our convention. On our travels a psychology book accompanied us—because of Norma.

She and I had been searching for some psychological means of fighting Loeb's influence.

"I once took an incredible psychology course with Carl Rogers," she told me. "I've heard that this summer he's teaching at Harvard. You should contact him."

I had gone to Cambridge and spoken with Dr. Rogers. Before we parted, he had handed me the assigned reading for his class. At the Harvard Coop I bought the first starred book on his list, his *Counseling and Psychotherapy*. Sol and I took turns reading snatches from it on our trip. It planted seeds in both of us that kept sprouting long after.

"If a guy who's a pain in the neck keeps hassling you, you can end up with an actual pain in your neck," Sol informed me as we flew from Dayton's in Minneapolis to Younker's in Des Moines. "Maybe my deaf ear means I'm trying to shut out some of the bullshit I hear your father tossing around."

"Could my sneezing have some psychosomatic base?" I wondered aloud. This possibility had dawned on me for the first time.

In mid-July I had several sessions with Dr. Rogers about the dynamics of change in a community. He stressed "the inevitability of gradualness."

"Rogers isn't talking technique, but philosophy," I reported to Norma. He emphasizes not what you say, but the feelings behind the words. I've been digging down deep to ferret out how I truly feel. Getting to know myself. It hurts."

"I know," she said, nodding. "He did that to me, too."

By August Sol and I had found the right ear specialist, the pioneer of an operation called "stapes mobilization." He examined Sol and declared him a fit subject for his revolutionary surgery. This involved scraping calcium away from the stapes of the inner ear so it could vibrate again. Sol underwent it.

Lo and behold, his left ear now worked. For a month Sol went berserk. He heard thunder crashing whenever he turned the ignition key in his car. When he flushed the toilet, Niagara was falling. Raindrops spattered as from a machine gun on the corrugated glass of the back-porch roof. Sol could hear again!

That fall we determined to make time for family and fun. Sol bought four season tickets for the Harvard football games. Usually flanked by two of our children, we became rooters for the Crimson. Sol, who had never graduated from college, let alone Harvard, shouted the loudest, belted out cheers and songs and booed most scornfully at the umpire. His hearty laugh and comments, completely partisan, rang out over our section of the grandstand. He counted no Saturday successful unless he left the stadium completely hoarse.

One Saturday we went to the game without children. That morning we had a date with Fritz Roethlisberger, dean of Harvard's Graduate School of Business Administration. In preparation, Sol and I had read his book on the Hawthorne experiment.

As consultants to Western Electric, Roethlisberger and a teammate had selected a group of workers at the Hawthorne plant and given them every benefit possible. They moved them to a better location, improved their lighting, gave them longer coffee breaks and piped in music. Beforehand, they discussed the changes with the workers. With each advantage, group output increased.

Then the consultants removed the benefits one at a time. Amazingly, output still kept on increasing. These workers had responded to the interest and concern shown them by Roethlisberger and his fellow researchers, rather than to the physical advantages. Following this experiment, many corporations throughout the United States had adopted a new emphasis on human relations with their employees.

Fritz Roethlisberger won us over on sight with his ready smile and the twinkle in his eyes. A chunky man of middle height, he introduced us to a tall, thin, self-effacing associate.

Very casually, Fritz then socked us with two zingers. First, he wanted to know, "What business are you in?"

We responded, then kept modifying our response from "manufacturing sweaters" to "servicing our customers, the retailers" to "servicing their customers, the public" to "making a buck." We spent years afterward, and our business underwent dramatic shifts, as we groped for the answer to Fritz's question.

"Would each of you draw an organization chart for me?" he asked next.

I drew a fanciful one, with Sol as the sun shedding rays of light on the organization and myself as a moon on the periphery. It drew a laugh.

Sol struggled long, trying to portray the facts accurately. The crisscrossed lines of authority between himself, my father, and Ted frustrated him. He looked up, troubled. Pandora's internal conflict spoke loud and clear for itself.

That same fall I gave up trying to cure the world's problems. I tempered my anguish over my parents' breakup. For more than a dozen years we had been mired in their muck. I had a growing awareness of the blessings Sol and I enjoyed. I ached for still another blessing—I knew not what—to further balance the scales.

One crisp October night Sol and I went for our customary stroll after dinner. I walked on Sol's right side, too used to staying near his "good" ear to vary from the custom. I had forgotten my mittens. Sol clasped my cold left hand in his right and drew both into his pocket after sticking his unused glove on my exposed hand.

"I don't have a gift for you," he said. "I didn't forget our anniversary. I just couldn't figure anything you'd really want."

"Don't fuss about it," I responded. "You'll get something for me when the right thing happens to strike you."

"I want you to pick out something for yourself," Sol went on. "I don't want the day to pass without our deciding on something for you."

"Please don't make me choose," I begged. "Half the fun of a gift lies in being surprised."

"Anything you want," he persisted. "You name it and, if I possibly can, I'll get it for you."

"Do you mean that, Sol? I asked. "Honestly, do you mean anything I really want?"

"Absolutely," he said. "Just name it."

"Well, if you're asking me my heart's desire—"

"Yes," he prodded.

"Oh, Sol," I blurted out, and surprised even myself, "I want another baby."

"I gave you my word," he said, smiling. "I left myself wide open."

We went home to celebrate our seventeenth wedding anniversary. Soon after, I became pregnant.

I had remained close to Norma. I respected her dedication to the *Sunday News*, and, thanks to her and the rest of its aggressive staff, the weekly was carrying punch; its circulation was growing.

Suddenly a bombshell struck! Blair Clark had sold out to William Loeb. The *New Hampshire Sunday News* was absorbed by the *Union-Leader*. Every *News* reporter promptly got fired. We and they felt betrayed.

Norma, who got married and left, was not the only one who acquired a new partner. From gossip in the New York showroom, Pa, we learned, was living with a woman he had met in Florida. He, she and her teen-age son occupied an apartment in Brooklyn Heights.

"I'd like you and May to meet Mary," my father told Sol one day. Ted had already met her.

Soon after, we went on invitation to a tall apartment house in Brooklyn. A quick-moving woman, only three years older than me, greeted us warmly. Small, homely, with straight black hair, Mary offered a distinct contrast to my stately, white-haired, still beautiful mother. She introduced her son, Maury, who was about to leave for a date. Affectionately, my father teased him.

Their airy apartment had blond furniture, India druggets scattered on the floor, bright paintings on the walls. It was so different from the home I had known, with its dark, conventional sets of furniture and heavy Oriental rug. The woman and the apartment both surprised us, but my father proved the real shocker.

He decided he needed more club soda. "I'll go down to the corner store," he told us. "It'll only take a minute."

"Snookie," Mary said, "be sure to wear your rubbers. It's starting to drizzle."

I took a second look at "Snookie." He shrugged his shoulders and made grumbling noises. Mary ignored them, ran to the closet for his rubbers and knelt to fit them over his shoes. Never could I have imagined my mother in a kneeling position, nor could I have imagined her husband as Snookie.

"And look both ways when you cross the street," Mary added. "You're always in such a hurry."

Snookie waved a contemptuous hand at her. He didn't fool us. She was babying him, and he was eating it up.

In late January, with subzero temperatures, a blizzard closed the Manchester schools—and the airport, until tall drifts could be cleared. My father, on an infrequent mill visit, was forced to stay over.

In the afternoon, Sol invited a dozen long-time employees to join him in his office for a drink with Pa. He included Joe, a short, slight lawyer who handled our local matters.

At the dinner table, Pa said, "This time we're staying in Florida for at least six weeks. Mary has relatives in Miami, and she'll have a good chance to get together with them."

"How I wish I could get Gene down there! That kid has had one cold after another. He can't shake them, stays skinny and misses school," I remarked. "What did the doctor advise? He told us to move to Arizona."

"Suppose Mary and I take him with us," said my father. Had I heard straight?

Gene was ready to pack his suitcase and leave with my father the moment he heard this proposal. Within ten days, he actually left. Mary would register him for mornings at a private school, so he could keep up with his studies. And she welcomed the chance to take him to the beach, to romp and picnic with him. "I promise to build him up," she told me over the phone.

She did. He came back tanned, rosy-cheeked, a dozen pounds heavier and a couple of inches taller. The Florida interlude broke up his chain of colds. In the year that followed, Gene gained thirty pounds and grew seven inches. And he kept singing Mary's praises.

Again in the summer, and again in the last month of my pregnancy, my father paid us a critical visit. Five years had passed since his upsetting visit to our cottage on Paugus Bay.

My father had not come alone. He had brought Sam, Ted and Jean. He had laid his groundwork earlier by presenting Sol with a book about Jimmy Walker. New York City's colorful mayor, it said, had wanted to "regularize his relationship" with actress Betty Compton. Pa, too, wanted to "regularize his relationship." He wanted to marry Mary.

"I've been living with Mary for more than a year. I'm not the kind to knock around from one skirt to another," he began. "She wants to get married. I've investigated her very carefully and I think she'll be a good woman for me. I've had Sam meet her. Sam, tell them what I've done."

"Your father has taken every precaution not to mix Mary or her son up in the business," Sam carried on. "She will sign a prenuptial agreement specifying this. Your father will make his personal arrangements for her security."

"That I can believe," Sol burst in with a laugh. "The ole man makes out like he's the biggest sport, but he still travels for a nickel on the subway. God forbid he should take a cab, even if it means getting caught in the rush hour. Mary will be well provided for."

Pa's shoulders heaved as he suppressed a chuckle.

"He has had me set up trusts," Sam continued, "by which he and your mother leave their shares of stock in equal parts to all their grandchildren. They will make the transfers in orderly fashion over the next twenty years."

"If my mother knows that this clears the way for my father to remarry, will she sign such papers?" I asked Sam.

"I believe she will look to Sol for direction," he said. "If she does sign, in return she will derive a lifetime income from the business."

"And what will Sol advise her?" I asked out loud, turning to my husband, as did Ted, Jean, Sam and my father.

The divorce had altered the balance of power at Pandora. Until the day he divorced her, my mother had remained loyal to my father. Through her and Ted, he had controlled sixty percent of the company stock. Now Sol would become Ma's chief adviser and could thus vote her stock. This would give Sol and me sixty percent and put us squarely in the catbird seat. If we so chose, we could force my father out of the Pandora management, even undertake to buy him out.

How did I feel about this proposal? First, I thought of how much of himself Pa had put into our business. Then, since Sol and I were expecting our fifth child and my brother had two, my parents would divide their forty percent seven ways. I did some quick mental arithmetic: Sol and I had forty percent; this plus our children's twenty-eight percent was sixty-eight percent. Ted had twenty plus twelve for his children, or thirty-two percent. Roughly, Sol, Ted, and I would end up as three equal partners. Eminently fair, I thought.

Ted sat by saying nothing. Jean left the room.

Sol finally broke the silence. "I'll have to talk this over with the ole lady."

Sam then mentioned that he had helped my father construct this package. "If you agree to it," he went on, "we'll sign and seal foolproof agreements that can never be broken."

Again a long silence. Suddenly I began to sneeze, sneeze, sneeze, as if I would never stop.

None of these upheavals fazed my unborn baby. Two weeks after the due date that creature, jumping, kicking, ever-stirring, still refused to make an appearance.

"How quiet that baby seems," I remarked one night, hand on my dropped stomach.

On a mid-August evening Sol and I had dinner out with our friends Eunice and Herman.

"Don't do what Betty did," Herman teased.

At 2:30 A.M. this local woman had given birth to a baby at home. The baby had plopped into the toilet bowl, and the mother had had to fish her out. Our doctor, summoned by her hysterical husband, found mother, child and cord waiting in bed for him when he rushed in.

"That poor doctor," I commented, "he still has to deliver me before he can take off on vacation." I sat crossing and uncrossing my legs. "I feel uncomfortable. Maybe it's the chopped-liver salad."

"How about getting out of here?" asked Sol. "Let's skip dessert." He claimed later that his watch read seven minutes to seven.

I sprawled clumsily on the front seat of our car, still shifting my weight from one side to the other. "Let's look in at the house before we go to the movies," I said. Our two younger children and my summer helper were at home; the two older children had left the month before for camp.

As Sol drove toward home in his usual flying style, I said, "I feel funny. Let's get home fast."

In front of our house, I jumped out of the car, headed for the front door, and rushed down the hall to the bathroom.

Through some flash of intuition, I bent over and held my cupped hands under my body. I felt the need to press. For seconds I crouched this way, my hands resting in the cold water.

Then something was coming out, where I could see it. It was the dark hair of a baby's head. As the newborn dropped into my hands, I could hear the church bells ringing the hour: seven o'clock.

"Are you all right?" Sol called through the bathroom door. "May, are you all right?"

"Just fine," I told him. "Sol, I'm having a baby." A moment later I straightened up. "It's a girl!"

"I'm calling the doctor," he yelled.

I cradled my baby in my hands. Beautifully formed, her head rounded, her body gently curved, she had not been distorted by labor or instruments. Her complexion was fair, not the usual red. But how quiet she was! Was she alive? Breathing? I thumped her back, feeling brutish as I did. She opened her mouth and mildly cried. I sat back, holding her well away, framed in my hands. I kept looking at her and realized I was grinning from ear to ear.

"I just got the doctor," said Sol on the other side of the door. He poked his head in. "Are you all right?"

"Want to see her?" I asked. "I'm feeling fine."

He came in and stared at the baby.

"We must be careful; nothing in here is sterile," I warned.

Sol touched her dimpled hand, looking helpless. "I'll see if the doctor is coming," he said. "Don't move."

"I won't," I assured him.

Someone in the kitchen had turned the water on full and was making an awful racket with pans. Footsteps sounded in the upstairs hall. Objects were thudding in the lower hall. What's going on, I wondered. In the basement the high-pitched voices of Ralph and Becky were babbling.

Placidly I sat through all this, a queen on a throne, admiring a rare jewel in my hands. The baby yawned and raised a tiny fist. Then I heard heavier footsteps and the low rumble of the doctor's voice.

He entered the bathroom and asked, "How are you?"

"Just fine," I told him. "Isn't she a beautiful baby?"

He removed his jacket and washed his hands in the basin, soaping them thoroughly. "I'll need some boiling water," he told Sol, who held the door ajar.

"How much will you need, Doc?" my husband asked as they went out.

"Enough to dip these surgical scissors in," I heard him reply. "My God, what is all this?"

Every burner on the stove was blazing, and water was boiling furiously in my four largest pans. In the oven my Thanksgiving roasting pan was baking water. Eunice and Herman had not only tried to boil as much water as possible but also emptied a dozen sheets from the linen closet in case the doctor might want them.

The doctor re-entered holding his small scissors ahead of him. With his gnarled left hand he took the baby from me. With his right hand he cut the umbilical cord and clamped it.

"Where can I put her?" he asked, wrapping her in a white bath towel he had extracted from the cupboard.

"Right next door, in the little back room."

After a flurry of noises he came back. "We've prepared the studio bed in there for you," he said. He held the end of the cord as I hobbled with small steps to the back room. Ignoring the baby, lying peacefully in her bassinet, he began kneading my stomach. "I'm working out the afterbirth," he explained.

I felt ignorant. Though this was my fifth child, I still didn't know where and how the umbilical cord was connected, the risks the baby or I had faced until it was disconnected, or exactly what "afterbirth" meant.

"Bring me a pail," the doctor called to Sol. By the time Sol came back, the doctor had worked out the afterbirth, which he cast into the pail. Then he turned to me, "Well, young lady, that's that."

He went to wash up, and came back drying his hands. "How do you feel about going to the hospital?" he asked.

"I'd like to stay home," I said. "It's much easier on the children. But I'll do whatever you say."

"I think you're better off in the hospital. If anything happens, they have all the equipment there. They're willing to take the baby, even though it means keeping her apart from the others. And it will give your good husband a chance to rest."

My good husband did indeed look exhausted. Still respectable in my brown maternity dress, and cradling my baby, still wrapped in the white towel, I was wheeled out on a stretcher. Sol rode along with us in the ambulance, and left once we were tucked into our beds. Before going to sleep, he wrote out a birth announcement for the Sunday *New York Times*. Our daughter had weighed in at seven pounds, seven ounces. Struck by the recurrence of the number seven that evening, he included us and our five children in the family count.

"Joyfully," he proclaimed, "Sol and May announce the arrival of the seventh Sidore."

Before and after Micala's birth, several dialogues took place concerning my father—whether he should be bought out or allowed to stay in the business. Sol explored the subject first with Skinny.

"If you want to kick him out, that's what he would deserve," my mother said, "but I don't wish him any harm. I don't know why, but I carry no bitterness in my heart against him. I can't bring myself to curse him or yell out against him. Leave him in, push him out—whatever you want, Sol."

Sol conferred with Sam.

"If he took advantage of you in the past, he's certainly made up for it now with the agreements he's proposing," Sam said. "If you analyze it, his problems lie with Skinny and not with carrying his share of the load as a partner in Pandora."

I was griping over some "minor clauses" in the agreements. My mother, as we knew, would derive her income directly from Pandora, rather than from my father. But he had tacked òn a clause about Mary. On his death she, also, would get a life income from the company—provided she did not remarry.

"What a mastermind!" I protested. "Even after he dies, he still tries to pin Mary down. Notice, though"—and this point irritated me—"how neatly he has transferred the support of two wives, not just one, directly onto our shoulders."

"I've spent long hours on these papers," replied Sol. "On the whole, Sam and I consider that we've struck a fair deal. I'll never forget the part your father played, especially at the beginning. I say he can stay. Do you go along?"

Reluctantly, I did.

Many papers were signed, notarized and duly affixed with appropriate red seals. The ink had hardly dried on them when my father married Mary.

EIGHT

Dropped Stitches

FIVE CHILDREN SWAMPED ME. I had managed with four and fancied myself neatly tucking this fifth into a smooth-running schedule. Instead, I sneezed. In the hospital my milk had run dry. Without capable help, my housekeeping overtaxed me. I sneezed. I tried to keep my finger on the pulse of the business, pumping Sol for information daily and editing the *Yarn* monthly. I sneezed. I fussed over my mother, my mother-in-law, friends, relatives and the League of Women Voters. I sneezed and sneezed some more.

Some of my problems solved themselves. Micala, or Mickey, thrived on formula and broke the records of all four breast-fed children for weight and growth. After a few months of help coming and going, a fine-looking widow with a healthy sense of humor answered my ad. Blanche had six children of her own, of whom only one teen-age son remained at home. She could leave each evening or sleep over, as it suited us. Accustomed to a large family and dispensing even-handed justice to ours, the new housekeeper immediately won our children's respect.

Once she came, I had more leisure. The sneezing, however, did not let up and, for the first time in our marriage, Sol and I argued.

My husband was working longer hours than ever. In the spring before Mickey was born, he had engineered the move of our mill from the fourth floor of one building to four floors in our newly acquired building. He had taken some mild razzing from my father on the luxury of a company cafeteria, on the conference room, on the too-grand size of the executive offices.

By fall Pa's razzing was much sharper. Once we had accepted his remarriage, once he felt sure he would remain at Pandora, he changed. From a mild fellow seeking our favor, again he became the tough customer we knew from the old days.

"Three times to New York in ten days, Sol!" I complained. "Must you put out every brush fire yourself?" May, I thought, you sound like one helluva nag.

"Maybe the ole man is showing off for Mary," Sol said. "If I let him get away with it at the start, I'll have twice as big a boogeyman to knock down next time."

"Can't you send Ted once?" I asked. "He surely doesn't look as tired as you do." That inner voice said, Hey, ease off.

"Ted can't buck your father the way I have to," Sol insisted.

I repeated my complaint to Dr. Thannhauser when I went with Sol for his next medical checkup. "Three times to New York in ten days," I said. "Can you talk sense to him? I can't."

"Never, but never," said the doctor sternly as he wagged his forefinger at me, "do you stop a man from doing what he has to do."

Sol flashed me a V-for-Victory sign. We dropped the subject.

However, he took one precaution. On our anniversary in October, he extracted from a side drawer in his sun-parlor desk a small white jeweler's box tied with gold ribbon. As he did, I glimpsed a duplicate box behind it.

"What's that one?" I asked.

"My ace-in-the-hole, young lady," he said. "I'm taking no more chances with you." He began to laugh.

Piqued, I lunged at him, but he pressed the first box into my hands. I opened it to find a ring of five matched opals. The phosphorescent fire in the old oval stones made me catch my breath.

That fall Sol finally installed the dye house. He had researched and selected dye kettles and dyestuffs, supervised auxiliary plumbing and the treatment of waste effluents, hired a master dyer, and set up a laboratory for the technician to match and sample shades.

Before Christmas he assembled all our workers and thanked them. "Your efforts have paid off," he said. "We've had a good year. As soon as the accountants close the books, I'll be handing out profit-sharing checks."

He did not slow down on outside activities either. As the rabbi's loyal supporter, he was embroiled in bitter controversy. Each month he came home from temple board meetings after midnight, seething and unable to sleep.

"Put that bunch on a back burner," I urged. "Get involved in something else."

In his own fashion Sol heeded me. He tapered off his involvement with the temple, but took on a committee working to add a gymnasium-auditorium to the community center. He hired carpenters to transform our unfinished basement. He helped my mother resettle in Manchester when Bertha finally conceded that Morris's key might never again turn in her lock.

He continued to feel overtired. Dr. Thannhauser gave him a next appointment, not in six, but in three months. The doctor had found his aorta enlarged.

"I can stay as active as I like provided I take one week's vacation every three months and a long weekend every month," Sol informed me. "Believe me, I'm going to follow orders."

That spring my father was still grandstanding. He would by-pass Sol and instruct our shipping staff to coddle his pet customers. Sol spent hours on the phone placating less-favored accounts. These calls interrupted tedious work in the dye house, where he was setting rigid standards for color-matching. Ted, buried in trials on new full-fashion machines, gave him little help.

Sol's health seemed to get worse, not better.

"You're to go away," Dr. Thannhauser told him on his next visit. "Go at once; go today. Don't bother to argue or stall. You must rest, do absolutely nothing but rest. You might have to stay away for a long time. Otherwise you're heading for collapse."

For the third time since I'd known him, Sol had pushed himself to breaking point.

"If I have to go, this month's a good time," he told me. "Knitting orders are all laid out for back-to-school inventory. Ted wants a chance to show his stuff. Let him have it."

"He can carry on, but I don't know if I can—not with the baby and all the other children. Can you take one of them?" I asked.

We settled on Ralph. He required little care; he would only miss kindergarten. If Sol went back to our honeymoon retreat, the innkeepers, by now close personal friends, would look after our small son. That very afternoon Sol loaded our station wagon with luggage and fishing gear, and he and Ralph took off for upstate New York.

I next saw him three weeks later in the Bronx. Holding seven-month-old Mickey in my arms, I had pressed the buzzer of an apartment in a block-long tenement complex. A stranger with a bristly red mustache and reddish stubble covering his cheeks had opened the door. He kissed me.

"Sol!" I exclaimed. "How's it coming?" I asked. "How's Ralph? How's your mother?"

"I'm much better," he assured me, "and Ralph's been having a ball. I'll never get over sleeping twenty-four hours straight the first day I got there—the one and only time in my life I've done such a thing." He interspersed his answer with long "brrr's" to Mickey, while her eyes opened wide, then gently tickling her until she giggled.

Sol had been fishing out on the lake when the call had come that his mother was dying.

"It was drizzling, so I had pulled that old battered felt hat down over my ears. They yelled to me from the shore but I didn't hear. When they finally got hold of me, I couldn't get here fast enough."

He had been doing eighty when a motorcycle cop stopped him.

"I explained why I was hurrying so. Darned if he didn't

escort me to the Yonkers city line, blowing his horn and going like hell. What a ride!"

With soft steps he led the way into the sickroom. Fatso's eyes were open and she recognized us, but I missed that instant glow of pride she always showed on seeing any grandchild. She did not reach out to fondle Mickey or to caress Sol or me. With colorless face, she lay withdrawn, now and then moaning in a low key.

"The doctor stayed up practically the whole night with her," Sol said. "He'll be back soon. The longer she lasts, he told me, the better her chances."

The buzzer rang. Sol's sisters filed in, each laden with bundles, each holding a small daughter by the hand. We shared a hasty lunch.

The buzzer rang once more. Bag in hand, the doctor passed us to go to his patient. When he finished his examination, he exchanged a few words with Sol.

"He thinks the crisis has passed," Sol said. "We can leave if we want to."

So Sol and I prepared to go our separate paths. Three more weeks would elapse before we met again, in Manchester. The next summons to the Bronx came two weeks after that.

This time Fatso no longer fooled the doctors, nor did we arrive while she still breathed. As we rushed to her bedside from New Hampshire, she died in her housekeeper's arms.

Sol's absence from Pandora accomplished one thing: he learned he was missed. First my brother, next my father, filled him in on everything that had gone wrong.

"That electric blue, that emerald green," Ted wailed. "Some dyer we have! The klutz never got the shades right or consistent from one dye lot to the next."

In these two colors the dyer had passed lots of yarn that did not match the original samples, that did not match each other, even some that had streaks.

"And nobody caught it," Ted groaned, "not in winding, backwinding or even knitting."

"You never noticed it yourself?" asked Sol.

Bodies, sleeves, collars and trim had to be assembled, slit, steamed, separated, brushed, flattened and then cut before being stitched into sweaters. All goods were processed in plain view on two factory floors.

Finally, in Merrow, the operators had loudly objected to sewing together backs and fronts that did not match, sleeves and collars still a third shade, bodies with streaks.

"You never caught it before Merrow?" Sol asked again.

"People may have mumbled a few words," answered Ted. "I thought they were making a fuss over nothing. Anyway, I was running all over the place trying to take care of everything at once."

Sol spot-checked stacks on the examining tables, where inspectors had refused to pass hundreds of electric-blue and emerald-green sweaters.

"I guess you did the best you could," said Sol, "but it's no use blaming dyers, winders, knitters or anyone else. And it's no use being Mr. Fix-it in the lab now; you can only do too little and too late. Let's see how we can crawl out of this."

"Ted should have forgotten his pride," he told me that evening. "He should have called for help the minute he smelled trouble. He's wasting his time with alibis."

In the New York showroom, meanwhile, my father was writhing. Customers were checking promised delivery dates on orders placed early in the season. They needed merchandise to cover advertisements or catalogs. Carl kept referring them to Mr. B.

"We promised Best & Co. delivery by June 10," my father told Sol. "I don't care who you steal it from. If we don't get the goods to them on time, my name is mud."

"We'll reknit the orders and expedite them through the mill," said Sol, "but we can't knit without the right yarn. We must hire Charlie."

Charlie, an outrageously high-priced dyeing consultant, flew up. In our laboratory he installed fluorescent lights to duplicate retail-store lighting. He instructed the dyer to match his shades under these, rather than by daylight. The dyer had preferred chemicals from a house other than our usual one. Charlie backed him up. While Sol and Ted stood by, Charlie and the dyer instituted a system to assure that one dye lot precisely matched the next. Usable lots of the two tricky colors were streaming into winding before Charlie left.

Once they did, the machines could knit again. The season, however, was far advanced before the plant regained momentum. My father insisted on filling Best & Co.'s orders first; smaller accounts got later deliveries. Disgruntled customers showed their displeasure by returning late merchandise or canceling orders.

By October, Pandora was left with an unhealthy inventory, a mountain of green and blue sweater seconds and the threat of far too much customer turnover the next season.

Following this debacle, no one questioned who ran Pandora. Sol did. He kept my father informed of each move but deferred less and less to him. He encouraged my brother, but called the shots himself. Sam, Sol's closest buddy, spoke to him daily and at length on the phone.

"You and Sam act like sweethearts," I teased one evening.

Their talks, however, helped my husband avoid petty squabbles with my father and take firm stands on issues. "First come, first served," Sol insisted once the season ended. Despite their pressure, no longer could my father or the salesmen get shipments out of turn.

Next, Sol backed Carl up in one of his perpetual tussles with Mr. B. "Best & Co. wants an allowance because we make one shipment to their main store and they do their own shipping to their branches. Look at their volume. They deserve it," Sol said to my father. "About money for their catalog, they're featuring four of our styles, so we can't get out of sharing the cost."

"Carl, with a funny expression on his face, looked from your father to me," Sol told me later. "Then he ran to the phone to give the buyer the glad news."

"You've stopped the soft-shoe diplomacy," I commented.

Sol had moved the spinning mill from Lowell to the top floor of our building. This division supplied yarn, mostly wool, for our own use. To fill our other requirements my father was buying increased quantities of synthetics from Du Pont.

"How about having Ted buy the yarn?" Sol proposed.

"You're talking about a couple of million dollars," my father said. "Do you think he's ready?"

"I know Ted made some bad mistakes last year," Sol went on. "He didn't smell trouble early enough, he tried to fix it himself, he was full of excuses. But he's got to learn."

He reminded Pa of the shellacking Pandora had taken once when my father had been away and the price of nylon had shifted a few pennies. Grudgingly, Pa conceded; while he wintered in Florida, Ted could handle the yarn purchases.

"New synthetics are springing up all the time," Sol pressed on. "This ties in with research and development, and that's where Ted shines. It goes further than your vacation. We may soon have to start spinning these novelties ourselves."

Reluctantly my father yielded. Once Sol gained his point, Ted began to travel to New York more frequently.

One more obstacle had to be hurdled that same year. As a condition of securing bank loans, we had to pay off all we owed by November each year and remain debt-free until February. In the three-month interval, we collected moneys due us for holiday merchandise and stockpiled inventory for the next season.

In our New York days, the lean season often found us scrounging for funds. By November Sol and I would have stripped our bank accounts and those of our children and borrowed on insurance and elsewhere to pay off the bank loan by the deadline. In Manchester, the normal cash flow of our business had grown to fill the vacuum. This year, though, thanks to Ted's misadventures, Pandora again suffered a cash shortfall.

Sol refused to concede that only my father could cope with the bankers. He and our accountant accompanied him to the next session with them. The accountant answered all technical questions about the statement. Sol presented graphs and statistics to plot our volume projections and probable financial needs for the coming year. My father confined himself to feisty comments.

Clearly, Sol had taken charge.

Involuntarily, my father hastened the process. Since he had turned playboy, he had been running—to dance floors, to fancy restaurants, to race tracks, to weekends away and to Florida vacations. Once he met my stepmother, she had been nimbly running beside him. Nature ground their running to a halt.

Pa's toes were tingling, constantly and ever more painfully. He tried his regular doctor, one foot doctor, then another, then an internist. From no one could he get relief from the pins and needles that pierced him each time he set his foot down. He had to grasp the railing firmly whenever he went up and down the subway steps. In the office he began to sit more and more. He tried lengthening his stay in the Florida sun. The climate suited him, but he came back north to even more torture than when he had left.

Sam wangled an appointment for Pa with one of the world's leading neurosurgeons.

"Irreversible," the great man declared after extensive tests. "A form of arthritis for which we have no known cure. I can prescribe nothing."

Shortly after, my father and Mary flew down to Florida. On their return, he announced that they had purchased a home there. His days as a kingpin had ended.

If Sol felt more comfortable in business, he also felt more comfortable in his community work. A nationally famous architect was drawing up plans for a new temple; the congregation was now earnestly involved in fund-raising. A spacious tan-brick gymnasium-auditorium had been added to the community center, a white wooden Victorian mansion.

The more comfortable climate extended to our home as well. One evening in June, Sol sat at his desk in the sun parlor. With a magnifying glass he was examining a mound of silver dollars he and Ralph had brought home from the local bank. One by one he was sorting the cartwheels for mint, year and condition. He looked up to see Sara Mae glide into the room wearing a bouffant peach tulle evening gown for her first prom. Proudly, Sol was eying her from head to foot as I walked in.

"A father serves one purpose," he told us. "When he sees his daughter in formal clothes for the first time, he has to whistle."

And whistle he did, a loud and long musician's whistle. Sara Mae flushed with pleasure. Sol jumped up to fetch camera and flash bulbs and snapped several pictures of her. Holding her skirt to its fullest, she waltzed out, only to return shortly with a shy escort. Sol walked the two of them to a car waiting at the curb.

"Just making sure she'll be home by midnight," he said when he came back inside. "We're getting there, Mug," he said, "getting there."

Why, in the year following, did my sneezing reach new heights? Many nights found me sleepless, prowling downstairs or sitting up stiffly in bed, afraid to move lest I wake Sol. In vain, I tried to puzzle out the causes.

Sol and I could count many joys. Before Labor Day of 1954, Sara Mae left for her freshman year at the Rhode Island School of Design. A solicitous boy friend from M.I.T. had materialized to chauffeur her, her suitcases and overflowing cartons to Providence. Surely Larry caused me no distress.

Gene would soon take off for his junior year at prep school. Ralph had returned from his third season at summer camp. Micala was about to take the leap from nursery school to kindergarten, and Rebecca was already at Webster School.

Sol's latest business venture had enjoyed an amazing start.

"We finally got rid of all the electric-blue and emerald-green sweaters," he had mentioned one day. "An undertaker carted them away with some other dogs we've been holding too long."

Then he mentioned the price: eighty-seven cents for sweaters that should have retailed for six dollars.

"At that price and after all those years, I wish we had sold them to the people in the mill," I commented. "Some of those sweaters could have passed for firsts."

Sol stayed thoughtful for a while.

"Runt, you've given me an idea. We ought to set up our own factory outlet," he replied. "At least we could recoup labor and material from our seconds and irregulars." He added, "Our building stands on a slope. A store on the north end could have its own entrance from the millyard."

Once the store opened, and it seemed to spring into existence overnight, our employees got substantial cash discounts on top of already low prices. They swarmed to the shop. So did townspeople and tourists. The Pandora Factory Outlet had such explosive growth that cars brought traffic in the millyard to a dead halt. In one heat wave that August, Sol spent hours passing out lemonade to the waiting crowd.

"We can't keep those tables stacked," Sol told me. "In the off-season I'm going to knit all our leftover yarn into our most popular styles. The store can use the merchandise, and we'll get rid of surplus yarn as well as surplus sweaters."

Heartily I approved. As always, our lean months mercilessly ate up any fat we could accumulate.

"When the rush dies down," he went on, "I'm knitting regular stock as well. Those nylon classics have skyrocketed. We'll plow back our profits into giving our employees twelve months of work."

At this I demurred. "You're taking an awful chance."

Out flew Sol's slide rule. In detail he explained the records he had kept for the past three years of every type of nylon sweater, by color and by size. A modest percentage of these units gave him a sound base for projecting future stock. Carl, my brother, even my father, he told me, had warmed to the prospect of filling early orders from stock already on our shelves.

Our business was prospering, our pressures loosening, our children blooming. Thanks to Blanche I could work for a few days each month at Pandora and could leave with Sol for weekends in New York or for week-long vacations. Why was I sneezing more?

Ralph had not been himself since his return from camp. He did not climb the apple tree in the back yard or don a catcher's mitt to field the apples Gene pitched him from the high branches. He did not tease Becky or Mickey or race his bike through neighborhood streets. He did not score baskets in the hoop attached to the garage or scale pebbles at neighbors' doors or windows. He did not even hop over the back fence. For days he had been doing nothing.

One sunshiny day when I saw him quietly curled up on a chaise, I felt his forehead, then summoned the family physician. I tried to get Sol, but he was unavailable.

I moved my son to the bed in the back room. He did not object, but lay limply staring at the ceiling. "Nothing hurts," he said. "I just feel tired."

After a while the doctor's car pulled up. His examination of Ralph seemed to go on and on. How many times did he have to hit that same knee with his rubber mallet?

"He's going to the hospital," he announced at last.

"What is it? What is it?" I asked.

As we crossed the street to the doctor's car, Sol pulled up.

"What are you doing home?" I asked.

"I have to go to Newark," he said. "Sam is dying."

"We're taking Ralph to the hospital," I explained. "Milton thinks it may be polio."

"And then again it may not be," interrupted the doctor. "In any case, he's better off in the hospital until we find out exactly what's wrong. Do you want to follow us?"

Soon we sat outside a small utility room converted into an isolation chamber for a too-sick and too-quiet ten-year-old. Every now and then Sol would phone the Newark hospital. Sam had been operated on—something to do with his pancreas—and he was doing poorly.

During the day we sat outside the threshold, barred from Ralph's room. Late at night we would leave. I marked time by crocheting an afghan. Sol sat with me, phoned Newark, went to work, then came back to sit some more.

"Yes, Ralph has had the polio virus," the doctor admitted on the fifth day. "So far it has left no effects. We must wait a little longer."

My numbness began to leave me and I could express concern for Sam. "How I wish I could see him alive this week," I said, "rather than dead next week!"

Our son continued to show progress. So we flew, by private plane, to Newark. Before noon we walked into Sam's hospital room. He looked pasty-faced, his dark hair flopping lankly on his forehead.

"How is Ralphieboy?" he asked.

"By some miracle, the virus should leave no traces," Sol told him. "We consider ourselves awfully lucky."

"Maybe you can bring me some luck," Sam said. Then he added, "No, no luck will help. I can't eat. Have you ever seen a goose stuffed before the holidays when they're fattening him for the kill?" He poked his forefingers into his cheeks to show how they had pried his mouth open with instruments. "They stick the food in and try to cram it down my gullet. I keep telling them nothing can go down."

With his pharmacy background, Sam had recognized cancer of the pancreas. Even before the operation, he knew it to be hopeless. I found Molly and talked with her while Sol sat with Sam for the next two hours.

We flew back in the afternoon and hurried to Sacred Heart Hospital. Our son smiled and waved to us. He would not be crippled by polio.

The next week I brought Ralph home; on the same day, Sol returned to Newark, for the burial of his dearest friend, forty-nine years old, our company attorney, our mainstay for the past twenty-three years.

"I never saw a funeral where so many men cried," Sol told me.

Within a year I walked down a hospital corridor once more. Sol had chosen the July Fourth holiday week to undergo surgery.

"A small growth at the base of my spine—nothing to worry about," he had reassured me after his spring medical check. "No rush, but Thannhauser says, 'Better out than in.'"

Seeing Sol white-faced in a white hospital room marked a first for me.

He grinned, held my hand and reported on the biopsy. "Benign! All the tests proved okay."

"You lucked out this time," I said, "but I've been trying to figure out why you ever landed in a hospital."

"You and Carl Rogers." He laughed. "Tell me why."

"You miss Sam," I said. "Every day you used to get on the phone and pour everything out to him. In the past few months you've had plenty to pour, but no outlet. All that garbage stays throttled inside you. Your body can't take it."

"You may have something there." He sighed. "Sure as shootin' I miss Sam. How I could have rapped with him all this spring!"

I had a suggestion. "You know this guy I've been going to at U.N.H.?"

Frederick Jervis was a psychologist recently named head of the Student Guidance Clinic at the University of New Hampshire. I had gone to Durham to see if he could help me figure out why I sneezed.

When I had extended my hand to shake his, he rose from behind his desk. Slim, with bright-blue eyes and fair, high-standing hair, he stretched forth his hand and groped for mine. He's blind! I realized with a shock.

A baseball player, blinded in the Battle of the Bulge, he had been rehabilitated by the army as a psychotherapist. He was married, had three children and had elected to make his home in New Hampshire.

I made an appointment for therapy but expected little. What could he, inexperienced, handicapped, offer me? To my surprise, I found myself making the round trip to Durham more and more often. Did I imagine it or was I sneezing less?

In our sessions I had described the aborted growth of the Manchester League of Women Voters and its struggles to influence the community, talked about the problems of our household, but invariably slid into business concerns. Dr. Jervis showed deep sensitivity to these. He confessed his bias: someday he hoped to specialize in systems, such as business management systems.

"You'll have to meet my husband," I had told him. "You're talking his language."

In the clinic I said to Sol, "Fred's wonderfully easy to talk to. While you're home recuperating, let's ask him to visit."

"Do you think anyone can fill in for Sam?" he asked.

"Give this man a chance," I urged.

One afternoon, a week later, Fred was deposited on our doorstep. I guided him to the sun parlor where Sol lounged in pajamas and bathrobe, introduced them and left, closing the curtained French doors behind me.

The two did not emerge for hours. I thought over the past year and tried to imagine what they were talking about.

Sol had taken three important steps to ensure a banner year for Pandora in 1955. First, during the slow winter months, he had knit 20,000 dozen nylon basics. For the previous two years this gamble with off-season inventory had yielded a windfall.

Second, he had leased Remington Rand's latest computer. That hardware had been installed for spring shipping, so that any kinks could be ironed out before the fall rush. "They claim it's easy to operate; we'll need no geniuses to run it," he had reported.

Third, he was testing Ted's ability to stand in for him. "I've promised Ted that this entire year he'll make every crucial decision on machinery as well as yarn."

"You're loading heavy responsibility on his shoulders," I had protested.

"I'm throwing him the ball," he answered. "I have to see how he runs with it. Problems arise every day in the nitty-gritty of running a business. Is he still trying to make believe they don't exist? Or, in the past few years, has he learned how to confront them?"

"A pretty expensive experiment!" I exclaimed. "Just when you have things running smoothly."

"What better time than now to try it?" he asked. "May, with your father fading out of the picture, I simply have to know how heavily I can lean on Ted."

All the leaning, I felt, went in the opposite direction, but I argued no more.

That year nylon had dropped dead. Out of a quarter-million sweaters, almost half gathered dust on our shelves. Stores clamored instead for the newest synthetic, Orlon.

In May, my father panicked and came storming up from the south. He had Carl summon three leading salesmen and lectured them on selling merchandise we owned.

"Yes, Mr. B.," said the New England man, but he only paid him lip service. The trio continued to push Orlon.

"Dump those nylons," Pa yelled. "Get rid of them at any price. The first loss is the best loss."

Shamefaced, Carl brought back only one offer, a ridiculously low one from a major discounter. Sol agonized over loyal customers who had bought the same goods at regular prices for back-to-school selling.

"When will Alexander's put them on sale?" he asked Carl. "At what price? Will they hold off at least until October 1?"

Carl extracted a promise from Alexander's that they would not offer the goods before September 15, but could not pry out the price.

"Ship, ship!" ordered my father.

Sol had to ship almost 100,000 nylon sweaters to Alexander's, but from a distribution center reduced to chaos.

The new computer had snarled all shipping. The right goods went to the wrong addresses, the wrong goods went to the right addresses, and some goods were shipped in quantities that bore no resemblance to quantities billed. Two Remington Rand technicians practically lived in our mill. Sol and Ted worked at their side during the day and many nights as well. Sol predicted it would take the balance of the year before the computer operated smoothly.

My brother, meanwhile, had made key decisions. Each year we usually added one new type of equipment. This year Ted had invested in two: four full-fashion and two interlock machines. Although these would fill gaps in our line, they required specific yarns in deniers we did not normally carry. Then, because Orlon clearly seemed a runaway winner, Sol had begun buying synthetic tow for us to spin it ourselves, and Ted was fumbling through the spinning and knitting processes of these unfamiliar fibers. Ted opted as well for one other novelty, Acrilan. Monsanto was launching this product with much hoopla. Since our sweaters would be advertised in *Seventeen* and *Mademoiselle,* as well as in trade publications, Monsanto would have to put us on a yarn quota, but promised a regular, if modest, flow.

Greater machinery expenditures, more yarn counts, treacherous synthetics—what next?

Over Memorial Day, Ted had asked Sol to host a barbecue in our back yard for both families and some out-of-towners. Ted's guests—a man, his wife and three sons—proved unique.

The children, triplets born prematurely, had been popped into incubators at birth, and their delicate eyes had been overexposed to oxygen. We were entertaining three blind seven-year-olds! Cheerful, well co-ordinated, the boys raced around with our children and Ted's, played games boisterously and devoured hot dogs and hamburgers. We prolonged the afternoon, sorry to see them and their parents go.

When everyone left, I asked Sol, "Les represents Bancroft, doesn't he? Surely Ted isn't being romanced into still another new yarn?"

"I've told you and I've told Ted—he's making all the decisions about yarn," Sol answered. "He has definitely decided on Ban-Lon. He's even leasing crimper attachments from Bancroft. We'll soon start to spin it ourselves."

"Orlon, Acrilan and now Ban-Lon? Even for the holiday season, Sol, we don't have enough lead time."

"I'm bending over backward to give him his head," he said.

"You'll bend over so far," I retorted, "you'll turn into a pretzel."

The scenario for the Year of the Triple Disaster had been written. By June it began to unfold.

The regular personnel could not handle the shipment of over 8,000 dozen units of nylon sweaters to Alexander's. Sol and Ted drafted Al, a controller lately come on the scene. The three men worked from closing until midnight for a week, packed the entire stock into cartons, wrote out labels and shipping instructions by hand, checked quantities and figured invoices.

Quickly and sadly, with his slide rule, Sol estimated what a beating Pandora was taking.

Al remained in the distribution center, trying to tame the balky computer. It was slow going. His phone kept ringing. He and Sol had to pacify retailers angry over late shipments, partial shipments and too many small shipments. Only headaches loomed ahead.

Sol expedited goods through the plant. "Each dozen's like pulling teeth," he told me.

The first lots of Ban-Lon had been rejected; they had not met specifications. Despite Ted's efforts and screams from the road men, the Ban-Lon samples reached them long after they had started their holiday trips. Next, Monsanto reneged on its promises. Expensive machinery and well-paid knitters stood idle, waiting for Ted to dole out Acrilan. Orlon, meanwhile, trickled in stingily from Du Pont and unevenly from our own spinning division.

Untried yarns in small lots paralyzed our dyehouse and diminished the flow of goods through the mill. Our piece-workers were affected; they were taking home skimpy wages. The superintendent in charge could not take the pressure; he quit at the height of the season. In manufacturing, too, headaches abounded.

So, what with calamities in inventory, computer mistakes and Ted's decisions, Sol had plenty to talk over with Fred.

Emerging at last, the two men found me in the kitchen. I noted their smiles and easy camaraderie.

"I want Fred for myself, but I want him for Pandora, too,"

Sol said. "Beginning in August, he has agreed to come to the factory once a month. He'll make himself available to me, to the other executives and for any group meetings I arrange."

Share-the-wealth Sol, I thought. Never had I pictured him using the psychologist on any but a personal basis. Shortly after, I left to drive Fred back to Durham.

"Therapists, I understand, rarely work with more than one member of a family," I said to him. "Right now I feel Sol needs you more than I do."

Fred confirmed that he would not counsel Sol and me at the same time. "Perhaps I can recommend someone else for you when you're ready."

He began to talk about the opportunity and the challenge facing him at Pandora. He looked forward to working with the man at the top and, through him, reaching all the way down to the people on the line. He felt that together they could evolve a more effective system of management.

"Hashing things over with Fred made me come to certain conclusions," my husband said later. "I'm elevating your father to chairman of the board, and doing it the next time he comes charging up from Florida. Whether he likes it or not, I'm going to be president. I do the work; I may as well claim the title." Bless you, Fred, I thought.

"As for Ted, I knew the risk when I gave him a free hand. He had to learn the hard way. He hasn't." He paused. "Anyone can make a mistake. Only a fool makes the same mistake twice. He's still blaming everyone but himself. I'm blowing the whistle on Ted."

Sol and Fred had indeed clicked.

My invalid returned to Pandora impatient to restore the factory to its normal tempo.

"How can any company make such a tremendous investment in a computer, new knitting machines, new spinning equipment and new yarns without a corresponding outlay for expertise to make sure everything works?" Al had asked him.

A top-notch executive experienced in data processing and distribution was hired. Shipments began to go out correctly and more nearly on time.

Ted had been filling in for the superintendent who had walked off the stitching floor. Sol insisted on an immediate replacement. He interviewed a technician from Brooklyn. Morty wanted to move his family out of the city; Ted seemed to like him. So Sol hired Morty to work under Ted's direction. The stitching room resumed its normal rhythm.

"Expertise helps," Sol admitted to Al, "but we must start with square one, the yarn, if we want goods streaming through every department."

About to tackle the spinning mill, he stumbled on Ted brutally berating its overseer, an invaluable old-timer.

"Don't pick on Henry if Orlon isn't moving fast enough," Sol reproached Ted.

"Sometimes it pays to hit someone in the face as hard as you can," Ted replied. "It keeps him on his toes. If you're wrong, you can always say you're sorry."

"Let's approach Du Pont," Sol suggested instead. "For twenty years they've used us as their guinea pig for every new synthetic. They owe us one."

Sol reached a man high in the Du Pont hierarchy. An expert, on loan, showed up shortly thereafter. In no time Henry's output of Orlon increased. Sol also struck a bargain with Monsanto. He agreed to be photographed as one of our industry's leaders in an advertisement. Sitting in a rocker, busily knitting on long bone needles from a ball of Acrilan yarn, Sol occupied a full page in *Women's Wear*. Monsanto came through on their commitment in exchange. From outside and inside, a steady supply of yarn began to fill the pipe lines once more.

Shortly after Labor Day Alexander's jumped the gun. The discounter put 100,000 nylon sweaters on sale at $2.95; our regular accounts were selling them at $7.95. Sol and Carl, brainstorming with Fred, had anticipated the move.

"All our early lots of Orlon have gone into promotion lots," Sol told me. "They may not have the same cashmere feel we're offering now, but they have enough of that buttery smoothness that customers will grab them up. Stores can buy them at rock-bottom prices and hedge their losses."

The strategy worked; the hubbub died down.

Nylon stock returned by retailers was immediately routed to the factory store. "Hallelujah for that store!" Sol said. "We can sell everything that makes a round trip, and at decent prices, too."

An old acquaintance of my father's had made a stab at disposing of our surplus synthetic yarn. With Sol's backing, Ted replaced him. He found a young go-getter who drummed up unheard-of accounts. They bought all the yarn we could spare and kept our spindles humming.

The spinning mill and the factory store would probably cushion our back-to-school losses, Al projected in October. We might break even for the year if we suffered no further losses in the last three months.

"Do we dare keep on knitting off-season and speculate without confirmed orders?" Sol deliberated one evening. "We're damned if we do and damned if we don't."

"For two years you were a hero," I reminded him. "If you want to go ahead, don't let anyone tell you why not to. Instead, figure out how."

Fred Jervis helped Sol lessen the risk. They gave Carl a research project. What styles were moving in greatest numbers over store counters in September and October? Carl contacted a dozen of our most faithful accounts, won access to their records and reported. By November Sol had issued orders for a skeleton program of Orlon classics.

I may have felt like a matchmaker in having brought Fred and Sol together. Before the summer ended, Sol and I had been confronted by another happy couple. Sara Mae and Larry had been going together for three years. She was about to start her sophomore year at R.I.S.D.; he was getting his master's degree at M.I.T. Enough courtship, he told Sol; he wanted to marry her.

"I guessed what he was coming for," Sol told me. "But when he said, 'I'm asking for your daughter's hand in marriage,' I found my eyes filling up with tears and a lump in my throat.

"I couldn't do to him what your father did to me," Sol continued. "Larry promised me he'd see to it that Sara Mae finished college. What could I say? They're getting married during the Christmas holiday."

"You once said, 'We're getting there,'" I reminded him, half smiling and half bawling. "Sol, we're there."

In December, ten days before his granddaughter's wedding, my father came north. Sol met him, because the two men had a date with the three banks that now jointly funded us. Pandora had repaid its loans that month and not, as usual, in November. Instead of staying debt-free for three months, Pandora might have to borrow again in six weeks.

"I have to give your ole man credit," Sol told me. "We went in to the bankers; he bellyached about the interest rate. Where we had paid three percent, the prime rate had gone up to three and a quarter percent. He wouldn't stand for that.

"He got them to agree to three and an eighth percent. On a million dollars that saved us $1,250 for the year. But do you know what he really accomplished? He got them so wound up they never gave us the inquisition I was waiting for."

"They surely wanted to know why we paid late," I remarked.

Pa had fielded that question neatly. Due to the new synthetics, we had to increase our inventory and prolong our season.

"The bankers bought this," Sol went on. "What a bill of goods your father sold them!"

The occasion for her grandfather's visit, Sara Mae's wedding, took place on a bright Sunday afternoon. I remember smoothing out folds in Sara Mae's long red satin coat over her frothy white gown, and fussing with her veil, my hands trembling. I also remember straightening out two slightly tipsy tiaras on her two maids of honor, her sisters Rebecca and Micala.

As we entered the synagogue—the new temple would not be completed before the next year—I remember the fragrance of hundreds of roses, and I remember Sol, looking far too pale, escorting his precious daughter up the aisle before he surrendered her to Larry.

We held the reception in the gymnasium-auditorium. I remember Larry and his ushers singing choruses from the repertoire of the M.I.T. Glee Club. I remember my father at one end of the head table resolutely ignoring my mother at the other end. Mostly I remember the sun's rays through the tall windows as they suffused the ballroom with a glow while bridesmaids in gold, dancing with their partners, circled a radiant bride and groom.

Midway between the meeting with the bankers and the wedding, Sol had honored my father with a cocktail party in his office.

He had invited Fred Jervis, the rabbi, with whom he had grown increasingly intimate, and Joe, our Manchester attorney.

Bright, quick and ever-obliging, this lawyer was shouldering an even-larger wedge of our corporate work. Visiting my husband's office, I would often overhear Sol on the phone informing Joe of minute company details.

"Still searching for a substitute for Sam?" I had commented.

"With one difference," replied Sol. "With Joe I've carefully spelled out a distinction I never had to mention to Sam—Sam understood it. Joe has agreed to one condition I've laid down. If ever any conflict should arise between the Blum family's interests and my interests, Joe clearly knows he's my lawyer first."

At the party, Sol had announced a new roll call of Pandora's officers. Mr. B. was named chairman of the board; Sol officially became president. Ted was advanced to executive vice-president.

"I gave Ted the title to sugar-coat the pill for your father," Sol said.

"How did it go over?" I asked.

"Ted looked pleased. Your father made his usual faces, then a wisecrack about being kicked upstairs," Sol answered. "Al said to me, 'Weren't you always president?'"

NINE

A Road Paved with Knitting Needles

ANOTHER YEAR, ANOTHER SEASON —a contrast with the one before.

"I don't see what can possibly go wrong," Sol told me one day in late summer. On his long fingers he ticked off all the good things happening at Pandora.

On his thumb, the runaway success of Orlon classics. They had taken such hold that our salesmen had surpassed all previous records.

On his forefinger, the great quantities of Orlon being fed to our knitting room by our own spinning mill and dyehouse. Ban-Lon had also taken off. Ted, with Sol's assent, had ordered three more crimpers. Our yarn agent was selling all the Orlon and Ban-Lon we could not use. We had dropped Acrilan from the line.

On his middle finger, the consistent stream of work progressing through the mill under Morty. We could take pride in the excellent quality of Pandora sweaters.

On his fourth finger, the correct, even early, shipments of merchandise, overseen by the capable man directing distribution.

As Sol got to his pinkie finger, he looked like a cat licking cream. "Get ready to travel, a biggie this time," he finished. "Honeygirl, for our twenty-fifth anniversary you and I are going abroad."

I whooped with delight. He briefed me on an international knitting fair being held in October in Leicester, England. The

American delegation would make its headquarters at the Savoy Hotel in London. After ten days, part of the group would fly to Paris for a similar stay. Both in England and in France we could combine business with sightseeing and fun.

In the next few weeks Sol spent most of his time projecting spinning, knitting, research and orders with Ted. My brother had knit children's patterns and swatches from exciting new synthetics. These had caught the eyes of Carl and Carl's newly hired Swiss designer, Maria. At the same time, Ted was searching diligently for outside customers to take up the slack on our full-fashion machines. He had located several interested men's houses.

Sol and Ted laid out enough odds and ends on the machines to complete fall shipments and keep the plant running during our absence. Marian, Sol's secretary, was compiling charts of Pandora's sales to retailers, region by region, for the past three years. Sol would balance this index with Carl's feedback from over-the-counter sales. On our return he would then carefully compute orders for off-season knitting. What could possibly go wrong?

Before we left for our second honeymoon, Sol insisted on a formal silver wedding in our home.

"We'll have family and friends around us. The children will take part," he said. "We have an occasion worth celebrating."

He had spoken to the rabbi about a rededication ceremony. I engaged an organist with a portable organ, hired a caterer, and hosted a dozen out-of-town couples that weekend. Monogrammed silver charm bracelets were presented to each woman present as a memento.

The last guest departed on Sunday afternoon. That very evening, Sol and I flew to New York, and joined the United States contingent on Monday morning.

We adapted to England easily. Each weekday Sol and the other knitters commuted to the Leicester fair; in London, I explored sights and shops with left-behind wives. In the evenings we went together to the theater.

On the last day, I went with him to Leicester, relishing the adventure of riding on a British train, and then walked through endless aisles at the fair, inspecting the latest in machinery, yarns and auxiliary equipment. We enjoyed a lunch with graduates and faculty from the Leicester College of Knitting.

Sol had hired a car to take us to Stratford. A one-armed veteran drove us in a specially fitted car. We noticed many amputees in the villages and towns on our route, and our chauffeur said that hardly a British family had escaped the war without a casualty of some kind.

Midway through our ride we came to Coventry. Earlier, we had gawked at pits and craters scooped out of the countryside. Here, though, an entire city bore war wounds, but with a difference. Coventry's blueprint for the future contrasted with yesterday's gaping holes. New buildings, rectangular phoenixes of steel and glass, were rising from the rubble. A billboard announcing a new cathedral was set among the twisted remnants of the old one.

At Stratford we went to a Pickwickian inn. Bright flowers in gardens and window boxes braved the October air and lent color to the street; nosegays decorated each dining-room table. That evening, in the velvet and gold theater, we saw *Hamlet* performed by skilled actors in rich velvet-and-lace costumes. Stark tragedy in a satin setting. After a hearty breakfast—Sol smacked his lips over the kippers—we took the train back to London.

Wherever Sol went, he handed out a gimmicky tie clip with the letters "YCDBSOYA."

"You can't do business sitting on your ..." he decoded for a far-removed kinsman we had looked up, a supermarket tycoon named Jacob Cohen.

We were entertaining him and his wife for dinner at the Savoy the night before we left for France. The two men roared.

"Send me a gross of them," Cousin Jack demanded.

Sol promised.

In our room at the Hotel Meurice in Paris we found roses from Prouvost, Lefebvre et Cie., international raw-wool merchants who sold us large quantities of Australian wool tow for spinning. At Du Pont's office on the Champs-Elysée we gazed with respect at swatches shown us by a uniquely gifted Swiss spinner. In innovative experiments he had mixed French angora with Orlon, simulated silk ribbon, and reproduced wool chenille in man-made fiber.

We took time out for the Casino de Paris, for the Bateau Mouche on the Seine, and for the French National Ballet.

In the midst of this whirl came a transatlantic call from Sol's brother. Sol shrieked with joy at Lou's announcement. His firm had bought him a seat on the New York Stock Exchange.

After three weeks of floating on clouds, literally and figuratively, we returned to Manchester. Only then did we learn the answer to Sol's question: What could possibly go wrong?

Grimly, Sol spelled out for me Pandora's latest cliff-hanger. Ted had devoted himself to creating samples for the men's houses. While developing and presenting varied and complicated styles to potential customers he had spent much time away from the daily operation of the mill. To Morty had been delegated the responsibility for completing the children's samples and working with Carl.

"What a reorder I took from Best and Co.!" Carl had bragged one day. "I only hope we have enough turtlenecks to fill it."

Morty at once by-passed Ted. He issued verbal orders to the knitting and spinning departments. Each time Carl exulted in another sales coup, Morty put another thousand dozen on the machines. He had kept the plant going at full capacity from the moment Sol left.

On Sol's return, Al cornered him. "Inventory is strangling us," he reported. "I can't make Ted sit down and listen. We've stumbled into such a tight money crunch, I see no way out."

"You must have some mistake in your figures," said Sol. "Look at the shipping records—our best season ever."

Early the next morning Al finally collared Ted. The two men walked through a factory glutted with Orlon slipovers, turtlenecks and cardigans; they saw storage bins packed with Orlon yarn. With Morty, they took physical count of every unit in the manufacturing pipeline and weighed every bundle of yarn. In the afternoon, bathed in cold sweat, Ted and Al marched in to Sol.

"You must listen," my brother said.

"We have no bank balances," Al stated. "We cannot pay off our loans in November. We won't have the cash even in December. Every cent is frozen in inventory."

Ted substantiated the inventory figures. Sol was finally convinced.

"How much money can we raise?" he asked me at home after filling in the details.

We marshaled our assets. Sol even cashed in his budding stock portfolio. He got a substantial advance from the man who bought our wool waste. Ted brought in whatever cash he could. Somehow we scraped together enough money to clear our bank debt, but, for the first time since we had moved to Manchester, Sol had to make a major layoff of help. Ted advised firing a fixed percentage in each department across the board. Sol refused. Laboriously poring through lists with Al and consulting Fred, he took into account seniority, skill and the worker's money needs. Giving some people leaves of absence, helping others get placed elsewhere, he finally pared the payroll from over 400 to under 350.

Five months later the miracle we needed happened. Our salesmen brought back order after order for the very Orlon sweaters waiting on our shelves. A further miracle: many stores wanted early shipment. We could pick finished merchandise, send it on its way and get paid off earlier. The yarn agent, meanwhile, had disposed of large lots of Orlon at profitable prices.

Money began to pour in. Sol paid off his insurance loans and restored our children's bank accounts.

With this strange twist of luck, one other benefit accrued to us as well. Pandora gained the reputation of having "the right goods at the right price at the right time."

The strain of Pandora's narrow escape from disaster told on me. Once again a stuffed-up nose was keeping me awake half the night. Once again I was prowling around downstairs with my mouth dry from breathing through it and with sodden tissues in my hand to catch the drip, drip, drip from my sneezing. One midnight I found myself sitting in total darkness behind Sol's desk in the sun parlor crying like a fool.

Fred Jervis recommended a therapist who headed the New Hampshire Child Guidance Clinic in Concord. "I interned under Anna," he said. "Let me ask her if she can fit you in."

Although Anna was overbooked, she offered me an appointment. A stocky woman, who peered over Ben Franklin glasses, she flashed me the kindliest of smiles. Yes, she would like to help me. She could give me random appointments, and as soon as she discharged the next patient, I would be assigned his slot of time. Meanwhile, she had a suggestion. She asked me to write out, between visits, whatever troubled me.

In a corner of her office stood a dollhouse in cross section. I remarked on the lifelike family figures in it. Tenderly, she spoke of little children who came to her and playacted with those make-believe people.

"They can get very angry with the dolls and throw them about or beat them up," she said. "They can let out all their feelings. It's all right. Those children know I love them just the same." Sadly, she added, "How much understanding and encouragement they crave! Some of them are so troubled."

I took some of my scribbling to my next appointment and read it to her.

"You write well," she said. "Save it. Someday you might put your writings together in a book."

As I grew to know Anna better, I compared her with my mother. Large and beautiful, Bertha had a "stucco self." Vain about her appearance, she extended this to her children and her home. She shrank from displaying emotion by touch or by words. In all the years that she and my father lived together, I had never heard one quarrel between them. Bertha's moment of sublime glory had come when she gave birth to Morris's son. No other event had attained that peak.

Anna, short and plain, dressed neatly but without fuss. She poured forth love. It emanated from her eyes, her lips, and the comfort of her kiss and caress. Anna gave me her total attention. With her I could bottle up no emotion. Willy-nilly every grain of feeling came tumbling out or got written down to be sifted and winnowed later. Sometimes my own words shook me.

One Sunday afternoon I took Sol to Anna's. I wanted him to meet this woman who had grown dear to me. The three of us talked in her comfortable living room.

"Please tell my mother what you were telling me," I said to Sol, who was rocking in an overstuffed chair.

"Did you hear yourself then?" he asked as he stopped his rocking.

When and by what permutation Anna became my mother I never knew.

Sol and I had long ago accepted Bertha as an ongoing responsibility. Unexpectedly, this grew heavier.

Dropping in one evening we found her quite distraught.

"What am I to do?" she asked Sol, her cheeks looking warm, puffy and unnaturally flushed.

Her landlord had sold the house. The new owner had given her notice to move and a date by which to vacate.

"I'll find another place, move, get chased out again, then have to move again," she said, on the verge of tears.

"Skinny, I'm going to build you a house," Sol promised, "where no one can ever kick you out again. I know a kind, patient architect who specializes in private homes," he told my mother. "He'll listen when you talk; he'll give you the house you really want."

Sol bought a plot of land only a few blocks from my brother's house and from ours. The architect responded to every wish my mother expressed. Shortly before her dead-line, Skinny moved into her own home, a ranch house connected by a spacious breezeway to a garage.

My mother's problem had been happily resolved. With Anna's guidance, I bared and resolved other problems.

"I feel like an onion," I told her. "We seem to be peeling off layer after layer."

One layer dealt with Sol's health. He had turned fifty. His father had died in his mid-fifties, his mother barely sixty. I now made it a practice to accompany Sol to each of his medical checkups.

"Everything is fine," said Dr. Thannhauser. "The aorta is a bit enlarged, but that's nothing to worry about—as long as you don't get yourself overaggravated."

"I try to follow your advice," Sol answered. "We go away on those four vacations a year. I've been taking more time off. I've been following the diet carefully."

"Ach," interrupted the fatherly, beaming doctor, "with the care you take of yourself, you're going to live to eighty."

If the old German physician relieved me of a wifely anxiety, Anna altered the image I had of myself as a mother.

"How do you spend your day?" she asked me.

Silently, I reviewed my movements hour by hour. "As a service station," I answered at last.

A large chunk of my day went into driving assorted children to and from extracurricular activities. After that session with Anna, the children and I delved into bus schedules and car pools. I tapered off my driving as they managed more and more transportation on their own.

With respect to chauffeuring I may have been doing too much for my children; in another respect I may have been doing too little. Easily and naturally, Sol fondled me and our kids. Reflecting my parents, I kept my hands to myself, never petted them. If I cherished Sol's touch, how our young ones must also long for tangible signs of affection! By a conscious effort, I began to reach out to pat them, gently embrace them, give them an occasional hug or smooch. They seemed to treasure it.

"We must look at children through rose-colored glasses," Anna preached.

It felt good to do so.

"I have blossomed into poetry," I announced one day and recited to her: 'A sneezer/Is a pleaser.'"

She laughed. We had been discussing whether I repeated my service-station pattern with others. Henceforth, we decided, each time I sneezed I had to ask myself, are you pleasing someone on the outside or heeding your insides?

Ted had come to Sol with a proposition. He believed in deals that involved partners. Some time before, nine investors had sought a tenth to buy untold acres of get-rich-quick Florida real estate. Ted had persuaded Sol to split this tenth share with him. Subsequently, we learned that our holdings lay in central, not coastal, Florida, were partly submerged and were hardly marketable. Now Ted was asking Sol to become a one-fifth partner with him in a local electronics firm.

"He says he'll feel more secure if I share a piece of the action," Sol relayed.

"So that Ted can feel more secure, we now own a one-twentieth interest in a Florida swamp. It may please him, but not me. Sol," I begged, "let Ted find his own partners."

Sol turned Ted down. My brother had no trouble locating a stand-in.

"Ted has invited us to a cocktail party this Sunday, where we can meet his new electronics partner," Sol said. "This guy just got his graduate degree in business administration last year, and he's supposed to be a whiz kid."

Ordinarily, Sol and I were not included in Ted and Jean's social life. That afternoon we walked over to meet Jerry. Jean, the solicitous hostess, hovered over him. Though self-conscious and awkward, he seemed to have been accepted by her and their friends.

"Am I glad we said no to Ted," I remarked after we left. "In this one deal, at least, Ted has worked out his own answer."

During this period my father's ego was steadily becoming more bruised. Sol's succession to the presidency grated on him. True, Sol kept him posted, regularly phoned him. Once a year we visited Pa in Florida; twice a year Pa came north. But Sol, managing wonderfully well on his own, sought his advice less and less. Pandora's reputation and profits flourished; along with them, Sol flourished.

Once again our knitting quarters were growing cramped and our shipping room bulging. So Sol bought a half-interest in another millyard building, four times as large as our first one. Joe had handled all the legal technicalities and given practical advice on terms. Ted was working with a layout consultant to ready a good part of the space as a distribution center. Sol also transferred the full-fashion division to the new building.

In the vacated space he installed an annex to the factory store. This proved only a stopgap. Because customer traffic still clogged the millyard, within the year he leased an empty building. Directly across the railroad tracks, it had once housed the bustling Amoskeag Locomotive Works. He commissioned Sara Mae, who was studying interior design, to lay out a greatly expanded retail store that would preserve the flavor of the old Amoskeag.

Sol and I talked at length one day about the future of Pandora. Using Fred's systems, we asked ourselves where we wanted to be five or ten years down the road.

"We've been knitting sweaters for the kids born in the baby boom," I said. "Those war babies keep growing up. We should grow along with them."

"You're talking about a completely separate junior division, with its own sales manager, designer and sales force," said Sol.

I had not pictured anything quite so grand.

"I go for the idea, but how will Carl feel?" Sol asked. "Carl has to find that other sales manager or it won't work."

Sol did talk to Carl and direct him to find an executive to head this spin-off.

In a white wicker armchair on his sunny patio, pins and needles dancing from his toes and an orange cat crouching on his knees, Pa flexed his muscles. He could not be confined to reading the *New York Times* or masterminding stock deals with Maury, his stepson. With each development at Pandora, he had to show he still packed clout. Himself the epitome of ambition, he derided Sol's ambitions. "Big eyes," he scoffed.

Though he showed concern in his own fashion for people who worked for him, he ridiculed the extent to which Sol went. *"Narishkeit* [foolishness]," he said.

Sol's decision-making process really riled Pa. Sol talked over every major project with each associate involved, especially with Carl, Al and Joe. He would inform Ted, but my father knew Ted's opinion carried little weight. Sol even talked to that "brain-shrinker," Fred. Worst of all, though, he listened to me. Unforgivable!

"I just saw Morris in Miami," reported an uncle of mine. "He says, Sol, you have to make Teddy your fifty-fifty partner."

"I thought we buried that ghost long ago," I said, turning to my husband.

"Pay no attention, Mug," Sol replied. "The ole man just can't sit still; he has to make waves."

I paid no attention. My days of pleasing my father, then sneezing, were coming to an end.

How well my sessions with Anna had worked I found out one day in June 1958. Sol and I drove down to Sara Mae's college graduation. In the crowded auditorium of the Rhode Island School of Design, we had no trouble picking out our daughter as the seniors marched in processional down the aisle and mounted the stage to receive their diplomas. Hers was the biggest belly in the graduating class; she had two months to go. On the ride home Sol and I were bubbling with the joys of the day. Suddenly I stopped short.

"Sol, do you realize you haven't heard me sneeze once on this entire trip?"

After twenty-five years of consulting experts and undergoing allergy tests, injections, medicines, nose sprays, X-ray treatments, and after just one year of working with Anna, I no longer sneezed.

Shortly before Labor Day, Sara Mae and Larry presented us with a granddaughter they named Pandora. Shortly after Labor Day, Ralph took off for prep school.

"Soon you and Sol will be alone, just the two of you," Anna commented when I next saw her.

"Already we're rattling around in that big house," I replied. "From seven of us sitting around the table, we're down to TV suppers for Becky and Mickey and a quiet dinner for Sol and myself."

We discussed a second career for me.

"I'd go back to work in the factory, but I don't want to cramp Sol's style," I said. "He's running an awfully good show."

I mentioned another reason for shifting gears, one that had lately dawned on me. "I'm like the letter Z," I told her. "All these years the feet have been walking forward while the head has been screwed on backward. More than fifty years ago my father fell in love with *strickmaschinen* in Berlin. Because of him I've been following a road paved with knitting needles."

Anna looked at me quizzically. "To me you seem very different from anyone else in your family. The accident of birth doesn't lock you into that family forever. And now ..." she prompted.

"I don't have to stay in the knitting business," I said. "When I look around, I see other roads."

At home Sol and I continued the discussion.

"Something to do with writing," I suggested. "Years ago you started me off on the *Yarn.* I've always enjoyed it."

"Manchester has meant a lot to us," said Sol, approaching the subject from his own angle. "The greatest gift we could offer our community would be a newspaper—an alternative to William Loeb and the *Union-Leader.*"

Wholeheartedly I agreed. Then I asked, "Won't it take a lot of money?"

"A worthwhile investment," he told me. "We have two sons. What a great thing, to offer them two separate businesses to go into!"

We mentioned the idea of a newspaper to Joe.

"Do you know of any other investors?" Sol asked.

"How about a crackerjack editor?" I chimed in.

Agreeable and co-operative as always, Joe promised to cull every contact to find investors with money and the right man to be editor.

Carl was also looking around for the right man, one to head the junior division. On our New York weekends we had interviewed a few candidates. None seemed to measure up.

They had, however, brought up stipulations about employment contracts, and Carl had mentioned safeguards for himself. We were ironing out these items over supper one night with the attorney who handled our New York affairs, when Sol, almost off-handedly, brought up an unforeseen development.

"Stock in our company is divided evenly into two classes," he began, "voting and nonvoting. For ten years Mr. B. has abided by the agreements we all signed in 1949. Each spring he has distributed five percent of his stock and Bertha's to the seven grandchildren—nonvoting stock." Sol paused. "This year he has made no transfer."

"This year he'd have to surrender voting stock," stated the lawyer.

"Exactly," said Sol.

"Do you want to go to court?" the lawyer asked, after a few minutes. "You have a case."

"Let's wait until the end of the year," said Sol. "He must be bluffing."

No stock had been transferred by June, when my father came north to receive a unique tribute. He was being honored for a lifetime in the industry.

"Morris Blum Celebrates Fifty Years in Knitting," read a headline spread across the centerfold in *Knitting Times*, our trade magazine. Friends and suppliers had bought pages for advertisements wishing him well.

Sol made a big to-do over him. In front of the mayor, company executives, local suppliers and friends, Sol presented him with a silver plaque commemorating the anniversary. The mayor gave him a gold key to the city. The *Union-Leader* sent a photographer; a picture and story appeared the next day. In New York, Sol staged a second reception.

"So much fuss!" Pa complained, but obviously he savored each moment.

Never once did Sol ask him, How come you're reneging on our agreement? Instead he clung to his belief that my father was only playing games, that eventually he would transfer the stock.

Family matters diverted my attention. Sara Mae became pregnant again. Gene transferred from his Midwestern engineering school to a prelaw course at our state university. One event befell us, too, that we could not take in stride.

In October 1959, the holiest of Hebrew Holy Days happened to fall on the eleventh, our anniversary. The phone kept ringing, with friends wishing us Happy New Year and/or Happy Anniversary. Late in the afternoon, the phone rang once more. Sol answered it. Then there was a dreadful, piercing outcry.

"Daddy, daddy," I heard Becky's high-pitched, tremulous voice asking, "what happened?"

I found Sol in the kitchen, his face buried in his hands, great gulps of crying racking his body.

"Lou has been killed," he sobbed.

Sol's brother, Lou, and two of his co-workers from the Stock Exchange had gone upstate for their annual pilgrimage at fall-foliage time. They liked to fish, hike, listen to the World Series and, as Lou put it, just horse around. Having enjoyed the weekend, Lou was driving them back on the New York State Thruway.

Suddenly, with no warning, Lou had crumpled over the wheel. The car went out of control, leaped the median dividing wall, and smashed head-on into a car going in the opposite direction. His two passengers and a woman seated beside her husband in the front seat of the other car were killed instantly. Lou could not be buried until a coroner completed an autopsy, which showed he had suffered a fatal massive coronary.

"One thing really bothers me," Sol told me after the funeral. "When Lou died, he dragged three people to their deaths with him. The moment he felt anything, he should have kept his foot over the brake, not the gas."

One thing bothered me, a quite different thing. Not only had Sol's parents died fairly young, but here also was Lou, dead at fifty-four.

With hearts still heavy, we started out on a trip Sol had planned long in advance. Three years after our first venture, we were going abroad again.

"What businessman does not go to Europe regularly?" Maria, Carl's Swiss designer, had asked, peering at "Meester Seedore" over her heavy prism glasses. She had sold Sol on catching the latest European fashion trends and on tasting Switzerland's splendors.

"The week before, I will just have reached my home from the fall showings in Paris," this maiden lady told Sol. "I will bring you samples and sketches. You must rest up for a few days; American men get themselves altogether too tired. Then I will show you and Meeses Seedore all around Zurich."

She made reservations for us, too, in St. Moritz, to experience the grandeur of the Alps. While there, she decreed, we must pick the wild flowers of the field and ride the funicular. Thence, by way of Lake Como, we went to Milan.

There, Sol met with the head of Snia Viscosa, the Du Pont of Italy. We toured the spinning complex, and saw swatches of interesting and markedly different textures: some with a random nub, others blending synthetic with shiny or tinsel thread. Sol wanted to judge the Italian mill's capacity to deliver any orders he might place.

On a stopover in London we enjoyed the theater and shopped the sweater market.

The shifting kaleidoscope of foreign cities, lakes and mountains somewhat cushioned the shock of Lou's death.

Back in New York, Sol's thoughts were further diverted. Carl introduced one more prospect to head a junior division. Ronnie had been sales manager of a nationally famed junior sweater house. He had left the previous year to buy an interest in a Philadelphia knitwear concern. Gossip had it that the bloom of ownership was wearing off, squabbles with partners were wearing him down and greener fields might beckon.

Average in looks, height and build, this man was transformed when he smiled. The sweetness of his grin, punctuated by double dimples and a glint in his eye, would charm anyone.

"He could sell wallpaper to Eskimos for their igloos," I told Sol.

Sol, too, was impressed and wasted no time in making him an offer. Ronnie accepted with provisos. He needed skirts coordinated with our sweaters and could recommend a master craftsman to manufacture sportswear. He also needed prices on shetland classics low enough to undercut any competitor.

After learning that Carl, too, felt he could sell skirts matching his children's sweaters, Sol agreed to the pricing structure. Although he had made slow headway with my father on adding a junior division, he now presented such arguments that Pa couldn't say no. So Sol met the skirt man, set in motion the legal framework for a separate company, and shook hands and sealed the bargain with Ronnie.

The joint efforts of the new executives made the skirt offering an instant hit in both size ranges. Sol followed through with loss-leader prices for Shetland sweaters. Ronnie gained ready admission to his many friends in the big stores. At the same time Carl negotiated for a larger showroom in the same building.

On our first trip to Manhattan after the New Year, Sol and I inspected our spacious new quarters. They included impressive offices for two corporate vice-presidents, Carl and Ronnie, and for their respective secretaries. The showroom, glittering with new furniture, had a unique feature. A line split it in the middle. The front half was carpeted in purple, for juniors; the back half, in pink, for children.

"Mason-Dixon," I whispered to Sol. In years to come, might this line mean conflicts between the two divisions? Would these two men fight for mill time for samples, for production time for stock, for sales effort by representatives handling both lines? Best to forestall any such possibility, I thought. But, listening to Sol straightening out some last-minute snaffles with Carl and Ronnie, I relaxed. If there were any flare-ups, these men would trust him, I felt.

"Mr. B. is still holding out," Sol reported, when we met with our New York lawyer. "Until the last day in December I had hopes he would come through."

"Once before I asked you if you want to go to court," the solemn attorney said. "You have a case."

Sol sat quietly, buried in thought. "My stomach turns at the thought of suing," he finally said, "especially within a family. Only lawyers profit from lawsuits." He laughed and added an apology to except present company. "Eventually the ole man has to come through." He looked over to me. "Let's take a calculated risk."

Ted and Jean were taking a few risks of their own. When she unpacked Ted's suitcase after one of his weekly trips to New York, Jean found lipstick on his shirt. The next time he left town, she decided, she'd go to a movie with Jerry.

"Kid stuff," I told Sol. "They're playing at 'tit for tat.'"

"Ted should travel," said Sol. "Travel ventilates the mind, broadens anyone's perspective. And he should take Jean along—get the two of them out of their rut."

So, early in the year, when Carl had to go on a sales trip to San Francisco, Sol insisted that he take Ted and Jean along.

And that fall he registered Ted for the quadrennial International Knitting Exposition in Milan. He was sending the couple on their first trip abroad.

Their itinerary was expanded to include Stuttgart, where Ted could meet two very hospitable German brothers from whom we had bought sophisticated knitting machinery, and Zurich, where Maria could show them around. Their last stop was Rome, a city Sol and I had yet to explore.

"Tell me all about your trip," I said to Jean, three weeks later.

"So much packing and unpacking," she complained.

Not only had Sol's ploy failed, but more shenanigans followed.

"Ted is going skiing in the Swiss Alps," Sol remarked shortly before the Christmas holidays.

"Bet he's going without Jean," I guessed. "Even with a footwarmer in her boots, her toes get numb when she just looks at snow on the slopes."

He was going with two bachelors.

While he was gone, his wife did not sit home. On New Year's Eve, for instance, Jean showed up at the Manchester Country Club on the arm of the attentive Jerry.

"Ted and Jean will work it out somehow," I said to Sol. "With Jerry eleven years younger than Jean, I can't get excited."

On Ted's return, he and Jean had a bitter falling out. For weeks she refused to speak to him. Gossip had it that Jerry was pressing her to divorce Ted and marry him. Sol and I were forced to face a serious situation.

"Suppose Jean marries Jerry," I said, "what happens to her stock in Pandora?" When Ted had been given his twenty percent, he had listed half in Jean's name, half in his own. "She takes her ten percent with her. We hold a stockholders' meeting, and Jerry represents her minority interest."

Sol and I pictured Jerry sitting next to Ted, posing embarrassing questions and further disrupting our already strained setup.

"I'd better get Joe's advice," Sol said.

He did, and Joe offered to call on Ted and Jean; he would sit down with them and make them talk sense.

After long sessions of soul-baring, Ted and Jean came to an agreement. She surrendered her shares to Ted in trust for their two children. In return, Ted vowed that, if they split up and she did not remarry, he would support her handsomely. While patiently working out these terms, Joe had somehow defrosted the ice between them.

Shortly afterward, Ted slipped in with a peace offering, a toy dachschund, under his arm. When he presented that tiny black puppy, Jean melted and cuddled it in her arms. Ted and Jean christened the dog Schnappsie and toasted him and the rebirth of their romance.

Joe, too, experienced an aftereffect. He opened up to Al one day, when the controller appeared in his office to pick up some documents.

"I've put myself in some spot," he said. "Since I persuaded Jean to transfer her stock, I've grown very close to those two. I didn't expect to get so involved with them."

Joe earned our gratitude for his part in effecting the stock transfer and reconciling Ted and Jean. Throughout that year of 1960, one other interest linked him to us: the Democratic party. Since the election in the first month after we moved to the Granite State, Sol and I had voted Democratic in a Republican stronghold. Joe had served on the Democratic State Committee, even run for office. Over the years, when Democrats passed the hat for hopeless campaigns, Sol had responded generously.

This year, John Fitzgerald Kennedy was going to beat the bushes in New Hampshire's first-in-the-nation primary. Through Joe, Sol was asked to extend the courtesy of a tour through our plant to him.

On January 25, Kennedy walked through Pandora. Years later, we dedicated the desk at which he sat to autograph leaflets. Framed on the wall behind that desk are JFK's letter of thanks to Sol and a photograph of the two men: Kennedy, pen in hand, sits at the desk; Sol lounges atop it, to one side, watching him.

The afternoon of the tour, at the Hotel Carpenter, Sol introduced me to Kennedy and the tall, elegant Jackie at his side. I complimented her on her stunning red coat with beaver collar.

"I got it at Ohrbach's," she confessed.

In the months that followed, we watched JFK's progress closely and anxiously. So did the *Union-Leader*. From February to November, in front-page editorials, morsels of hurtful gossip, and evidence of Jackie's extravagances, Loeb took all the pot shots he could.

On the afternoon before Election Day, Kennedy returned to Manchester. He stood on the bandstand in Victory Park facing the *Union-Leader* building and talked to an overflow crowd.

"I believe there is probably a more irresponsible newspaper in the United States, but I can't think of it," he said. "I believe there is a publisher who has less regard for the truth than William Loeb, but I can't think of his name."

The pent-up fury in his words lingered and rekindled a fire in Sol and me. Manchester needed that alternative newspaper. We would get it going.

Riding on the coattails of Kennedy's victory, reliable Joe came through with four other investors willing to put $5,000 each in a newspaper. One owned a radio station and sought a foothold in another medium. One was a brother of a former congressman callously bruised by Loeb. A third, an idealistic Democrat, thought the gamble for an objective voice worth $5,000. Don Madden, the fourth, had experience in newspapers, television and public relations; he had managed Kennedy's successful press campaign in New Hampshire. Don agreed to edit the newspaper as well as put up cash. A weekly, he figured, would not overstrain our $25,000 capital, provided we reached a minimum level of paid advertising.

"You're going to the Inauguration," Don said to Sol. "The

first issue will be coming off the press just about the time you get back."

In January, we journeyed to Washington to see John F. Kennedy take the oath of office. Wedged with other well-wishers into a reviewing stand, we stamped our feet and ignored the freezing cold as we thrilled to his words. I introduced Sol to a man I knew, a Massachusetts political figure who commuted to work in a Manchester mill. Ziggy and I had raised funds for a local mental-health clinic. What a dynamo he had proved himself in that drive! Casually, he introduced us to "Chub" Peabody, a future governor of Massachusetts. Then Ziggy and his attractive wife offered to team up with us for the Inaugural celebrations.

Through a paralyzing snowstorm we crawled by cab from one gala event to the next. Near midnight, wet with snow, we straggled into one of the balls and watched John and Jackie Kennedy dance together.

Back in Manchester, as we drove home from the airport, Sol said, "Let's stop off at the paper."

Lights still shone inside as we walked into the modest offices of the weekly on a downtown side street. Don Madden caught sight of us. Wordlessly, he handed Sol a copy of the first *Manchester Free Press*.

The weekly was beset with problems from the start. How to achieve a minimum level of advertising, a dependable staff and a respectable circulation immediately challenged Don. Apart from newsstand sales, we were mailing the paper free of charge to 30,000 homes for the first year. Later we would launch a subscription drive. Based on this guaranteed circulation we offered advertising rates far lower than the *Union-Leader's*.

The newsstand sales proved negligible. Skyrocketing costs for printing and mailing exceeded our forecasts. The *Union-Leader* combined pressure on some customers with bribes or special rates for others, and held fast to its principal accounts. Later, it lowered its rates, to woo diehards or would-be prospects from us.

Our space salesmen came and went; they could not survive solely on the commissions they earned. When ads languished, Sol appealed to the other investors. They placed what insertions they could, but these were too small and too seldom to fill the vacuum.

Reporters, steady ones, also proved hard to come by. Veterans preferred the instant feedback of a daily to a week's wait before they saw their stories in print. Over one weekend, a capable reporter disappeared when her husband was unexpectedly transferred to New Jersey. A former *Union-Leader* man, Kevin Cash, might or might not show up. Years later, he was to write and publish a book, *Who the Hell Is William Loeb?* Dark-bearded John Rees worked a few weeks, while he wooed, and later wed, Grace Metalious, of *Peyton Place* fame; abruptly he quit.

That spring I commuted to Boston University for a journalism course and transformed myself into a reporter. I started with a five-inch column called "Knit & Purl." My coverage expanded to the social "Weekly Whirl," to school, industry and diocesan news, and, later, to straight stories of murders, suicides and even a kidnapping.

"Sideways Sullivan Strikes Again," read my account of a school board meeting. The head referred to a committeeman who faced front and due west across a long oval table while he harangued the chairman and jabbed away at him with his right arm pointing due north. "Teachers Contracts Renewed," read the *Union-Leader's* account of the same meeting.

Don welcomed my reporting.

"My price is right," I teased; I was accepting no pay.

Don put in many eighteen-hour days. He hustled for scoops, researched and wrote powerful lead stories, supervised reporters' assignments, pounded the pavement for advertising, trained shifting help, did make-up and composition, delivered proofs to a printer thirty miles away, checked the mailing lists and mailing service, and dreamed up circulation gimmicks.

I typed at the office evenings as well as days. I was working too hard and too long, knew it and couldn't stop myself; I treasured every minute as a reporter. From comments, I knew that readers were poring over our copy.

Sol came in at night to perch on a high stool, consult with Don and wrestle with the latest figures. With the help of his slide rule he would project long-range trends for income and outgo. When our meager capital faded away, he canvassed the other investors for more money. One by one they dropped out. Sol and I, bitter-enders, refused to drop out.

First, we put up an extra $5,000. Later, it took infusions of $10,000 to keep the paper alive. By fall we could foresee that the *Manchester Free Press* would swallow up an investment of $100,000 for 1961. We persisted. I kept on reporting; Sol kept on supplying funds.

TEN

Foot on the Brake

FOR OUR THIRTIETH anniversary, in 1961, Sol and I explored Israel and stopped off in Rome, where a friend had arranged a tour of the Vatican and an audience with Pope John XXIII. On our travels we had climbed to new heights. At home we were to plumb new depths.

My brother gave us the first inkling; he was avoiding Sol. For twenty years he had sought his approval, got his okay before tackling any project. Now he made excuses to go out of town, to visit either the Manhattan showroom or Brooklyn contractors. In Manchester, he appeared at the mill sporadically.

"Ted's car stays parked for hours in the alley behind Joe's office," Sol told me one noon. "I saw it when I went to work this morning. It was still there when I came home for lunch. I don't know what to make of it."

"Don't take it personally," I consoled him. "He has trouble. Jean really wants out. Evidently something is still going on with Jerry."

Sol looked puzzled. "Maybe I should feel relieved that Ted can confide in Joe, but the whole setup bothers me."

To this cloud my father added a heavy shadow. He phoned one day in December to announce a visit north.

"Pick me up at the airport," he instructed, "and get me a motel near Boston where we can eat a quiet supper without people butting in on us every minute." He offered no explanation.

We did as he requested. Then, at dinner, over a Scotch, he came to his point directly.

"Teddy has developed into a fine businessman," he said. "He has to get his chance. If I hold my breath waiting for the pair of you to give him a break, I can turn green and purple."

He paused to gauge our reaction. I was tracing designs in the white cloth with the tines of my fork; Sol was methodically cracking the knuckles of his left hand, then his right.

"I have all my voting stock," Pa announced. "I'm transferring my shares to Ted."

"You can't, Mr. B.," said Sol.

"You signed agreements with us," I burst out.

With a wave of his hand my father dismissed this, not even glancing toward me. "What one lawyer can make, another lawyer can break."

As we started eating I let the implications sink in. Whoever controlled the voting stock controlled the company. If my father lined up his voting stock with Ted's against Sol's and mine, we four would be deadlocked. Then what? The balance of power would rest with my mother's shares.

Sol began talking of a man's honor. "Not just the word you give in business, but the word you give anyone, whether banker or family, humble or high."

"Aaaaa ..." my father snorted, with a heave of his shoulders and a twist of his lips.

The discussion continued. Words and gestures came from my father; we did not buy what he was selling. Sol and I found ourselves talking at, not to, him; our words likewise had no effect on him. After three hours Sol called a halt.

"Two goddamn stubborn fools," Pa spluttered.

"Shall I send someone for you in the morning?" asked Sol, striving to keep cool.

"Do me no favors," my father cut him off. "I'll get my own ride." He didn't say with whom.

When Sol walked off to claim our coats, I had a breather alone with my father.

"You're going to kill the goose," I told him, "the goose who has been laying your golden eggs."

The shadows grew heavier and blacker on the morrow. Shortly before six Sol made his customary call to let me know he was coming home. His voice sounded glum. With Bacardi in hand I greeted him at the door.

"Here's a drink and some hors d'oeuvres for you," I said. "And I'm running your bath. I refuse to talk business until you've decompressed."

"I can stand some spoiling," he answered.

After his bath, he sat at one end of the big kitchen table; I sat on a chair at his left. He toyed with his lamb chops and rice.

"Your father showed up early. Guess who he had pick him up in Cambridge?" he asked. "Joe! Joe picked him up; Joe helped your father into Ted's office; Joe hung around all day."

"How could Joe do this?" I wanted to know. "I thought Joe clearly understood that he's our lawyer first."

"I thought so, too," Sol said.

Ted had called the ole man's buddies from all over the mill. My father had held court with Henry, Julius, Harry from the dyehouse and a half-dozen others. Together they had slugged away at a bottle of whisky. Sol had glimpsed them through the door between his office and Ted's.

"They made believe I didn't even exist," he told me.

In the afternoon my father had called for Al. He quizzed the controller at length about the year's statement, the cash balances in each of our three banks and the accounts payable still outstanding.

"Next, they closed the door between our offices, and the ole man, Joe and Ted stayed holed up for hours." Sol brooded over the incident. "What the tarnation are they cooking up?"

Despite a hectic stint of interviews and stories for the *Free Press*, I had already pieced together some fragments of Ted's melodrama. Now I took time out to phone several knowledgeable friends and to question my mother in detail. Unwillingly, she yielded a few items about "poor Teddenu."

Jean had definitely decided to divorce him. Yes, she and Jerry felt deeply about each other. Unable to sway her, in a veritable frenzy, Ted had flown to Florida. I could easily imagine the scene between father and son, could almost hear my father's spiel.

"This woman, that woman—one skirt is as good as another," he must have started. "But where does it say you have to play second fiddle to Sol forever? Did Moses write it in the Ten Commandments?"

In the past, Ted had let Pa's words slide off his back. This time Pa had a punch line. "I haven't given up one share of my voting stock. I'm saving it all for you."

A different story! Under different circumstances. Obviously, Ted listened.

They must have outlined some opening moves. First, Ted must talk to a lawyer and find some loophole in the agreements. Ted, friendly with Joe, had become even more intimate after the Miami visit.

Next, Ted must begin to wean my mother away from Sol and me. Increasingly, in the days that followed, this strategy became evident. In the past I had had to implore Ted to please look in on his mother. Now the same Ted began spending an inordinate amount of time with Skinny. Suddenly she gained another admirer; Joe, also, was dropping in on her regularly. Sol and I knew because we balanced each visit from Ted or Joe with one of our own.

One afternoon I found her sitting in her favorite armchair gazing vacantly into space, utter despair written all over her face.

"I thought all the pain I suffered with Pa would save my children from ever having to go through what I did. How my poor Teddy is suffering! May," she said, and sighed, "I don't know how to move, what to do."

"What's happened?" I asked her.

"Teddy has a gun hidden in his dresser drawer. If he has to, he told me, he's going to use it on himself."

"Don't fall for that baloney," I said, although none too convincingly.

I told Sol when he met me at the *Free Press* office.

"Hitting pretty low, isn't he?" he said.

"A dozen years ago, when my mother had to choose between a husband who had walked out on her and a devoted son-in-law, she put her faith in you, Sol," I said. "I wonder whom she'll choose between a son-in-law and a son who threatens to kill himself."

"Let's do something about it before it's too late," said Sol. "Let's visit your father in Florida. Maybe we can still talk sense to him."

Pa's seventy-fifth birthday in 1962 became the occasion for our trip. In Miami, we found him in his wicker armchair on the patio, while Mary fussed with plants and the tiger cat dozed in the sun.

"Where do you want us to take you out tonight?" asked Sol.

Pa looked pleased, mentioned his favorite Chinese restaurant and bid Mary make reservations.

We chatted about each of our children, our two grandchildren and about his health. Each day the pains in his toes grew more excruciating, he told us. He and Maury had maneuvered some smart swaps in buying and selling stocks. He was laughing about them when Mary, all spruced up, came out again. She confirmed his trading triumphs, pouring compliments on Snookie for launching his stepson as a capitalist.

At a window table overlooking the bay, the five of us, including Maury, enjoyed a tasty meal and agreeable conversation. At its end a waiter brought a cake, holding it aloft with candles burning; other waiters joined him in a pidgin-English version of "Happy Birthday." We sang along, while Pa pretended boredom.

Leaning heavily on my arm, with the others out of earshot, my father set out with me for the entrance lobby.

"You know," he said, "I can't fuck any more."

Words failed me. Did people his age still expect to? Was he looking to me for pity?

"Not so good for Mary," he said.

Dumbstruck, I kept on walking with him to join the others at the door.

"I see my father more clearly," I told Sol later that evening in our hotel. "Imprisoned in his armchair, drenched by the sun, only spectator sports with Maury and no bedroom sports with Mary—no wonder he wants to set off giant fireworks, to prove he can still light up the whole sky."

"There's more to it than that," said Sol. "He can't let any outsider, even me, be top dog."

"I was hoping this madness would blow over," I replied. "Maybe he's shot his bolt."

"Don't count on it," said Sol. "I think that from the very beginning he has always had his son in mind."

My thoughts went back some forty years, to Pa the Patriarch at the hospital when his Crown Prince was born. I had to agree with my husband.

The next morning we three settled down to serious talk on the patio. Mary kept herself occupied inside. Far from a breathing spell, we witnessed a mighty build-up of conflict. My father, it developed, was having corporate minutes and documents researched to prove that Sol himself had breached our agreements.

"We'll look for it and we'll find it," he claimed. "We'll find all the proof we need."

"The law examines a person's intentions," countered Sol. "Never have I made a major move, Mr. B., without talking it over with you and getting your consent. I've lived up to every letter of those agreements."

"Talk is cheap," said his partner. "When you don't have each thing in black and white, I have you with your pants down."

"You're not getting away with this one," said Sol.

My father's face grew dark with rage. No longer did he try to sound reasonable.

"You schmuck," he railed, "you can tear up the paper those agreements are written on and throw it in the garbage pail."

"I got to get kissed if I'm getting screwed," said Sol.

As my father struggled to destroy the status quo at Pandora, Sol struggled to keep it intact. He was motivated emotionally as well as ethically. He still looked on Ted as a "kid brother" and longed to help him preserve his marriage. In the next few weeks, he managed to initiate a dialogue with him. He urged Ted to move with his family to New York.

"In a small town people have long memories; in a big city nobody watches your every move," he told him. "You and Jean have been through a bad trip. This happens in many marriages, but couples survive, pick up the pieces and carry on. You should start fresh in a different setting."

Ted pricked up his ears.

"Your father and I got along pretty well over the years because we operated in separate territories."

In the New York showroom, Ted could serve a useful business function. One other advantage: in New York, Ted would rank Number One. Jean need not compare her status with anyone else's. She had complained to a mutual friend that Sol and I hung together and hung heavy over Ted. Such pressure would be far removed.

Ted looked receptive.

"Right now there's something else I want you to do. Do it for me, Ted. Do it because you have a sense of fair play," said Sol. "I want you to talk things over with Fred. Go for a half-dozen sessions. He can surely help you with some of your problems."

Ted balked. The notion of psychotherapy conflicted with his sense of manliness. He soon found an excuse: Jean had agreed to move with him away from Manchester. She let herself be persuaded that their marriage, after twenty years, deserved a second chance. She welcomed a change in scene. So, together they took off for Manhattan, together selected an apartment on Fifth Avenue facing Central Park, together packed up their household and pulled out.

"Maybe this will do the trick," said Sol. "Ted plans to stay close to home for the next year, travel as little as possible and try to run the mill by phone."

"That means you'll be doing his job as well as your own," I said.

"I don't mind," he remarked. "I'll enjoy getting back into everyday operations."

"You'll be working twice as hard, and Ted will be phoning twice as hard," I said, "not just to the factory, but to my mother. And his buddy, dear Joe, shows more and more concern for her welfare. He still keeps dropping in on her."

"Are they setting her up for something?" Sol wondered.

All too soon, Sol and I were to know.

Morris wanted a date with Bertha; he would fly north expressly to meet with her. Skillfully, the stage had been prepared. At the mere prospect of seeing Morris, Bertha palpitated like a young girl.

Her great day arrived. Morris came to Manchester and, after fifteen years, spoke to Bertha once more.

"When can I see you?" he asked over the phone. They set a time.

My mother asked Sol and me to stay at her side when he came. We sat waiting on her cheerful breezeway. Bertha, eyes on the driveway, opened the door herself for her guest, and then got busy serving tea and cookies. As we drank, she kept her eyes averted, never looking directly at Morris; he stared, never letting Bertha out of his sight. We exchanged some small talk, then fell silent.

"It takes a big man to make a big mistake," my father began, his eyes fixed on her. "What a fool I was!"

She flushed beet red. We also stared at her. Incredulous, I saw that Pa did not have to say much more. With that "confession" he had her, as of old, under his sway.

"Are you telling us," Sol asked, "that you want to call it quits with Mary?"

"Too late for that now," my father answered. "I was a fool, but we don't have to stay foolish all our lives. You and I," he told my mother, "we must stick together for the sake of our son."

"Such a devoted family man!" I put in.

"Stop trying to make me feel guilty all the time," he said, shutting me up. Then he launched a masterful pitch about the two of them safeguarding their son's birthright. By this time Ma's eyes were riveted on him.

"I'm giving all my voting stock to Teddy," he concluded. "You have to agree to do the same."

"You do that, Skinny," said Sol, breaking the spell, "and we'll land feet first in the courts."

"*Strasse mir nicht* [threaten me not]," answered my father. "I don't shiver that easy."

"He's steering you right into trouble, Ma," I said.

Before Morris left, though, he had Bertha's word that she would at least think it over. For weeks and months after his one-hour blitz she did, indeed, do just that.

By long-distance phone my brother continued to bombard her. He cast doubts on how long his patched-up marriage would hold together. Schnappsie had died. Jean had taken it very hard, had viewed the dachshund's death as an omen. My mother passed his gloom along to us.

"You and May have each other," she told Sol as we sat with her one evening. "My poor Teddy has nobody."

"You go back on your word to me, Skinny," Sol replied, "and I swear I'll never speak to you again."

"I can't do this, I can't do that," she cried. "I don't know what to do."

I gave her no help. Ted kept phoning. Joe kept dropping in. Ripped apart by divided loyalties, she developed a rash over her whole body that would not go away.

One forenoon I hammered away at a typewriter in the *Free Press* office. I was writing a three-part history of the Maine–New Hampshire Catholic diocese and had just unearthed a startling fact. Manchester had had a black bishop, the first in the United States. I looked up to share my discovery with Don, but my view was blocked.

"Ziggy, what are you doing here?"

"Thought I'd drop in," said Ziggy, whom I had last seen at Kennedy's inauguration. "Happened to have an errand nearby."

In Washington, Sol had talked to him about our new weekly. Since then he had been following its progress. "How's the paper doing?" he asked.

"The baby's still breathing," I told him, avoiding any hint of the $100,000 reserve Sol had set aside for this second year to keep the oxygen flowing. I related some of our ups and downs, stressed our growing prestige, and gave him figures on our slowly increasing base of advertisers and subscribers.

"Can I treat you to a sandwich?" he asked.

Over the meal he told me about how he had advanced from personnel director, the job he had held when I met him, to general manager for the same firm, one that spun, dyed yarns and wove fabrics. The owner stayed away more and more, dumping total responsibility on Ziggy's shoulders but not releasing real authority to him. Ziggy's honest Polish face mirrored unhappiness.

"By the way," he said over coffee, "I hear your brother has left for New York."

That evening I told Sol about my lunch with Ziggy.

"By this stage I can smell when I'm being propositioned," I commented. "Ziggy was applying for Ted's job."

"A good man," Sol replied. "Someday I may take him up on it."

Sol was working harder and spending longer hours on the factory floor than he had in years. Though Ted tried to run the mill by phone, his attempts proved a fiasco. Sol had to step in, fill in and smooth over needless snafus. He did not complain; he enjoyed the personal contacts.

One day he recounted an incident that had tickled him. He was squiring a visitor from Czechoslovakia around the mill; many foreigners came to tour our model plant.

"Iris jumps up from the loopers and runs over when she spots me," he said. "She's flashing her engagement ring for me to admire."

Spontaneously, he grabbed her and gave her a bear hug.

"She was tickled. She knew I wished her well," he said, "but that Communist from behind the Iron Curtain—his eyes almost bugged out of his head."

He laughed and tried to predict what the gentleman would report to his party bosses. I laughed along with him, but still worried that he was working far too hard.

"You need time for people like Iris; you need time for long-range planning," I said. "Instead, you're knocking yourself out." Then I asked, "Did you think any more about Ziggy?"

Not long after, Sol invited Ziggy to lunch; then he invited him to meet Fred. Within the month, he had hired Ziggy as his staff aide. Ziggy took charge of spinning and dyeing, in which he had extensive background, and later took on the full-fashion division in the other building. He, Al and Sol formed a natural trio, huddled with our mill supervisors, went out to lunch together. Almost instantly Ziggy had become one of the gang.

"I was telling Fred what a difference it makes to have Ziggy there instead of Ted," Sol reported to me several months later. "Not that one or two of the old-timers aren't bucking Ziggy—that's only natural. But the rest of us are welding ourselves into a great team."

That summer Sol may have been reaping rewards for having Ted in New York; by fall, his body was doing penance. I heard about it after the November election, when he had his semiannual physical.

As Dr. Thannhauser put him through the preliminaries, Sol chatted about our vacations and his diet. He mentioned that Sara Mae was expecting her third child, Gene was doing well as a government intern in Washington, Ralph had gone off to the University of Pennsylvania, and Becky was at Woodstock. Only Mickey remained at home.

"Ach, how empty your house must seem!" remarked the internist as he checked Sol's weight. "Very good."

With zest Sol spoke of the *Free Press*, his joys and triumphs in watching our weekly get healthier.

"Each month our loss grows less; with each issue our influence grows more. Within a year we should reach the break-even point."

Proudly he told how Tom McIntyre claimed we had helped him win his Senate seat in the recent election. In an off-year, when our state had gone Republican by a landslide and the *Union-Leader* had loosed a volley of hurtful publicity against him, McIntyre, a Democrat, had won. The votes of our Manchester subscribers had turned the trick.

The examination continued while Sol spoke. "Everything sounds good so far," the doctor noted. "Let's get the chest X-rayed and a cardiogram. That slight enlargement of your aorta—we'd better take a look."

"What's the verdict?" I asked when the two men walked back in twenty minutes later.

"Not so fast," said the doctor. "First tell me"—he turned to Sol—"what's going on in your business."

"Our junior division is doing beautifully. Sweaters are doing well; sportswear has really taken off," Sol began. Then anger crept into his voice. "I'm doing my darndest to keep that factory running smoothly, but my partners—my so-called partners—keep putting up stumbling blocks."

My father had, unannounced, signed two company checks that withdrew huge amounts of cash from two Pandora accounts.

"With surprises like this," Sol had asked him over the phone, "how do you expect me to operate this business?"

"Maybe you shouldn't be the one operating this business," retorted my father.

"They're forcing me into litigation," Sol told Dr. Thannhauser.

As for Ted, Sol was still stewing over his latest stunt.

"My brother-in-law loves little bits of businesses here and there, and always with partners."

Ted and two men from a competing firm had bought a knitting mill in Pennsylvania. To conclude the deal, he had used Pandora's lawyer, Joe, and our New York accountant, hopelessly compromising both men. The checks my father had drawn, I had suggested to Sol, might have been used to finance Ted's slice. My irritation matched Sol's as he spoke.

The doctor silently heard him out. "Young man, I'll give you two pieces of advice," he said at last. "Keep as active as you want, provided you take your vacations."

"That's fine," said Sol. "What's the other?"

"About your business"—and here the doctor paused—"tell your associates to go to hell and tell them more often."

Ruefully, Sol began to laugh. "A bit late, but you're probably right."

"From now on you're to come back every three months, not every six."

Dr. Thannhauser put his arm around Sol as he walked us to the exit. In a soft undertone, he repeated, "Tell them to go to hell."

"I'm scared," I said as we drove home at Sol's usual high speed. "Only once before did he ever have you come back in three months instead of six. He's trying to tell you something."

I wondered if Sol should cut down his hours at work.

"You don't want to hold me down, not now," he protested.

"What if anything should happen to you?"

"You're to take over," he snapped back.

He slowed down. Half facing me, he spoke very deliberately. "The men will see you through." Almost as an afterthought, he added, "Al's the one."

Al represented an unknown quantity to me. Never had I exchanged more than pleasantries with him.

"If anything should happen to me," I countered, trying to offset such heavy going, "you must marry again, Sol. You should never live by yourself."

At this he burst out laughing, his laugh reverberating through the car. "Don't you boss me around enough while you're alive?" he asked. "Are you telling me what to do when you're dead?"

That Christmas our older son surprised us by bringing home the girl he hoped to marry. We fell for Linda even as Gene had. A few weeks later our younger son gave us a different surprise. Quietly departing from his second semester, Ralph enlisted in the infantry. He was sent first to Fort Dix, then to Fort Gordon. He notified us when he had completed his basic training, and we arranged to fly down to see him.

Sol telephoned Ralph's grandfather. To me, Sol had said, "No matter how we feel, he's still Ralph's Peep." To my father he said, "If you want to see Ralph before he's shipped out, come to Augusta this weekend—your last chance for quite a while."

Pa came readily. The four of us had an uneventful dinner, at which we spoke not one word of business. My father joshed Ralph, but not too cuttingly. Another Dr. Jekyll/Mr. Hyde, I was thinking as we saw him off the next morning.

Later we talked with Ralph. He had graduated with the highest scores in his class and had had an offer to remain at the base as an instructor. He had turned it down.

"They'll send you overseas," I said.

"So what!" Ralph answered.

"He might land in Iceland or Germany," Sol said, stretching his arm protectively over Ralph's shoulders.

"He might not," I said.

Within a week, Ralph was shipped out to Saigon.

Sol and I watched the war in Vietnam escalate from a trickle into a torrent even as we watched our close-to-home hostilities escalate in the same way.

The escalation on the home front was prefaced by a stink bomb going off in the rear of Sol's station wagon while it stood parked in front of our house.

"Crazy kids," I said, "thinking up wild stunts."

"I wonder," said Sol.

A deluge of memos began to stream across his desk. They reached their greatest volume on Monday mornings but swelled at odd times during the week. Issued in Ted's name, couched in legalese, they bore out my father's threat. The memos spelled out charges of Sol's mismanagement, of his disregard of some technicality in the 1949 contracts, even of dishonesty. The memos challenged him as chief executive officer.

Several memos dealt with the company foundation. One noted that in 1958 Sol's signature appeared on two donations: one to Community Chest, another to the United Jewish Appeal. Nowhere in Brookshire Foundation minutes had Mr. Sidore been authorized to grant those checks, both for substantial amounts. Was he enhancing his own standing in the community at the expense of the other trustees? Another asked for a detailed report on his trip to Snia Viscosa in Italy. He had not filed such a report. What practical outcomes justified the expense?

"They're hoping to needle me to death," said Sol, bringing home an inch-high sheaf of memos one evening, "but I'm going to fool them."

"They've only reached 1959 so far," I remarked.

"No use stalling any longer," Sol decided. "They're building their case with higher and higher stacks of these. We have to get our own lawyer."

"If we have to, let's do it quickly," I concurred. "Time doesn't favor us."

Sol sought the best lawyer we could possibly get. Our neighbor, Max, helped him. In long tête-à-têtes over the red roses that climbed the white picket fence we shared, Sol had confided in Max. A powerful personality, head of a large shoe factory in town, Max sympathized. He arranged for us to meet his own attorney, Ken Graf.

Like conspirators, we kept the date in Max's finished basement. Outside, the sun shone bright; inside, every blind was drawn and copper lamps illuminated the large room. Max introduced us to Ken, a man with bullet head, crew-cut hair and piercing blue eyes. As we sat around a massive oak table, Sol presented our story. Ken scanned our agreements, grilled us both, and shuffled through some of the memos Sol had brought. He took his time.

"It seems to me you have a case," he said at last, very deliberately. "We'll do all we can to reach a settlement, but I'll apply for a court hearing just the same."

Thankful that he had accepted our case, we placed ourselves in Ken's hands.

"I don't think my father will walk into a courtroom to fight us," I said.

"I'm tired of thinking," said Sol. "Let's play it by feel."

Ken filed our case in court. Because the calendar was crowded, we would have to wait until spring.

My father had no forewarning; our lawsuit caught him off-balance. Even more infuriated that we had refused to knuckle under, he orchestrated a louder and more strident March of Memos.

Ted informed my mother of the court action and told her he could no longer visit her, even overnight; he had to avoid New Hampshire lest our attorney serve him with a summons. He also told her Jerry had followed Jean to New York, and his marriage had fallen apart. As Ted filled my mother with his crises, she could no longer withstand the pressure. She promised to vote his way.

"If you do that," Sol had warned Skinny, "I'll never speak to you again."

He now refused to speak to her.

Tidying up Mickey's room one morning I happened to look out the window and noticed a car parked in our driveway. I had heard neither a bell ring nor any door open and shut. Racing down the carpeted steps, I stopped abruptly. A sound had come from the sun parlor.

I ran in. The papers on Sol's desk, always in neat piles, seemed in disarray. A figure spoke from behind the desk. "Hello."

"Joe!" I exclaimed. "What the hell are you doing?"

"I was driving by when I suddenly remembered an urgent phone call I had to make," he said. "I knew you wouldn't mind if I used your telephone."

"Why here? Why didn't you use the one in the kitchen?"

"I came in through the front door. I rang the bell," he explained, "but no one answered and I thought it would only take a minute."

I escorted Joe through the kitchen to the back door and out to his car.

"I have some advice to give you," I told him. "Ted listens to you. Tell him to get a lawyer of his own—a good one. Divorce yourself from the situation. Don't try to stay everyone's pal."

"You're absolutely right," said Joe.

Ted did get his own lawyer. Sol told me about it a few weeks later. The attorney now representing my brother had spent two years at Dartmouth while Joe was there and, like Joe, had graduated from Yale.

That summer Becky tried a daring experiment: she flew off to an agricultural school in Israel. Mickey was spending the season at her usual camp. With no children at home for the first summer since 1936, Sol and I had time together—alone. We welcomed the breathing spell. Before making any plans, though, I consulted Ken.

"I want to go back to work at Pandora," I told him. "I want to stay at Sol's side. That guy is not supposed to aggravate himself, and they're getting under his skin."

"I would not advise it," he said. "You've stayed behind the scenes for many years now. Going in at this juncture could be used against you. Do nothing out of the ordinary."

Doing the ordinary involved much letter-writing. Sol wrote long pages of small talk to Ralph. I put out a weekly newsletter, *Fourpenny Pilgrims*. The Pilgrims were our scattered children; the fourpenny, the four-cent stamp required to mail it.

As a diversion, one Sunday in July we visited Dr. Thannhauser, who was convalescing from major surgery in Wolfeboro. On a broad veranda overlooking the lake, he entertained us by playing two records. On each a coloratura soprano—first Maria Callas, then Joan Sutherland—sang the same operatic arias. Animatedly he compared them and explained why he preferred the "more substantial" Joan to the "shallower" Maria. His housekeeper poured English tea and served a luscious apple torte. It was a refreshing afternoon.

Two months later, we stared, unbelieving, at his death notice in a Boston newspaper. Amidst the huge crowd at his funeral service, we recognized only his office nurse.

For her freshman year in high school, Mickey chose not to go to a school where she would be known as the fourth Sidore. And we were happy not to have to part with this last child yet. While she attended Central High, we took time off to visit other prep schools for her.

That fall we often took her and one of her pals with us to the Harvard football games. One October afternoon we invited Fred Jervis and his wife, Jan. In sixteen seasons of football games, that afternoon stands out. Directly opposite us, across the playing field, sat John F. Kennedy. The bright sunlight cast a glow around him, accenting each vigorous move, each graceful turn. We watched him smile, gesture and comment to aides and Secret Service men.

We saw him again that evening, at a Democratic fund-raising dinner in the Boston Armory, for which Sol had reserved a table for ten.

Sol sent a message to the President reminding him of their previous contact at the Pandora factory before the New Hampshire primary, and asking if a blind war veteran, one of our guests, could shake his hand. Quickly word came back: "Okay." We rose to watch Fred, escorted by Sol, meet, exchange a few words and shake hands with Kennedy.

During the Thanksgiving weekend, I worked in the *Free Press* office. On a high stool not far away, perched over a drawing board, sat Sol. So far this year we had invested considerably less than for the same period the year before. Each issue that fall had shown a profit, which would further shrink the 1963 loss. Projections indicated that we would break even in 1964. Sol was double-checking the figures.

Suddenly Don Madden called from the composing room: "My God! Kennedy has been shot!"

Sol and I and everyone we knew went around dazed for the next few days. We kept our eyes on the television set. We saw Jackie with the mortally wounded President in the open limousine. We wept to see her, standing tall, with a heavy black veil hiding her face, on the walk to the funeral mass. We shuddered at the riderless black horse in the procession to Arlington. We were shocked when Jack Ruby shot Oswald. It was a harrowing time.

Sol sat down a few days later and wrote his "Message from Management" for the December *Yarn*. It read: "A small bit of each of us died when President Kennedy died. A small bit of each of us should live, acting in his image to keep his memory alive."

I believed Sol. I believed a small bit of him died with JFK.

By December Sol could no longer put off finding a replacement for Dr. Thannhauser. The New Hampshire Department of Health had made a routine chest X-ray of every employee at Pandora. As a result, we had been notified of an abnormality in Sol's heart and were urged to consult our physician.

Sol made a date with the young internist who had taken over Thannhauser's practice. After the examination we waited in his office for the doctor to summon Sol. The specialist, instead, walked out to him.

"I don't like the way your heart sounds. You're to go home at once, get into bed and stay there for at least six weeks," he ordered. "I'm prescribing digitalis for you."

I drove home; the doctor had forbidden Sol to touch the wheel. Sol appreciated neither my driving skill nor the medical diagnosis.

"I'm getting a second opinion," he said. "I can't believe this guy—an alarmist. Besides that, I can't stay in bed for six weeks, not at this time."

Our local doctor arranged an appointment with Paul Dudley White. The famed heart specialist found no dramatic change from Thannhauser's records, and suggested Sol follow his normal routine.

I felt utterly confused. I did not sleep well those December nights. I kept waking up to listen, to be sure that the man lying at my side was still breathing. Sol developed a shrill whistle with each breath he took in his sleep. The sound gave me goose pimples. I never spoke of it to him.

Our holiday week with our two girls in ski country did not revive his spirits. And the weather didn't help; it rained steadily. Sol complained about the inn being crowded and noisy, about having too little to do.

"Forgive me, Mug," he said one evening as we listened to the band. "I just don't feel like dancing."

One bright spot came when we exchanged gifts. For me Sol had a white Swedish hand phone shaped like a question mark. He got a charge out of an outrageous black-yellow-orange vest of Bahamian fabric I had had custom-tailored for him.

He wore it on New Year's Eve back in Manchester. In his oxford-gray flannel suit, he looked appropriately con-servative when we arrived at several parties. Then he unbut-toned his jacket, flung it open and stuck his thumbs in the armholes of the flamboyant vest. He dazzled everyone.

In the midst of the partying, Gene tracked us down to tell us that he and his beloved Linda were formally announcing their engagement. They made ours a truly happy New Year.

Sol transmitted tidings of Gene's engagement to Al when he went to work on Thursday, the day after New Year's.

"But I never got the rest I needed in the week we were away," he told Al. "And to come back to these!" In disgust he held up more memos. "They must have worked overtime all vacation week to figure out these beauts."

"He made a joke of it," Al told me later, "but he looked sick after he got through reading all of them."

That evening Sol sat in the sun parlor trying out a new Polaroid. He took several shots of Mickey, had me take one of him and Mickey, then sloshed through the snow to share them with Max, next door. On his return he wrote a letter to Ralph.

"I'm going to enclose some of these shots," he yelled out to me.

My phone rang shortly after nine the next morning.

"May, don't get upset," came Al's voice on the other end.

"Is he gone?"

"No, he's all right. They've taken him to the hospital. Do you want me to meet you there?"

"First, I stopped off at the post office to mail a letter to Ralph," I could hear Sol telling the doctor when I paused in the doorway of his room in Sacred Heart Hospital on January 3. "Then I drove into the millyard, on my way to work." Sol was speaking through an oxygen tent. "Suddenly, as I got to the Waumbec Mills, I felt this terrible pain in my chest and shoulder blades. I put the car in low gear and my foot over the brake."

Sol saw me and held out his hand to clasp mine.

"I was coasting along and motioned to a fellow driving toward me that I needed help. He just kept going; he didn't understand. I can't blame him."

Oh, Sol, are you still finding excuses for the other fellow? I thought.

"Just as I got to the mill I was able to bring the car to a stop, and I can't remember a thing after that."

He did not know that the plant nurse had rushed out, that she had administered oxygen and stayed with him until the ambulance came. He did not know of Al's frantic telephone calls, to me and to track down the doctor and summon him to the hospital.

Presently Milton Utell got ready to leave his patient and motioned me to step outside with him.

"Shall I call Ralph home?" I asked.

"You may as well," he said. "What harm would it do?" How casually he phrased it, not to fuel my alarm!

"How about a consultant?"

"Good idea," he said. "Let me get Paul Dudley White."

While a nurse ministered to Sol, I got on the phone. I spoke to Sara in Cambridge; she would come up at once. I spoke to Gene in Washington. If he would contact Senator McIntyre, I would get in touch with the Manchester Red Cross; perhaps between us we could get Ralph back quickly. Becky was still home on vacation. I asked my mother to keep an eye on her and Mickey.

Between calls I sat at Sol's side. He would try to talk, even joke, despite his pain. He called often for the doctor.

"I'll take a baseball bat to that nurse if she doesn't bring me some water," he told Milton when he came.

"He can have all the liquids he wants," the doctor instructed the nurse.

She brought water and a straw. Sol could swallow only a sip.

Sara Mae phoned from the lobby. I went down and held ten-month-old Jonathan while she visited with Sol.

"I'm staying over," she said when she returned. "Do you still have the crib in the attic? I'll go put it together."

I went in to tell Sol that the Red Cross was bringing Ralph home. He figured out that Vietnam was exactly halfway around the world.

"Will they send him home by the Pacific or Europe?" he asked. "I can't wait to see that guy."

"What do you call what happened to Sol?" I asked the doctor when he next returned.

"Probably an infarction," he replied.

"Infarction?" I repeated. "Doesn't that mean that his heart broke?"

"That's one way of putting it," he said. "Let's wait for White," he added. "He's coming the first thing in the morning."

Gene, on his arrival, found me yet again pacing the corridor. He held me close, and then sat almost steadily at his father's side. He left only to keep in touch with the Red Cross about Ralph.

Early the next morning I looked in on Sol. Gene was already sitting beside him, and the doctor was there.

"How is he?" I asked Milton.

"Still hanging on," he said, "and the longer Sol can stick it out the better his chances." I remembered a doctor making the same speech about Sol's mother.

We went downstairs to wait for Dr. White. The eighty-year-old heart man came on the dot, had no patience with waiting for an elevator, but bounded up four flights of double landings like a frisky colt. Puffing, our knees creaking, we followed. Gently, he twitted us.

"Finding it kind of steep?" he called back over his shoulder.

White looked at Sol, then at his X-rays. He used medical jargon that confirmed Milton's diagnosis. He gave us not one morsel to nourish any hopes. Once he left, I found myself pacing like a caged beast.

Intermittently, I went to Sol's room. Gene had learned that Ralph had been routed via San Francisco. He and Sol had reckoned how long Ralph's flight would take. "Monday at the latest," said Gene.

Soon Sara Mae appeared with Becky, who looked fragile, and the sturdy Mickey.

"Your father smiled at me," I told them. "Maybe I'm thinking with my heart, not my head, Sara, but he's still holding out."

By Sunday morning even my faintest hope had evaporated. Sol looked worse; he was filling up with uremic acid. I could hardly force myself to sit with him. Gene had far more stamina. He stayed; I paced the corridor.

I fancied my head strapped to a butcher's block. I waited for the cleaver to fall and chop it from my body. I imagined myself jumping outside my skin and dashing away from my own flesh when the blow struck.

In the afternoon Don Madden stood in the corridor with a questioning look.

"What will we do," I asked him, "if Sol doesn't make it? Will you go on?"

"Now more than ever," he said. "I want to prove we can swing it. For Sol's sake, we've got to make a go of that paper."

Now more than ever I, too, wanted to prove we could swing it.

"If we can keep the losses to $25,000, as we did last year," I told him, "the way Sol and I feel about the *Free Press*, we can subsidize it indefinitely."

"That won't do," he answered brusquely. "I wouldn't want it that way. The paper can't be 'kept.' It has to make it on its own financially. I'm going to try my damnedest."

He and I both looked in on Sol, then I watched Don's tall, spare figure retreating down the hall.

"Don't get hysterical," I commanded myself, feeling my familiar world caving in on me.

I forced myself to pace with measured tread from one end of the corridor, past the nurses' station, to the other end. There, I very deliberately counted to ten before I turned around to pace back again.

Toward dusk I became aware of a tall man in a bulky tan overcoat standing by the nurses' station. He seemed to be waiting for Sol's nurse to beckon that he could enter. Could the Red Cross have brought Ralph back already? I started toward the figure. As I approached, I glimpsed tortoise-shell eyeglass frames and in another second recognized the outline of my brother's face.

"Ted!" I called.

He had not heard me coming. He turned toward me, his face expressionless. He said nothing.

"Is there any way for us to get together?" I asked him. "If Sol ever gets out of here alive, can all of us work side by side?"

Still expressionless and saying nothing, he turned his back and walked toward the elevator.

On Monday morning Becky looked in on her father. "He seems so tired," she said. "so monumentally tired."

Mickey came in after school, her bare legs red above her mud-streaked galoshes. "Soft, mushy snow," she told me before she went in to see Sol. When she came out, she said, "He's asking for Ralph."

Late Monday night Sol asked again for Ralph.

In Japan, Ralph's plane had been grounded overnight by fog. He did not arrive until four in the morning. When he came, Milton sat with him for a long time. Ralph could not be consoled. His father had already died.

Sol lived for eighty-six hours after he first blacked out. For eighty-six hours we still had him. We had him until ten minutes before midnight on Monday, January 6, 1964. He died because part of his heart, the aorta, had become too enlarged and had burst.

ELEVEN

Idling Machinery

SOL'S DEATH NUMBED ME. I made all the funeral arrangements, but as I plowed through these details I was filled with
a sense of unreality.

In the temple I listened to the rabbi conduct the service,
but I could not grasp his words; my thoughts strayed.
Looking down at my hands clasped in my lap, I became
aware of my black dress. For years I had worn no black.
Where had I suddenly found mourning clothes?

I looked about me. My children and grandchildren surrounded me. They, too, wore dark clothing. How quickly all
of us had conformed to the amenities! How rigid, how
utterly futile!

Mickey, her bangs long over her eyes, sat on my left, pale
Becky on my right. Sara Mae and Larry had brought their
two older children. Gene had Linda close beside him, her
hand in his. And from the other side of the world Ralph had
come. These nine, gathered together from every corner,
seemed real to me, the only real beings among the hundreds
who filled and overflowed the sanctuary. The voices intoning
the Amens sounded like the chorus of a Greek tragedy.

Even the rabbi seemed unreal as he followed the identical
procedure he used at every funeral service. His eulogy filled
a predetermined number of minutes. At predictably pegged
intervals the voices of the choir sang out. As always he

concluded with the Twenty-third Psalm. And at the precise moment that he reached the word *shepherd*, he executed his usual departure from the pulpit.

"You told me you would fight for composure, not break down. A dignified farewell, you said, was the least you owed this man you loved as a brother," I found myself silently shouting. "Do you have to go through standard operating procedure like a mechanical, wound-up toy? In our barbaric culture do we leave no room for the spontaneous gesture, for the outpouring of grief? Not for you and not for me. Keep face, keep a brave front."

The service ended. I rose with my family and, holding firmly to Mickey's hand, led the macabre march behind the coffin to the exit.

Cars waited for us at the curb. Becky and Mickey entered the first one with me. Suddenly my father's face appeared at the open door. He poked his cane in, trying to enter. I shook my head no.

The chauffeur closed the door, and again we led a procession, this time to our house.

"What can we do for you?" Becky asked me during the ride.

"I should be comforting you, not you worrying about me," I told her.

"Let us help," she pleaded.

"A little privacy," I said. "I need it so."

Once we got home, I retreated to my bedroom. The children greeted a throng of visitors, answered the telephone, served tea and shielded me—sometimes from seeing people, sometimes from seeing more than one or two at a time.

When my bedroom door opened to admit a close friend, I could hear the subdued murmur below. Once I heard the loud voice of my father rising above the others as he made some snappy comeback. I sat on a footstool, my face buried in my hands. I tried to force myself to face my aloneness.

Instead, I was thinking about Sol and his footstools. Dr. Thannhauser had once instructed him to sit with his feet elevated. So we had footstools all over the house.

Toward dusk I went downstairs for a cup of tea. My brother stopped me.

"I just wanted you to know how sorry I feel, how very sorry," Ted said.

"Is that all?" I asked. "I thought you might have some way to resolve our problems."

He hesitated for some seconds. "I just want to express how very sorry I feel," he repeated, and walked away.

I had my tea and climbed the stairs again. Dazed, I began to pace the floor. Sol and I had known and loved each other for thirty-six years. How could I now undertake to start a new life? How anemic it would seem beside the richness I had known!

Ralph came up to tell me my brother wanted to see me. I went to the landing, nodded to Ted and, seeing my mother near the stairs, beckoned to her to join us. In the bedroom we three faced each other.

"I will let you come into the business," Ted told me, "provided I become president and I have final say on every matter."

I said nothing.

"I will take care of your interests just as I take care of my own," he continued. "I will even permit your children to come into the business and treat them as if they were mine."

"May," my mother put in, "Teddy told me he would make regular reports to you. After all, you are interested in the newspaper; you could work on the newspaper."

"I'm glad that Ted will make regular reports to me," I said, "because I, too, will make regular reports to him. I intend going into the business; I intend seeing what I can do to keep it going—the way Sol set it up."

Silence.

"After all, I have a considerable stake in this business," I said.

More silence.

"I hold the majority stock," I went on. "I suggest we split up the corporations, Ted, so that you have some, like the dyeing or the real estate or the factory store, and I have others. Let's share the presidency."

"No way," said Ted. "I become president; I have final say on every matter. More than that, you must drop all lawsuits."

My mother started to plead with him. He hushed her, turned and left. In despair she looked at me; then she, too, left. I went back to my pacing with Sol's words echoing in my skull.

"You're to take over," he had said.

"You're to take over" had thumped in my head as I had paced the hospital corridor.

"You're to take over." Once he died, his words had swelled to a great crescendo.

Passionately, I wanted to, for his sake and for my own.

"No, never," blared an equally loud message, from my father and my brother.

I was distracted from my brooding by the door again opening. Anna. I led the way to a corner of the giant-sized bed. As we sat in one corner we rumpled the quilted aqua spread that exactly matched the tufted aqua headboard. In the darkening day we looked out at the empty field across the street. Anna's arm went around my shoulders. I placed my cheek next to hers; it was wet.

"Nan, why are you crying?"

"I feel like crying," she said.

"You're crying but I'm not," I remarked.

"You're very brave," she explained. "You're trying to keep the tears back for the sake of your children. You walk with your head up."

"I cannot eat; I cannot cry."

"We were brought up that way. We were taught to carry everything inside."

We talked a bit longer. Involuntarily, I loosened emotions I thought frozen deep inside.

"I couldn't stand seeing Sol die." I told her about my head

on the butcher's block and the cleaver chopping it off. "I still feel like a spectator standing outside my own body."

Anna sighed. "Let some time pass."

"People call a mate your better half," I said. "Half of me has died, Anna."

"Let some time pass," she repeated.

She returned the next morning to find me still pacing.

"I cannot rest, Nan; I cannot sleep."

I did not confess that I was hoarding every sleeping pill the doctor had prescribed for me.

"I have a solid lump here," I said, placing my clenched fist between my breasts, "and I want to keep it that way where no one can touch it."

"Why?" she asked.

"So long as I live I can keep Sol there, forever whole. I don't want him to melt away, to dissolve in my bloodstream."

"Why?" she asked again.

We stayed quiet for a long time.

"Maybe you're right," I admitted at last. "So much remains unfinished."

Anna must have lifted some veil of grief. I began to talk to and hear some of the people around me. I saw Ken when he called on me that day.

"Are we going ahead with the lawsuit?" I wanted to know.

"What lawsuit?" he asked. "You have no lawsuit. Who will testify? You've lost the chief witness."

Grimly, I went back to pacing. People kept calling. Among them came Al. Becky brought him up.

"Do you feel like a walk?" asked this soft-spoken, serious man.

I nodded. We left the house of mourning for the stillness of the gray outdoors. For the first block we may have chatted idly. Turning the next corner he posed a question: "What do you plan to do?"

"I would like to carry on the business," I told him, but could say no more; I had choked up. "I want to," I said after a while, "but I see no way to do it."

"Are you worried about raising the money?" he asked.

"Of course," I answered. "Why do you ask? Do you think it's possible?"

Poker-faced, he responded, "Oh, sure, I think we can swing it." While I hung on every word he outlined a plan for raising money.

My father had sworn never to sell out to Sol. Less than a year before, Sol had come up with a formula for a buy-or-sell price. Scribbling numbers for hours and developing pages of statistics, he had labored to propose a fair figure. With more numbers, he had outlined a payout in three years.

"No, sir." My father had curtly brushed him aside.

If Pa had refused Sol, why would he sell out to me? Al seemed to think it possible. Al even seemed to think it desirable.

After three minutes, I had made my decision. I was going for broke.

On a dreary morning, my children, Al and the rabbi stood with me around a cemetery plot wet with soft snow. The rabbi chanted the Kaddish and the prayer for God's mercy. A gravedigger turned up damp earth with his spade. Before I surrendered the bronze urn with Sol's ashes, I kissed it. One of the children took it from me, and each of them kissed it in turn. Our tears and sniffles dripped on it. The gravedigger planted it deep in the gaping hole. We each cast a spadeful of loose earth over it. The workman filled the rest. With the back of his shovel he tamped the ground level.

We returned to the house to break bread together.

"Maybe I should go away for a few days," I said as I sipped some tea and caressed the cup to draw warmth for my cold, stiff fingers. "I long for the sight of an ocean or a mountain."

"I'll take you wherever you want to go," Ralph volunteered.

"Someone told me of an inn in Manchester, Vermont. Maybe I'll be able to get some sleep there. I can't sleep here in the same bed that ... "

"Let me replace the bed while you're away," Sara Mae said.

"I should go into Sol's office," I said to Al, while I watched the others eat sandwiches of cold cuts. "I've got to begin picking up the dropped stitches. Just give me a week to myself."

Al replied, "I'll keep in touch with you."

"Ken told me to call a meeting of the stockholders right away," I added.

"I'll send out notices for ten days from now, for the Tuesday after you get back," Al promised.

"Let's have the meeting here, in this house," I directed him.

Over winding, wet roads Ralph drove me to the other Manchester. The retreat, quiet and old-fashioned, had a view of Mount Equinox. Our rooms were warm and comfortable, the meals ample, our hosts pleasant.

But I could not eat, could not sleep, could not rest; worst of all, I could not cry. When I passed a comb gingerly over my tight and tingling scalp, I felt as if a snaggle-toothed rake were scraping and plowing through living, crawling earth. I could wear no jewelry but my wedding band. I lived on tea and bites of buttered toast.

I recall only bundling up and climbing a gentle hill for a better view of the mountain. At some point Ralph took off to visit a school chum at Williams College. When he returned Sunday, he heard me being paged for the telephone.

Al was calling. "On Thursday evening your father ordered a few of the executives to come to his room at the hotel. Ted and their attorney sat with him while he talked to them. All day Friday in Ted's office they were meeting and talking with key men, one after another. They haven't stopped over the weekend."

They began the very day Sol was buried, I was thinking. Bastards—they're not even giving me the few days I need to mourn for my beloved.

"To some they're making promises, to others conveying threats. They're cutting you and your family out of the picture entirely. I think you had better get back here."

"I'll leave right away," I said.

Snow had fallen during the night, and Ralph took extra caution. I asked him to drop me off at my mother's and wait for me. I let myself in and found her in her armchair, sitting and staring into space.

"I did it," she said when she saw me, "I'm the one who killed Sol."

"Sol killed himself," I answered. "He and he alone bears responsibility for his actions."

"I murdered him," she repeated.

"Don't make yourself the star of a drama," I told her.

"I got a notice that you're calling a stockholders' meeting next week," she said. "I'm not going."

"I have to know where we stand," I said.

"I'm not doing one more thing," she replied. "I've done you enough harm. From now on count me out of it."

On Monday morning I rose early and, on impulse, put Sol's sos black onyx ring on my middle finger. I hadn't worn it since my sixteenth birthday. I found myself pressing my thumb against the inside of the ring, as if to draw courage from it. I went to the garage and backed out Sol's station wagon, with his sos license plates. Driving it into the millyard, I parked it in Sol's accustomed berth alongside the front entrance. I pulled open the green wooden door and walked down the long corridor to his office. People kept stopping me to shake my hand or offer sympathy.

I removed my coat and hung it on Sol's rack. Clumsily, I opened the folding doors behind his desk that concealed his working-space shelf. I seated myself in his chair, a large bentwood rocker that nestled in the curve of his crescent desk. Al came in to greet me.

"I saw my mother last night," I told him. "She blames herself for Sol's death. She says she won't do a thing to harm me further. Joe and Ted held a session in the hotel with my father one night, then got to her house after ten o'clock to talk to her. She told them the same thing she told me. She won't vote Ted's way, she won't vote mine. She won't vote at all."

"If she abstains, we stand deadlocked," commented Al. "We must tell this to Ken." He went on, "This conflict had better be resolved quickly. If we stall or bicker too long, our whole team can fall apart. Without good management we can't run this business."

"How about an executive meeting this morning in my office?" I asked. "Let's have it right away. I'll invite each man personally."

Al and I checked the list of the dozen executives Sol usually asked. "Ronnie and Carl are working on samples in the mill this morning," he remarked. "We should include them."

"I really don't know where to start," I began, when everyone had arrived, "except to say I intend taking an active part in this business. As many of you already know, it is not entirely strange to me."

I reviewed my role from the company's founding, through my first Macy's order, to the launching of Pandora. I talked about my road trips, the move to Manchester, the war years and my last road trip.

"In 1944, pregnant with my third child, I left the factory to stay home," I continued. "Sol, though, wanted me to share his work. He came up with the idea of a company news-paper. 'Issue it every month,' he said, 'and you can keep your finger on the pulse of this business.' I've issued it now for almost twenty years.

"Sol and I knew about his heart condition. 'If anything ever happened to you,' I told him, 'I would just throw up my hands.'

" 'You would not,' he replied. 'First, a business like ours can run for a long time on its own momentum. Then, we have made plans; you would carry them out. Remember, more than eight hundred people and their families depend on us for their bread and butter.'

"One day Sol's heart did give out. I can't believe ..." I broke off, my voice quivering, but steadied myself. "I don't want to believe he's gone. I can't bear not to live up to what he expected. He expected Pandora to blossom and to prosper.

"No one can ever fill his shoes," I concluded, "but each of us, in his or her own fashion, can give it the best try we know how."

As the men started to break up, many stepped forward with words of reassurance. I mentioned my intent to walk through the factory and to talk to each of them and their people. Alone, with my pulse wildly beating, I sat in Sol's rocker.

Later that day I walked through the seven floors of the factory, employees halting me every few feet. I made the rounds from under the rooftop, where spinners and reelers worked with filaments and bobbins at long frames, to the subbasement, where men in rubber boots sloshed around the iron-grilled floor of the dyehouse. In the cafeteria I joined Carl as he ate his lunch.

"I'm still stunned by how fast everything is moving," he said. He glanced at his watch. "Your father must be leaving for Florida right around now. By the way," he added, "Ted's lawyer appeared in the showroom the other day and asked Ronnie and me all sorts of questions."

His words jolted me. In the past year—and not from Sol—Carl and Ronnie had heard of our lawsuit, then rumors of buyouts. Now strange lawyers were wandering on the scene.

Amidst threats of upheaval, the two sales managers must wonder where they stood. Without faith in their future at Pandora, they could panic. Perhaps I should fly to New York to repair or forestall any damage.

On the street floor I pondered this as I watched the girls on the tag-and-box line. The sweaters kept passing by on the conveyor belt. Each bore a label with the Pandora logo; each went into a box imprinted with a still larger logo. My childish scrawl repeated itself on sweater after sweater, box after box.

How long ago, Sol, you had insisted that I handwrite that logo! On the roof of our building you even erected a blue neon sign, twenty feet high, proclaiming Pandora to all the world in my script.

I fled from my signature and the mill to walk the half-mile to the distribution center and cover employees there. Then I crossed the railroad tracks to the factory store. Everywhere, I could feel warmth and compassion from people who had known Sol reaching out to envelop me.

On my return I repeated Carl's remarks to Al and my sense of urgency about going to the New York showroom.

"Before you do, we have a date with Ken," Al said. "We have to draw up a schedule of all moneys you can possibly raise, then prepare a package acceptable to bankers and creditors."

Al went through this exercise with me the next morning. The figures totaled substantially over a million dollars.

We presented the schedule to Ken in the afternoon. He listened intently as Al ticked off item after item.

Key-man insurance, a half-million dollars that Pandora had carried on Sol's life, topped the list.

All Sol's insurance policies came next.

All stocks and investments held jointly by Sol and me would be cashed in.

All our savings would be withdrawn.

Our children's savings accounts would once more be used as collateral for loans.

Al would investigate getting larger mortgages on company real estate.

He would seek loans from other business connections.

All the rest I must borrow from friends. This might mean putting myself personally in debt for the next five years or longer.

Al and I had figured out where the money might come from and when and how I could repay these loans. Ken accepted our proposal matter-of-factly. The two men assumed that my buying out the other interests made good sense. My getting into debt did not disturb them. Ken, like

Al, took for granted that my presidency would prove both practical and feasible. They astounded me.

"As soon as you have researched your sources thoroughly," Ken briskly concluded, "I'll approach the other stockholders. Then we'll see how we can advance the situation."

TWELVE

Keep Knitting

AN UNEASY TRUCE prevailed during the next few weeks. My
father remained in Miami, my brother in New York. In
midmonth I managed a one-day good-will visit to the showroom; otherwise I stayed close to Manchester. Painstakingly I
began to research my sources for funds. At the same time I
assembled copy for a memorial issue of the *Yarn*.

"During the eight-year period from 1955," I typed, "these
corporations had the greatest growth in their history. The
demand for Pandoras on a national level increased. Sales
volume had its greatest percentage of increase. The number
of employees grew from 388 in 1955 to 850 in 1963."

I stopped for a moment to steel myself. It struck me that in
three short years, the volume of the junior division Sol had
initiated had already equaled the volume of the twenty-year-
old children's division.

"To him, the 850 families who depended on Pandora for
their livelihood were important. Giving them steady work,
security in their jobs, every fringe benefit possible, scholarships for their children, keeping them informed—these
were important."

Let someone come along, Sol, who puts the dollar sign
first, I was thinking, someone who abuses or even misuses
our people, and what would Pandora stand for then? Who is
going to succeed you and what you believe in?

Via the grapevine from New York I learned that my father
and brother were loudly proclaiming they would never sell a

single share of their stock to me. "With May as president," my brother had stated, "Pandora won't survive one year."

For my part, I would never sell out to them. The business, I felt, would go down the drain with my brother and some of the manipulators around him. Joe had often hinted that he should become a director of our company. Sol had ignored him. Would Ted?

Doggedly, I pounded the keys, made phone calls, wrote letters to insurance companies, lawyers and banks. Ugly thoughts distracted and tormented me.

Why had I ever allowed Sol and myself to go into business with my father and mother way back in 1931? I should have listened to Sol's mother and kept a safe distance from them.

Why had I agreed to stay in business with them—not for a year or two, but for thirty-six years? In 1944, I should have insisted on a split rather than let my father blackmail us into giving Ted a share.

How and when could I have helped Sol pursue his true love, building construction?

The visit to New York had presented several hurdles. To appear on Monday morning at 1407 Broadway meant leaving Manchester on Sunday night. Ralph was spending time with Gene in Washington, and I did not choose to leave Mickey alone. At fourteen she had lost her father; now she was losing half her mother.

"I hate to leave you," I said. "How about Bobshe staying over with you?"

Eighty-year-old mother of my cleaning woman, Bobshe had arrived from Poland in the distant past on a visitor's visa and had neglected to go back. Often she came to our house with her daughter. When she did, we would find that she had baked delicious braided bread or tended our plants or darned socks.

Bobshe spoke no English. We had to communicate with her in sign language. Slim, with white hair, fair skin and rosy cheeks, she could answer only with a sweet smile or a willing shake of her head. No idle chatter.

"Super!" exclaimed Mickey.

For twenty years, once a month, Sol and I had checked into a particular New York hotel. "I can't go back there," I had said on the phone to Harriet. She offered to make a reservation for me elsewhere.

"I dread going alone," I had said to Sol's secretary. Marian agreed to travel with me.

In the city, Marian was to trace a missing bankbook, get forms to close out some accounts and meet me later. Briskly, I strode off to the showroom, and with each step I reflected on the unknowns I faced.

What would I find in the showroom?

With Ken's help I had prepared a temporary basis for working with my brother. Would I see him? Would he listen?

How would Carl and Ronnie react?

Other questions unnerved me even more. To what end was I going through all these motions? Of what use was trying to raise all that money? What chance did I stand when I bucked my father?

Ted showed up very briefly that morning. I presented him with five memos. The first read, "May I please have copies of all communications to and from bankers, lawyers, accountants, etc., and reports of all conversations with them pertaining to the business activities of the corporations?" Two others conveyed the same message as to all checks he had issued and all directives sent to executives. A fourth noted his lawyer's appearance in the showroom and asked about the man's objectives. The last expressed my concern over the lateness of samples and asked if I could assist him in any way.

Hastily, he shuffled through them. "Very interesting. I'll take them under advisement. I'm already late for an appointment." He smiled benevolently, gathered his belongings and departed.

His absence should have smoothed my mission. Instead, first one sales manager, then the other, pounced on me.

"Our quality concerns me," said Ronnie. A prime customer was sending a shipment back claiming the garments ran short. "We must check every measurement on our full-fashioned sweaters. Besides that, May, if the mill doesn't get my designer's sample requests through faster, we'll never get our fall line out in time."

Waving a competitor's price list, Carl claimed that our bathing suits had been overpriced. Also, some holiday goods had been delivered far too late. "That shipment will be making a round trip," he predicted. "Besides, we're getting a big return from Hudson's teen department. The pants don't fit right."

That afternoon we discussed how to announce Sol's death to the trade.

"So many customers come in and ask about him. They want to know who will replace him," said Ronnie. "As soon as possible we must get a notice out to the trade."

"I don't agree," argued Carl. "We must ride out the storm and let our products speak for themselves."

I mentioned the memorial issue of the *Yarn*, coming off the press in late January. Sentiment about the past, each of them curtly stated, had no meaning for retailers. Buyers wanted guarantees that, in the future, they could continue to rely on Pandora.

We reached no decision. I left New York completely demoralized.

"How can so many things go wrong at one time?" I moaned to Al on Tuesday. "They came up with a half-dozen lulus that stumped me." Despairingly, I enumerated them.

"Let's take these troubles one at a time," Al said. "About the barrage of returns: every year customers try this right after the holidays. They're looking for any excuse to return surplus goods before they take inventory in January."

"What about quality and wrong sizing?" I asked. "If we don't have quality, Al, we have nothing. We don't deserve to stay in business."

"We had a problem this past holiday season," he explained. "Usually we knit all our own sweaters. But bookings came in extra heavy." At the last minute, Ted had tried a Brooklyn contractor, who had stuck us with bad lots. "We'll take back what we have to," said Al, "but never again do we use that mill."

"How about the junior samples? We'll never have them ready on time," I said. "This year of all years Ronnie must come up early and with a winner."

"Don't fall for that gimmick of the mill not co-operating," replied Al. "Every season we have to keep after Ronnie, but he comes through. His designer is hedging," he explained. "If her line doesn't click, she's setting up the factory as her alibi.

"Now Carl, with his bathing-suit prices—just another alibi. Each house," Al went on to explain, "has its own loss leaders. We can't compete with everybody on every item. He's laying groundwork in case sales fall short of projections."

"Talk to me about the late deliveries," I persisted.

"We knew it, and took the chance. The goods may come back; then again they may not. As for the slacks, we must check. I'm telling Carl to have Hudson's return one pair." He outlined the procedure we followed. The pair returned and some pairs selected at random from stock were tried on live models as well as on dummies. The fit determined whether we accepted the return or not.

"The further I stay away from New York," I said, "the healthier I'll feel."

"Don't say that until you speak to Ken," Al answered.

Ken, it seemed, could report some progress. My brother's lawyer had indicated a willingness to talk.

"I must have scared him the other day with our memos," I told him. "But I don't put too much stock in what Ted or his lawyer says. What will my father say or do?"

"You'll find out on Friday, January 25," said Ken. "All of us are to meet in New York to try to resolve this."

It committed me to tackling New York once more.

Thanks to Al, I had learned my first lesson. Taking troubles one at a time pruned each down to manageable size. Next time I would not tremble as easily.

On Wednesday of that same week I lunched with Fred Jervis.

"How could Sol stand it?" I asked. "How can anyone stand being constantly on the spot? I feel I'm smack in the middle of a pressure cooker—one about to explode."

"I see. Why don't you get used to being in the middle?" asked the blind man. My second lesson.

My third lesson came from Ken.

On a windy Friday morning, flanked by him and Al, I walked into the posh offices of my father's legal team. I came with raw skin, wondering what fresh bruises my father might inflict. Al carried a schedule of assets and the company books. Ken brought his surgeonlike ability to cut through to the core of an issue, his impatience with trivia and his tenacious grip. He set an unforgettable example for me.

The opposing lawyers named an impossible price bound to unthinkable conditions. Ken attacked each item with the skill of a Yankee horse trader. Al stayed at his elbow, furnishing whatever information he needed. Our New York accountant—the same man I had known from my father's garages forty years before—wigwagged from one faction to the other. Joe watched from the sidelines, as did Sara Mae and Gene when they showed up later.

I sat in a tiny side office, my mother nearby. Suffering from dangerously high blood pressure, she had just spent a week in the hospital. Quietly, uncomplaining, she sat and occasionally scratched the stubborn rash that completely covered her swollen arms and legs. At the other end of the suite my father and brother also sat in an isolated cubicle, and ignored us. I still tortured myself with unanswered questions.

Takeover implied a willing seller as well as an able buyer. Never mind my brother. Had Ken and Al sized up my father accurately?

If they ever reached agreement on a sale, what would the price be? My father would drive a hard bargain.

If a price was fixed, who would buy and who would sell?

The purchaser would have to pay the full amount immediately—cash. None of us trusted the others. Could my brother raise the cash? I doubted it. Could I? Al said I could. I must have faith.

My thoughts were broken at intervals by Al or the children. They would pop their heads into my space to give the latest progress report. Now and then Ken would stalk in to define a dispute and learn my preference. The wrangling did not let up.

At five o'clock Ken called a halt. "Let's stop for dinner," he recommended. "We'll meet with clearer heads later."

The atmosphere had changed when we reconvened at eight o'clock. Ken had set a price. Ted and my father had actually agreed. The price? Exactly what Sol had proposed only eight months before! In cash, of course. Ken had hammered out a further understanding. I had first option and ninety days to exercise it. Before midnight, the lawyers shook hands on their pact.

The preliminary bout had ended. Ken had steered me through to the main event. My respect for him turned to awe.

Late Saturday afternoon I reached home, and almost immediately Mickey pedaled her bike into the driveway and burst in. I looked at my youngest, with her too-broad shoulders, her too-thick thighs and her too-long feet, and I couldn't wait to hug her and shout my good news.

"You didn't believe Ken could pull it off," she twitted me. Then she added, "I have to hurry."

She and her friend Cheryl were going to a mixer at the community center. Would I prepare a quick bite for her while she ran upstairs to change?

"Tomorrow, I'm serving you breakfast in bed," she told me as she ate. "We have to celebrate your big day."

She sat on the edge of my bed on Sunday morning. While we talked I could see her father coming to life again in her hazel-green eyes. She and Cheryl had had fun the night before, meeting boys from Lowell, Lawrence and Haverhill.

"I'm turning into a shuttle bug," I said, talking about my own travels. "Twice in the past week I've commuted to New York. More trips are ahead. Al says we must visit the bankers next." Perhaps I should rent a studio apartment in Manhattan.

Mickey mentioned her own priority: school. During the past fall we had made the rounds of four prep schools in four states. She had been accepted at her first choice, a Quaker school in Bucks County, Pennsylvania. Come September, should she or shouldn't she go?

"I want you to go," I told her. "Your dad wanted you to go."

"I feel funny leaving you all by yourself," said my four-teen-year-old.

I dared not keep her near me. This fledgling, too, deserved her chance to leave the nest. I must not prop myself up by leaning on her.

"We'll make the most of the next few months," I promised.

That morning, for the first time in weeks, I became aware of the scale. I stepped on it; it did not balance. Farther and farther down I slid the weight; at last the beam seesawed. In three weeks I had lost seventeen pounds!

Three weeks, seventeen pounds—the numbers had a familiar ring. Then I remembered. On our honeymoon, Sol had gained seventeen pounds in three weeks.

Involuntarily, I let out a howl. Weeping softly I stayed in the bathroom. I stayed until I had done with tears and bathed my eyes in cold water.

Two other times since Sol's death I had been able to loosen up and cry. The first time came when I cleaned out his desk. In a drawer I had come across a familiar white jeweler's box tied with gold ribbon. I closed the drawer, ran from the room, and took a walk—for fifteen minutes. I couldn't stay away. I undid the wrappings. Inside lay a charm, an old silver thimble with turquoise stones encircling its base. Sol had already prepared his gift for my March birthday. I stared at that exquisitely wrought antique, then sobbed until I could sob no more.

A few days later I emptied the clothes out of his dresser. As I unrolled a pair of his knee-high socks, something metallic dropped out. I stared at my silver ring with the five matched opals, the one Sol had given me on our anniversary after Mickey was born. I had missed it since our vacation last summer. Evidently I had just misplaced it in packing. I could almost picture Sol, with his hand cupped, extending the ring to me. I cried and cried.

Except for those three crying spells, too few and far between, I had had no release for my turmoil. I poured out my emotions on paper. Recently, I found this among my writings:

"Since Sol died, I haven't been a woman.

"Walking, sleeping, eating, waking, I've been a carrying case of memories—tightly locked in my chest. I've become a thing of neuter gender.

"For thirty-six years, one month and nine days, I was a woman, Sol's woman.

"I resent the words I must use to describe this.

"Years, months, days, hours, minutes, seconds, split time into two dimensions. How can you express the continuity, the depths stretching seemingly to the external, the roots that twist and interlace?

"How can the typewriter capture my teardrops in Q, W, E, R, T, Y? My words seem puny."

I had to get ready for the meeting with the bankers. The moneymen had to accept me as Pandora's president. Pandora's ability to borrow money had to be protected.

Al had never met with them; I surely had not. Over the years they had filled me with an accumulated terror. First my father had constructed a mystique about bankers—such ogres that only he could confront them. Later Sol had spoken of how sharply they had grilled him and my father at some of their sessions.

I had my own misgivings. Would my sex handicap me with hard-nosed bankers?

Al and I talked over ways of addressing the problem. If we could score with the toughest banker, John Obeda, the others would probably fall into line. I suggested we contact a New York attorney who had handled corporation work for us after Mr. Miller had retired.

"He claimed he knew big wheels in banking circles," I recalled. "Let's ask his advice."

This man confirmed his connections, claiming that he intimately knew bigwigs in the very bank John represented.

"Drop in on him casually," he counseled. "Just pass the time of day. No attaché case, no formalities. Take a reading of the temperature."

In the next few days I had occasion to return to New York. Ralph's leave had ended and he was taking off for San Francisco, en route to Vietnam. A school chum of his joined us for supper. Back and forth went their kidding while I sat with a fixed smile on my lips. Later, Ralph promised to send tapes home regularly; he assured me his new recorder was stowed securely in his baggage. He kissed me good night and good-bye, because he was leaving in the small hours.

All that evening and all that sleepless night only one thing kept going through my head: "Dear Lord, please bring him back in one piece."

Al joined me in New York the day after. We "dropped in" on Mr. Obeda. He greeted us most cordially. Then he asked Al a pointed question about our balance sheet. Al, as the lawyer had suggested, had brought no records to supply an answer. The banker bridled; his smile faded. He asked about probable profits for 1962. Al had neither prices nor even approximate figures. I hazarded a guess that we would probably show a nice gain. He sniffed and asked for the inventory figures. Al, the zealous record-keeper, had left every one of his green-lined graph sheets in Manchester.

Obeda blew up. He raised his voice to bark out guidelines

to us, the data we should present at future meetings. He cut our "chat" short and dismissed us harshly. We left like two beaten dogs slinking away.

"What a mistake we made!" I told Ken the next day. "We were totally unprepared. I won't ever let that happen again."

"May is right," said Al. "I felt embarrassed after we got started."

"I'm ready to go back and tell him off," I said, still smarting. "So brutal!"

"Stop talking nonsense," Ken broke in. "Concentrate on one thing. Whatever you do, how will that advance the cause? What do you hope to achieve?"

I outlined a half-dozen lines of attack.

"You're jumping all over the lot," Ken said. "Stop a minute. Think. What do bankers look for?" He answered his own question. "They'll want to see the capital structure left undamaged by the takeover. Next they'll look at your top management. Your three main officers are gone. Who is left to run the company? Last, how do your customers feel about Pandora? Have you maintained your position in the marketplace?"

I calmed down. For the next hour we sought a way to attack on the triple front Ken had mapped out.

"When we've got this package ready," I told Ken, "Al and I are coming right back to you. You're going to make like you're John Obeda and we'll rehearse." He did not say no.

I considered the last question first: How did our customers feel about Pandora? Carl and Ronnie could brief me.

By my next visit to the showroom Ronnie had previewed some of the fall 1964 junior samples with a valued customer. "She loved them," he reported. "She was ready to write with a heavy pencil."

"When you meet with the bankers," Carl put in, "the children's division will have actual paper to show them."

Carl had a point. Department-store orders would furnish our most effective testimony. The three of us reviewed last-minute changes in back-to-school lines and ironed out final arrangements for the February sales meeting. Before I left I asked Carl to ready proof of customer acceptance for our bankers.

Next I tackled the problem of management. With our three main officers gone, who would run Pandora?

"How can we picture the executive team, their depth, their talent?" I asked Don Madden. "The more I tie in with these men, the more I realize how valuable a legacy Sol left me."

Don suggested a "New Management" issue for the February *Yarn*. The cover would show the men's photographs, fourteen of them, with mine the fifteenth. The text would tell each executive's years with the firm, his duties, his career ladder and history. I began interviewing them right away, and the *Yarn* cameraman took their snapshots.

The problem of a healthy capital structure remained. A third of the takeover funds would be generated by key-man insurance. So I took a trip to Boston to expedite the processing of payment.

A keen young insurance agent had me sign documents releasing the insurance money. I braced myself then for a sales pitch that I, too, sign up for key-man insurance.

Instead, he looked up from his papers, and said, "Forgive me for asking something strictly out of order. What do you want it for? Why do you want to stay in this business? You can be well fixed and have no money worries for the rest of your life."

I blurted the first answer that came to mind. "What would I do with the money?"

Driving home, I had to admit the logic of the man's question. I could force my father and my brother to buy me out. If they could not raise the money, as evidence each day confirmed more strongly, I could force the sale or liquidation of the business. All of us would end up with substantial cash.

And what would I do with my time? The image of myself as a rich widow repelled me. So did the role of community do-gooder.

With time as well as money I could shift from reporting to publishing the *Manchester Free Press*. For three weeks in January, I had handed in my Knit and Purl column; then I had stopped. Don could replace neither me, nor my column, nor my plentiful copy. Other responsible reporters drew salaries. Any added expense would tip the scale away from the break-even point.

Don could not put in any more hours, could not fill every slot himself. He would accept no more money from me. Six months after Sol died, the paper was to fold.

I wore blinders for all but one course: to buy control of Pandora.

The education of a businesswoman proceeded rapidly in the ninety days after Sol died. Al had prodded our accountant into completing the 1963 statement early. I was in luck. That particular year showed better-than-average profits. Sol had repaid our bank loans early. Our cash flow and ratio of liquid to fixed assets appeared healthy. Al contacted our local bank. Yes, they would give us larger mortgages on our buildings.

The rest, raising almost a million dollars, depended on me. I pursued each lead like a woman possessed. The dealer who bought our knit waste advanced me a sum in six figures. Years later he confided that he had mortgaged his home to do it.

"Nothing would satisfy you then but total involvement," he told me. "I respected you for it. I did all I could to help you on your way. I knew you would make good."

"Would you have done the same for Ted?" I asked.

"I would have loaned him something," he said, "but not what I loaned you."

Our distribution center was owned jointly with a textile-finishing firm, which occupied the entire basement. The company was represented by an extremely sharp Albanian gentleman.

"I can advance you money in May," he said with his clipped accent. "Until then, I will endorse a note for you at the bank."

Years before, Sol and I had learned that our honeymoon lodge had burned to the ground. Impulsively, Sol had picked up the phone. "I know the insurance will never cover your loss," he had told the innkeepers. "Will a loan of $50,000 help you rebuild?"

A far grander hotel rose from the ashes of the old one, and in no time our friends had repaid us. Now I asked them for a loan. Their check came in the next mail.

Al loaned me money; so did other executives.

Ziggy said, "Anyone who could gamble all or nothing, down to your last penny, the way you did—I had to go all the way for you."

One morning I walked in to find a $10,000 check on my desk. Unsolicited, it had come from my secretary and her husband. I sat in Sol's rocker and cried like a fool.

Two of our top salesmen offered to let their commissions, a combined amount of $100,000 stay uncollected for a year, interest free. A third man, our California representative, called. "I've taken out a $50,000 bank loan," he said. "You don't have to pay it back for a year."

Al set up an appointment with our bankers for the second week in February. In advance he mailed them our statement. I invited Carl to accompany us.

On the day preceding the meeting, I flew to New York to hand John Obeda a preview of the *Yarn*. In our one-to-one encounter he visibly softened. I thanked him for setting Al and me on the right track. He beamed, patted me on the back and escorted me to the elevator.

Promptly at ten the next morning, four Pandora people faced seven moneymen.

They had studied our statement. They took pleasure in the black figures and Al's promise of more black figures coming up. They knew my personal financial position and foresaw no impact on corporate finances. Carl let them inspect originals of retail orders from Marshall Field and Best & Co. I handed out copies of the *Yarn*. Six of the bankers studied it while Obeda smiled knowingly at me. They could not help but be impressed by the caliber and depth of management.

Each of the seven had his own barrage of questions. With occasional input from Carl or our accountant, Al and I fielded them all.

One of the bankers, a toweringly tall man, invited the entire group to luncheon at a nearby restaurant. Sitting at his right and craning my neck to look up at him, I received an unexpected compliment.

"In all my years, yours is the finest presentation I've ever seen," he told me.

Why had I ever thought of these people as boogeymen?

Now that our credit line was secure, how about our sales organization? Before the end of February, thirty representatives would gather in Manchester for our annual sales meeting. Coming from every region in the United States, they would mix with the New York showroom staff, designers and a dozen factory managers.

By prearrangement with Ted, I would welcome everyone at breakfast on the first morning; he would make closing remarks at the banquet on the second evening. In the interim my brother would mingle freely with men he had known for years. Should I brace for trouble?

On the appointed day, I greeted our guests at the hotel. Once again I warmly thanked the three "big hitters" for their financial support, especially our California man. Our Ohio man handed Al a check for $10,000. Another asked if he could help.

"Right now it looks as if I may not need it," I told him, "but your support means much to me." It was surely encouraging to have sophisticated road men step forward with hard cash.

One circumstance jarred me, however. Ted was floating around with a coterie of his friends—Joe and three other men I recognized. Was Ted considering some venture, with these men as potential investors?

As I welcomed the assembled group the next morning, I suddenly became aware of Ted's head in the audience. He quietly sat through the program, which followed its usual format. First Ronnie, then Carl, showed their lines. Both used daughters of employees as models. The sales force applauded each style and each model. Ted joined in the handclapping, especially for one small tyke who meandered all over the runway.

At the coffee break, I noticed an incident that jarred me further. Ted corralled Dulie and spirited him away for a long interval.

In the afternoon, senior salesmen held workshops, "showing" the line to a half-dozen others, grouping and regrouping the numbers, figuring out how to get "big bucks" from buyers.

The full-fashion superintendent pulled me aside at one workshop. "Your brother had a long talk with me," he said. "He asked how I felt about all the changes."

"What did you say?"

"Whoever heads the company commands my loyalty," he replied. "Then Teddy said, 'That's fine—just the way it should be.'"

Was my brother feeling out technicians and executives about defecting? Pirating just this superintendent plus Dulie and Ronnie could cripple us. I had had a nightmare that on the very last day, before affixing his signature to the last paper, my father would back out. Should I also have anticipated mischief from Ted?

Each sales manager had reserved that evening for conferences with individuals on changes in territories, limits on overdraws, or better account coverage. Before Carl started, I told him and Al my suspicions about Ted.

"I happen to know that one of our men," said Carl, "is searching for a showroom for Ted. You're right. Ted is sounding out people to see who will go with him."

Early next morning I telephoned Fred Jervis, spilling out my fears and trying to probe the possible damage Ted could do.

"Speak to him directly, if you can," Fred urged. "Try to get into conversation with him. Find out the way he's thinking."

I did not catch sight of Ted, however. He did not show up at any of the workshops.

That afternoon, I had to pick up Harriet at the airport. She had located a studio apartment for me in Greenwich Village. Before I furnished it, I had asked her to come up and inspect furniture I already owned. By repositioning, adding or replacing items, I could change my background. Sol's ghost might haunt me less in less familiar settings.

That evening, sixty-six of us gathered at a popular Chinese restaurant for the sales banquet. My brother arrived late; there was no chance for casual conversation because the formalities had begun. Two saleswomen got gold service pins for twenty years with the company. Two salesmen got lapel pins for joining the Million Dollar Club. My brother closed the evening by repeating an off-color joke, making some innocuous remarks and handing out "We Try Harder" buttons (in many languages) that he had lifted from an Avis counter. One moment he was encircled by smiling faces and reaching hands; the next he had disappeared before I could talk to him.

By the last morning Ted had vanished completely. A designer talked about and illustrated the fashion forecast from Paris; a Du Pont official outlined a publicity campaign for its latest synthetic; Harriet detailed Pandora's advertising commitments. Some rookies took a tour of the factory. And it was over.

First, I felt great relief. I had been accepted; the lines had been accepted. Later, I suffered an awful letdown.

True, each man and woman had extended sympathy to Sol's widow. But these people had absorbed the shock. Sol had come; Sol had gone. How swiftly they had adjusted to life at Pandora without Sol!

Before February ended I knew when, where and how I could collect the cash necessary for the buyout.

"I don't need ninety days," I told Ken. "All the pieces have already fallen into place."

"Excellent," he said. "I'll set a date for the closing."

Later in the day he called back. The New York lawyers had other commitments. After mid-March they would discuss setting the date, no earlier.

"I do not believe them," I muttered to Al. "My father has some tricks up his sleeve, some maneuver to upset our understanding."

"Nothing of the sort," said Al. "Ziggy saw Ted in the city yesterday. He's leaving for a Caribbean vacation with Jean. He's not planning to start up any business of his own for the next year or two—just devote himself to her."

"His pals have had second thoughts about backing him in his own business," I translated.

"Do you want to use him as a consultant?" Al asked. "He told Ziggy that only he can develop holiday samples on the new Alemannia machines. He feels like an artist with an unfinished creation."

"We'll struggle along without him," I answered.

My suspicion of some last-minute hitch from my father or brother lingered nevertheless. In the uneasy interval I took over one more chore of Sol's, one he had mightily enjoyed: I handed out profit-sharing checks. One Tuesday, from early morning until shortly before midnight, when the third shift punched in, I distributed 750 of these, one for each employee who qualified.

The following week I received Ralph's first tape. I heard that he had read Sol's last letter, the one mailed the Friday before his death.

"Someday I'll show it to you," Ralph promised. "Dad packed a lot of news in there."

He had been transferred to the Hotel Metropole, in the heart of Saigon.

"Just a minute," he went on. "Some fireworks are going off outside and I want to see what's happening."

A long, empty silence followed; then Ralph's voice came on again.

"The other half of the Metropole has just been bombed," he said. "I have a buddy there. I don't think he made it."

The tape ended abruptly. He sent it half-empty. As I listened, I found myself twisting my fingers. They were turning red and white.

"Please, God," I begged. "You can't take two at one time."

God must have heard me. Almost two years passed but, all in one piece, Ralph came home!

On an afternoon in late March I arose from a twenty-minute rest on a blue paisley-covered sofa in my office. This sofa had replaced Sol's conference table and chairs. From home I had brought a pair of Bohemian glass lamps adorned with fair-haired, busty ladies. There were blue paisley drapes at the windows, between which stood a round walnut table, suitable for luncheons. I had shipped Sol's bentwood rocker to the New York apartment; to a close friend I had given Sol's crescent desk. They were replaced by a simple desk and chair.

As I walked down the corridor, I realized I was wearing my own ring, the one with the five matched opals. Outside the factory entrance was my own car, a blue Oldsmobile. Becky, during her vacation, drove the Buick station wagon with sos plates to New York for my use there.

Acting on Carl's advice, I had shunned any formal trade announcement of Sol's death. Instead, I was personally meeting customers. Carl would notify me when large re-tailers were due in the showroom. I would fly down to meet and socialize with them. The next morning I might go see a Long Island contractor and lunch in Brooklyn with a yarn supplier. Overnight I stayed in my Greenwich Village apartment.

To no one did I confide that, unable to sleep, I rose in the middle of the night, sat in Sol's rocker, and fancied myself cuddled in his lap, my head on his shoulder, his strong arms around me.

On April 4, once more flanked by Al and Ken, I walked into the Madison Avenue lawyers' offices. Gene met me there; Sara Mae brought my mother. My father and brother cold-shouldered me.

Again each faction occupied a separate cubicle. Again I heard endless bickering. Again I felt the urge to scream. I looked over to see Ken putting on his coat and hat.

"Where are you going?" I heard my father's attorney call out, while my stomach did a somersault.

"I came here for a closing," I heard Ken say, "not to renegotiate."

The lawyer whispered something to his associate; they ran after Ken and caught his sleeve before he got to the door. Reluctantly, he turned back, shed his coat, and settled one more irritating detail. Then they dug in to dissect every word in every sentence of the agreements yet again.

At dusk they adjourned until the next day. Gene told me at dinner that Ted was going into the dyeing business with Charlie, the expert we had summoned so many years ago to extricate us from the electric-blue and emerald-green mess.

"I offered to break our business up," I recalled. "I offered him our dyehouse. He turned me down."

The next day, the hassle continued. By late afternoon, I could sit still no longer. Getting up and approaching Ken, I beckoned him to my side.

"I must either scream or leave," I told him. "I'm going out to buy a hat."

"Go ahead," he said. "If I like it, I'll give it to you for a present."

I trotted over to Lord & Taylor, where I found a natural straw, one that suited me. It cost $37.50. Hatbox in hand, I went back to the law offices after a one-hour reprieve.

Ken was smiling and chatting amiably with the other lawyers. Incredible! The deal had been consummated!

For months after, as a memento, I kept his check for $37.50. He had liked the hat.

On Monday morning, we spent hours signing papers dealing with the original partners, my brother, and seven grandchildren. I handed over cash for stock certificates. The others handed over stock certificates for cash.

Ken, Al and I shook hands. The children and I embraced. My mother sat alone. My father, leaning heavily on Ted, hobbled out. Neither man looked at us. I never saw my father again.

After April 7, 1964, I was not invited to visit him in Florida or permitted to have any contact with him. Even in death I did not see him. When I attended his funeral in 1968, his coffin was closed.

On April 7, 1964, I became Pandora's third president. A volume of legal boilerplate six inches thick attested to this.

One day in late April I paused outside the factory door and looked at the millyard. Suddenly I heard a bird sing and turned my head toward his chirping. A hundred yards away I noticed a tree showing the first fresh green of spring. A sweet-smelling breeze riffled my hair.

How good to be alive! I thought.

For an instant I felt guilty; then the joy of the season surged up again.

How good to be alive!

My elderly dandy from the Atlantic City knitting exhibition, do you understand now what a nice lady like me is doing in the *shmatta* business?

I helped found and nurtured the growth of this company, Pandora. I learned how to knit and purl in a tough school. I weathered many ups and downs in a highly competitive industry.

I earned my standing—the hard way.

And you, Chris, with your panel on women in business, do you understand how I got there?

Yes, it was through my family.

Yes, it was through death.

Yes, it was on my own.